Doubts and Decisions

for Living

VOLUME II

The Sanctity of Human Spirit

Author's Books
(As at 2016)

Non fiction

The Nature of Love and Relationships **2011, 2016** 2nd Edition
Doubts and Decisions for Living:
  Volume I: The Foundation of Human Thoughts **2014**
  Volume II: The Sanctity of Human Spirit **2014**
  Volume III: The Structure of Human Life **2014**
Relationship Facts, Trends, and Choices **2016**
The Mysteries of Life, Love, and Happiness **2016**
Marriage and Divorce Hardships **2016**
Gender Qualities, Quirks, and Quarrels **2016**
Relationship Needs, Framework, and Models **2016**

Fiction

Persian Moons **2007, 2016** 2nd Edition
Midnight Gate-opener **2011, 2016** 2nd Edition
My Lousy Life Stories **2014**

Doubts and Decisions
for Living

VOLUME II
The Sanctity of Human Spirit

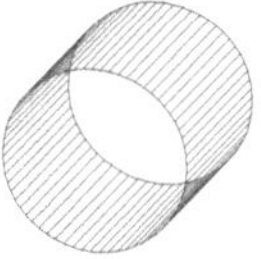

Tom Omidi, Ph.D.

Library and Archives Canada Cataloguing in Publication

Omidi, Tom, 1945-, author
Doubts and decisions for living / Tom Omidi, Ph.D.

Contents: Volume I. The foundation of human thoughts
Volume II. The sanctity of human spirit
Volume III. The structure of human life.

ISBN 978-0-9783666-6-7 (v. 1 : pbk.).
ISBN 978-0-9783666-7-4 (v. 2 : pbk.).
ISBN 978-0-9783666-8-1 (v. 3 : pbk.).

1. Conduct of life. I. Title.
II. Title: Foundation of human thoughts.
III. Title: Sanctity of human spirit.
IV. Title: Structure of human life.

BJ1581.2.O45 2014 170'.44 C2014-903378-8

Cover page design by Tom Omidi

Published by Eros Books,
Vancouver, British Columbia
Canada

contact@erosbooks.net

Printed in the United States of America

For my children

"And you…!?
"When will you begin that long
journey into yourself?"

Rumi

Table of Contents

Page

Prologue 1
Introduction 7

PART I: Psychology and Spirituality
Chapter One: Boosting Our Spirit 15
The Scope of Human Needs 17
Recognizing Our Unconscious Needs 21
The Spiritual Sensations of Self-actualizers 22
The Unity of Psychology and Spirituality 27
The Main Personal Dilemmas 29
Preparing Our Minds and Attitudes 31
Chapter Two: Knowing (about) Ourselves 35
Spirituality 37
Potentiality 40
Individualism (Integrity, Compassion) 44
Relationships 48
Contributions 53
Growth 56
Social Responsibilities 59
The Integral 'Self' 60

PART II: Science and Divinity
Chapter Three: The Spirit in Human Spirituality 69
The Role of Religion 71
The Role of Science 72
The Role of Personal Life Philosophy 73
The Role of Spirituality 74
Shortfalls of the Present Spirituality Approach 75
Chapter Four: Spirituality and Philosophy 87
The Ultimate Truth 93
The Truth about the Universe 94
The Truth about Humanity 95
The Truth about Our Personal Lives 100

Table of Contents (Cont.)

Page

PART III: Potentialities and Limitations
Chapter Five: The Spirit in Human Potentialities 109
The Makeup of Our Potentialities 111
The Functions of Our Potentialities 113
Chapter Six: Genetic (Career) Potentialities 117
The Reality of Job Markets 119
The Implications of Unfulfilling Professions 120
Chapter Seven: Divine Potentialities 125
'Self' Dilemmas 129
Who Cares 'Who We Are?' 131
What Are We Here for, Really? 134
Chapter Eight: Insight and Foresight 143
Potentialities and Opportunities 143
Potentialities and Interests 145
Potentialities and Confidence 146
Potentialities and Fairness 149
Potentialities and Perseverance 151
The Integrated Treasures of Potentialities 152
Chapter Nine: Life Limitations 155
Social and Economic Limitations 155
Natural Limitations (Physical and Mental) 159
Personality Limitations 161
Self-imposed Limitations 161
The Ultimate Limitation 163
Timing Limitations 167
Self-assessment 170
The Final Judgment 174

Table of Contents (Cont.)

Page

PART IV: Struggles and Victories
Chapter Ten: Quest for the Truth 179
Our Main Struggles 182
The Awareness Intersection 185
Human Logic's Reliability 192
Chapter Eleven: Beliefs and Convictions 203
Abstract Experiences 205
Real Experiences 212
A Sense of Victory 222

PART V: Common Sense and Self-awareness
Chapter Twelve: The Conflicting Roles of Our Doubts . 229
The Nature and Level of Our Doubts 232
The Scope and Effects of Our Doubts 233
Our Doubts about Human Nature 237
Managing Our Doubts and Decisions 241
The Benefit of a Doubt 249
Chapter Thirteen: 'Cultured' Common Sense 253
Developing Our Common Sense 256
The Value of Out Thoughts 259
Life's Dilemmas and Decisions 263

PART VI: Doubts and Decisions
Chapter Fourteen: Positives Doubts 269
1. Social Doubts 271
2. Personal Doubts 275
The Case of Self-doubt 278
3. Interpersonal Doubts 281
4. Supernatural Doubts 283
5. Spiritual Doubts 288

Table of Contents (Cont.)

Page

Chapter Fifteen: Negative Doubts 293
The End of Doubts 298
...The Beginning of Decisions 306
Chapter Sixteen: Decisions plus Destiny 311
Types of Decisions 315
Decision-making Factors 317
Decision-making Conditions 321
Decision-making Elements 323
Decision-making Criteria 328
A Warning for the Youths 330
Epilogue 333

List of Tables and Diagrams

Table 3.1: The Main Characteristics of Spirituality 85
Diagram 12.1: Level, Nature, and Type of Doubts 233
Diagram 12.2: Domain of Intelligence and Thoughts 246

Prologue

Something extraordinary seems to have happened in the last few decades to make most parents too concerned about, and attached to, their kids, much beyond the customary levels in the previous generations. For one thing, the rivalry among families to give their kids the best of everything has put most parents on edge, as they strive to indulge their kids and be the best parents they can be, to the point of often appearing too liberal and submissive. The rising social chaos and complexity is another factor that makes us anxious and more protective of our kids. We hope to give them enough confidence and guidance for handling the disappointments they must face. Parents of my generation were not so concerned and attached to their kids and they did not show their love and worries adequately, if at all. They were perhaps too relaxed, but their approach seemed more practical, natural, and in line with humans' inherent need to find their own ways of living. We learned much faster to become self-sufficient and get ready for life's hardships. But now, things have changed and we have been drawn into this overly liberal and protective mentality toward our kids. Still we do not get the right results, while we keep wondering whether we are fulfilling our duties. We are not sure whether our approach is appropriate and our guidance is helpful to them. Actually, the outcome so far indicates that youths have been too spoiled for their own good. They have indeed become more confused about the purpose of life. They do not learn about humans' inherent limitations and potentialities, or about the sanctity of human spirit that must be strengthened only through self-realization, and not selfishness. Instead of learning humility, which is the seed for exploring our spirituality and individuality, youths are encouraged to find their identity, happiness, confidence, and success through aggression, arrogance, greed, and sexuality. They are driven by fashion, fantasy, and superficiality. In this environment, it is doubtful that anybody can grow a moral mentality or any sense of spirituality to lift his/her spirit.

Our intention to guide our kids also fails due to our raw ideas about success and happiness. We doubt the meaning and means of capturing these elusive goals ourselves. Yet, we not only keep defining them erroneously, but also feel entitled to them automatically despite our shoddy lifestyles. On this matter, both parents and society have ruined the youths' chance to grasp life's realities. They grow up with high expectations for all kinds of privileges and happiness, which they believe should result from their shallow pleasures without building a pious mindset. Thus, they get confused and overwhelmed when they face daily turmoil. They have no clue or patience about the huge amount of efforts and sacrifices needed only to maintain a simple life, never mind attaining that elusive happiness that only a few people with real understanding of 'self' might achieve.

We also like to build our kids' foundation of thoughts, spirits, and knowledgebase about the oddities and values of the prevalent life structure. Yet, we have not even fixed our convictions, have no real notion of spirituality, and cannot stay objective about the vanity of our modern lifestyles. We cannot help anybody when social and personal limitations have crippled our own lives. Without changing our mentality and refining our values, we cannot build our spirits or help our kids build theirs amidst the chaos we have inherited and forced to accept as the best option for living.

Learning about ourselves and grasping the vanity of our values is difficult for most of us. Yet, gaining this basic level of wisdom is the only way to build both our own and our kids' spirits. We must find our sense of spirituality outside the prevalent lifestyles without recourse to religious teachings, away from the positive thinking propagandas that mislead us, and by avoiding our own personal prejudices, which are usually the most limiting factor for helping our kids.

Nevertheless, exploring human spirit and hoping to build it naturally in ourselves or our children is a daunting task. For one thing, our genetic traits, rearing environment, and personality hinder a person's capacity to explore his/her divine potentialities, grasp spirituality, and feel the essence of his/her being. Moreover, the unrelenting social influence on people, especially youths, makes the goal of independent thinking and soul-searching almost impossible. We are all too attracted to the rewards and promises of modern life and we crave social acceptance wholeheartedly. Thus, we hardly find time or motivation to attend to the deeper aspects of our being, i.e., our spirit and 'self,' which are ambiguous dimensions of humans, anyway, and quite an abstract topic.

For enriching my kids' lives, I tried to provide them with a rather calm and comfortable environment, all the privileges that other kids enjoy in modern societies, and an allegedly liberal, open communication channel. My goal was to help them build strong, independent minds to grasp the hassles and beauties of life realistically, away from the debilitating notions of the illusive world engulfing them. By learning about various obstacles and traps of our prominent life structure, I hoped they would be ready to face hardships positively, make the right decisions, and succeed in pursuing a simple lifestyle with the least amount of frustration and setbacks. They needed a solid foundation of thoughts and a reliable knowledgebase about the structure of life, but also the right beliefs, personality, and outlook to bear disappointments and proceed confidently. Most important of all, I hoped to inject optimism in their heads and tell them about the power and sanctity of their spirits. However, it proved a tough chore.

Discussing spirituality with our kids in a sensible format, perhaps as a hidden personal potentiality and the conduit for freeing our spirits, is tough for everybody. In particular, unreligious parents like me, with no sacred stories to support our beliefs, have a bigger challenge discussing some vague notions of spirituality to invoke our kids' spirits. On the one hand, religious families have a better chance to inject their faith in their kids' heads and naively believe they have satisfied their kids' spiritual needs too. On the other hand, unreligious people usually have a better chance of ultimately finding their own spirituality and reviving their spirits more honestly and naturally.

Ironically, exploring our spirit and spirituality is a natural urge, mostly as an inherent by-product of self-awareness. The more we learn about our inner nature as a human, the more our sense of spirituality emerges and the freer our spirits feel. Self-awareness and spirituality are on the same continuum, but gaining these levels of enlightenment requires determination, sacrifice, and patience to go through a long process of learning and exploring. Still, it would be an easier task for people with curiosity about life and 'self' than it is for religious fanatics with a set mentality and reluctance to search for the truth independently. Brainwashing kids' minds with religious stories would only restrict their chances for self-awareness and finding real spirituality. Especially youths must learn to think independently and find their own inherent potentialities, including divinity, gradually, the same way they learn about all other facts based on their instincts, research, logic, and intelligence.

At the same time, youths must know about the daunting effects of social norms attempting to raise people's spirits in artificial manners, e.g., through shallow slogans about positive thinking or living in the now. Society's attempt to spread positivity in the population only cause more confusion and stress for everybody. These slogans are mostly for subduing our minds, exploiting people for economic purposes, and promoting idle ideologies and life philosophies. Many of the positive thinking slogans in the recent era in fact harm us when they often do not match our unique personalities and/or the overall workings of human psyche. They hurt us, as we fail to accomplish all those illusive dreams that positive thinking and modern living promise. Our illusions distract us from learning and facing the harsh reality of life in the 21st century head on. Instead, we only hide behind a vast veil of desires, and then get frustrated and complain when our fantasies do not bring us the happiness and authentic positivity that only our liberated spirits can offer naturally.

Thus, this volume of *Doubts and Decisions for living* delineates the task of building our spirits and spirituality by firming up our personal beliefs and gaining our natural positivity. Ultimately, we should explore our own sense of spirituality in order to strengthen our spirits independently without recourse to religions or the prevailing positive thinking methods. We must restore our identity by resisting all kinds of social forces and personalities that always attempt to manipulate our souls. We must honour the sanctity of our spirit that is overwhelmed by all the superficialities surrounding us.

Happy reading
Tom Omidi, Ph.D.
Vancouver, 2014

Introduction

Each volume of this trilogy is largely about one of the three main functions of humans, i.e., thinking, feeling, and doing. Our life-long, excruciating doubts and decisions arise from our thoughts, feelings and actions too. Volume I focuses on the 'thinking' function mostly by studying humans' philosophical dilemmas and our motives and means for building the foundation of our thoughts. Volume III explains the 'doing' function, as we traverse hesitantly within a preordained structure of life. We try to cope with the peculiarities of socioeconomic environment by doing the right things and making the best decisions.

This book (Volume II) explores the 'feeling' function mostly by reviewing the role and vigour of our spirits for guiding our authentic urges, accessing our sacred senses, and finding peace and happiness. Our spirit also provides the energy and insight to withstand our erratic thoughts and stressful encounters. We feel lonely and helpless when life's setbacks overwhelm us and our spirit sinks. Building and maintaining our spirit is, however, quite onerous nowadays for many reasons discussed in this volume. It is becoming more difficult every day to stay positive and keep our hopes high when we must live in such substandard societies and deal regularly with corrupt and egocentric individuals.

Nevertheless, understanding the realm of our spirit and learning how to empower it through a personally defined spirituality is the only way to survive life's hardships and perhaps find a relatively peaceful life too. As another natural wonder of the universe, fortunately, our urge for spirituality is deep within us like a conduit for appeasing our spirits. Of course, attaining this private sense of divinity is a personal challenge, which neither religions nor scholars can explain to us or help us with. We must set out to grasp it on our own in a hard way. Then, we can draw on this natural source of inner power and intuition to establish our personal beliefs, build our identity, and keep our spirit intact. Otherwise, we would just stagger along with the cocky crowd without knowing who we are and what the purpose of our living is.

An inherent link exists between our spirit and psyche, but it must be reinforced through self-awareness and developing a personal sense of spirituality. It begins with exploring our urges, psyche, and needs, which we must tune collectively in order to revamp our deluded mentality about life and being. Through a soul-searching process, we must somehow come to terms with our neglected and pained spirit and feel our link to the universe. This self-awareness satiates our curiosities (and doubts) about living and reinforces our convictions. We learn to build a rather positive attitude about life and people, despite all the injustice and cruelties out there, and we become better and humbler human beings. Accordingly, our notion of spirituality develops naturally and independently, which feels authentic and sensible. At the same time, our invigorated spirituality bolsters both our psyche and spirit to redefine and enrich our lives, as explained in the following chapters.

The brief discussions of spirituality in this volume reflect its importance for building our beliefs and spirits, and for satiating our curiosity about existence. Spirituality is also an important subject for developing the foundation of our thoughts and gauging the validity of our lifestyles. Yet the present state of spirituality and the approach it has taken so far would not help the public much. This point is clarified in Chapter Three. Thus, if a reader is interested to know the author's position regarding spirituality in advance, s/he may read Chapter Three first. Nevertheless, this book does not get into the depth of spirituality, which is an enigmatic and sensitive topic.

Many spiritualists' ideologies sound quite attractive and they may be even useful for curbing people's need for feeling and expressing divinity. Yet, we require a more natural mode of spirituality to help us understand 'who we are,' and reach a relative sense of peace and freedom within our chaotic socioeconomic environment. In fact, a progressive type of spirituality, based on intelligence and scepticism, would probably be the best way to defeat the global gullibility that religions and rulers of the world have injected in the public's minds. It is merely some spiritualists' certitude and persistence about the absolute truthfulness of their ideologies that hinder the task of exploring spirituality and ruin the effect of their words and efforts. We should be careful not to get carried away by some illogical claims and certitude about the existence of God or another life form for humans beyond their earthly being. Some shallow spirituality claims should not misguide us again now in a different manner as religions have done for centuries.

Besides the theoretical explorations about spirituality in this book, the author's interpretations, based on personal experiences and feelings (as presented in Chapter Eleven), are included merely as references for building his foundation of thoughts. In a sense, the spirituality topics and quotes in this book are only philosophical conjectures and nothing more.

Part I explores the psychological and spirituality dimensions of humans and attempts to explain the link between them. Chapter One explains how satisfying our varied needs can empower our spirit and sense of spirituality, or conversely disrupt even our basic touch with our psyche and the self. Chapter Two describes the task of learning *who we are* by exploring the seven elements of 'self.'

Part II delves into topics of science and divinity in hopes of finding a rationale for our spirituality choices and means of developing it. Chapter Three discusses various concepts of spirituality and delineates the need for discovering our own sense of divinity independently away from religions and social influences. Chapter Four explains spirituality as a main pillar for both human identity and the foundation of our thoughts. Accordingly, our search for the truth—mainly for managing our lives—requires both a solid foundation of thoughts and a strong spirit to withstand the pressures of living.

Part III discusses human potentialities and limitations as a platform for building both our careers and spirits. We must use our divine potentialities to understand our personal and social limitations and expand our self-awareness. Chapter Five explores the nature and purpose of our potentialities. Chapter Six discusses our career related potentialities as a means of making a living, with the risk of dampening our divine urges in the process though. Chapter Seven discusses the role of our potentialities in pursuing our interests, building our confidence, and facing social unfairness. Chapter Eight discusses both self-imposed and social limitations as obstacles for using our potentialities and building our spirits. Chapter Nine explores the nature of life's limitations.

Part IV explains humans' main struggles and ultimate victories despite all the setbacks and disappointments in everybody's life. Chapter Ten discusses our quest for the truth as part of our attempt to strengthen our spirit. Conversely, our spirit drives our quest for the truth. This natural drive in humans for finding the truth and the 'self' by itself proves the existence of our spirit. Chapter Eleven explains how our beliefs and convictions evolve and empower our spirits, which in turn reinforce our willpower and beliefs. Some of the author's important life experiences leading to his beliefs and convictions are also discussed in this chapter.

Part V discusses common sense and self-awareness as the main tools for managing our doubts and decisions effectively, and for keeping our spirit intact. Chapter Twelve studies the conflicting roles of our positive and negative doubts. Chapter Thirteen discusses the nature and types of our doubts and decisions.

Part VI discusses life's major decisions and doubts for building our outlook on life and finding happiness. Chapters Fourteen and Fifteen explain our positive and negative doubts in some length respectively. Chapter Sixteen explains the factors, conditions, elements, and criteria for making our major life decisions.

The quotes from various scholars used in this trilogy are merely for reflecting other viewpoints on related topics without prejudice. They are plausible opinions expressed liberally in public domains on such philosophical topics and have thus become relevant for general review purposes. Although the author does not necessarily agree or disagree with them, he believes they are interesting points that readers might be interested to check in those books for further detail and reflection.

PART I

Psychology and Spirituality

CHAPTER ONE
Boosting Our Spirit

Courage, confidence, happiness, and optimism spring from a well-groomed spirit. In itself, a high spirit reflects the soundness of our choices and actions. Thus, we have the power and responsibility to boost our spirit by choosing a simple lifestyle in sync with humans' natural needs. Otherwise, our rising superficial needs suffocate our spirit, while we embrace the prevailing social values and set crooked objectives for our lives. For example, we naively believe that pleasures and extravagance can lift our spirit, whereas they actually dampen it by making us more needy and phony every day. Most people know these facts and the importance of keeping their spirits fresh and free. However, we forget that nurturing our spirits requires perpetual attention, wisdom, and sacrifice. Although an innate, divine dimension of humans, our spirit deteriorates very fast if neglected. It must be constantly monitored and empowered with our inspiring thoughts and deeds.

On the other hand, our spirit has the mandate of driving us to become a 'self'-fulfilling human being. Satisfying our innate needs, such as self-actualization and spirituality is a strong, subconscious urge driven by our spirit. Yet seldom anybody gets a chance to fulfil these needs, because we only follow the crowd for defining our lives. We feel obliged to struggle harder every day out of greed or even for basic survival, financially and emotionally, mostly because we seem trapped or do not know any better way of living. Even worse, we often cherish our mentality and lifestyles that satiate only our sexuality, neediness, and arrogance. All along, our goal is to find that illusive happiness that our naïve fantasies and narcissistic ambitions are supposed to bring.

In all, the rising social pressures and our pleasure-seeking mentality prevent us from pondering our deeper needs that can fuel our spirits. We are too mesmerized by our illusions to see the real world or even the sporadic clues about it. We are unwilling to accept that for attaining even a relative peace of mind, we must grasp the real purposes of living, revamp our needy mentality, and follow a simple life through a slow, peaceful process of self-awareness. There is no other way for salvation. Only through this long learning exercise, we may discover our inherent limitations and potentialities, which in turn provide tremendous opportunities for self-fulfilment and real happiness. Obviously, creating the right mentality and circumstances for exploring our innate traits and potentialities is difficult. Self-actualization studies, as briefly explained in this chapter, offer one method for doing that. But before setting sail for that long destination toward enlightenment, the more taxing task is to overcome (or at least acknowledge) our superficial habits and needs and evade the illusions we have come to love so dearly in the perceived world. Regarding the world of illusions, the Chris Hedges comment is interesting:

"A culture that cannot distinguish between reality and illusion dies. And we are dying now. We will either wake from our state of induced childishness, one where trivia and gossip pass for news and information, one where our goal is not justice but an elusive and unattainable happiness, to confront stark limitations before us, or we will continue our headlong retreat into fantasy. Those who cling to fantasy in times of despair and turmoil

inevitably turn to demagogues and charlatans to entertain and reassure them. And these demagogues, as they have throughout history, lead the crowd, blinded and amused, toward despotism." Chris Hedges, *Empire of Illusion,* Alfred A. Knopf, Canada, 2009, back flop.

The Scope of Human Needs

We have three types of needs: Physical, psychological, and spiritual. The physical type is comprised of tangible, basic needs that are evident since birth as our means of survival and bodily growth. These needs are intuitive and usually satisfied as a matter of habit. They stay in our conscious mind and impose direct, strong impulses, e.g., hunger, for satisfying them. Not only we recognize the signal, but also know how to deal with it, e.g., we know that it is time to find food and eat it. Our physical needs' direct, simple stimulus keeps us aware of our deficiency. Furthermore, we have been taught largely how to recognize and satisfy these primary needs.

The psychological needs, on the other hand, are hardly obvious to us like the basic needs, and they are too complex to pinpoint and study. No direct, simple, or automatic signals or stimuli warn us about many of our psychological needs or deficiencies. They are mostly our subconscious needs and we are at best only indirectly and subtly aware of them. Some of them, like loneliness, are felt rather readily. Even then, we feel helpless to handle them or deliberately neglect satisfying them. Sometimes we do not know how to fulfil those needs, and sometimes satisfying a need requires an outside source beyond our means. For example, 'love or belonging' is a strong psychological need that a person can fulfil only through another individual or group. In all, grasping and fulfilling most of our pressing psychological needs become quite cumbersome, compared with our basic physical needs. Thus, they cause deep personal deprivations, insecurities, and defects.

Our psychological needs are genetic or the influence of our rearing environment. The mere existence of these needs affects the psychological imbalance of almost all people at some degree. But as society and relationships get more complex so rapidly, the intensity of psychological needs are rising fast and the nature of their development in each person is getting more difficult to diagnose and cure. For example, the need for love develops in different intensity and format depending upon individuals' experiences since childhood. Furthermore, our misleading cultural and social teachings cause additional stress, deeper illusions, and psychological deprivations, e.g., when people keep seeking love obsessively as a tangible commodity that everybody can find and acquire. We imagine that our need for love can be fulfilled as naturally as we are taught to satisfy our basic needs. Our family and culture merely teach us to depend vastly on the illusions of love, power, pleasure, and similar symbols of happiness.

Abraham Maslow has offered a model of personal needs tree. At the bottom of this tree are basic needs like food and shelter. As these needs are satisfied, one moves up to the next levels such as belongingness, social, and status until one reaches the highest level of need in this hierarchy (tree), which is self-actualization. A higher need in the tree emerges, mostly subconsciously, as soon as the lower ones are satisfied. In a sense, this model suggests that humans would never be satisfied until they satisfy their highest level of needs, i.e., self-actualization.

In line with Maslow's model, our needs become more of the psychological nature as soon as we go past the very basic needs. Our need for compassion, love, belongingness, recognition, and self-actualization are all highly complex and psychological. Thus, they have a great potential for causing our sense of insecurity, suffering, and confusion, because satisfying these higher needs is extremely difficult and often depends on other people's view of us. We often feel helpless and at the mercy of outsiders to fulfil our psychological needs. While not evident routinely in our daily lives, we feel the impact of our psychological deficiencies, sometimes even without being able to link our anxiety directly to any specific psychological need. The most prevalent clue of psychological need deficiency emerges in the form of loneliness or restlessness feeling, even when loving family members and friends surround us. When such signals emerge, we attempt to at least understand the psychological need behind it, although satisfying it properly usually proves extremely difficult. Often, we might ignore the source of our unrest, not understand or misinterpret it, respond to it incorrectly, or feel helpless to do something about it.

Every day, more scientific proof emerges about the importance of psychological health not only for keeping our sanity and heightening our mental capability, but also for maintaining and improving our physical health and growth—and for building our spirits. The crucial point, however, is that we must learn about these needs mostly for coming to terms with them, instead of getting more needy or expecting to satisfy them all the time. We must learn to expect the chance of not satisfying some (or often most) of these needs, e.g., love, all our lives and still live with such deprivation rather constructively.

We all know about the body-mind connection and the importance of psychological health. Some scholars put even a higher emphasis on the relationship between physical and psychological health to the extent they believe that the cure for terminal diseases like cancer might be found more readily in psychological treatment instead of conventional therapies.

In *The Ageless Body, Timeless Mind,* Harmony Books, New York, 1993, Deepak Chopra M.D. states the following:

"The biochemistry of the body is a product of awareness. One of the greatest limitations of the old paradigm was the assumption that a person's awareness doesn't play a role in explaining what is happening in his body. Yet healing cannot be understood unless the person's beliefs, assumptions, expectations, and self-image are also understood. Although the image of the body as a

mindless machine continues to dominate mainstream Western medicine, there is unquestionable evidence to the contrary. Death rates from cancer and heart diseases are probably higher among people in psychological distress, and lower among people who have a strong sense of purpose and well-being." Ibid., page 20.

And in another book, he says:

"If I have a patient who is afraid, I can grasp his hand reassuringly and he will feel better; this happens even under anaesthesia. You can grasp the patient's hand at a difficult moment in surgery and see the monitors for blood pressure and heartbeat register the calming effect. The heart and the brain, it seems, are connected much deeper than where molecules are. One sees the truth of this whenever a baby is cradled in its mother's arms. Within a few minutes, the two of them will be breathing together, even if the baby is asleep, and their heartbeat will start to synchronize (they will not match beat for beat, since the child's heart rate is faster than the mother's). This body-mind connection is invisible, but who would call it unreal? It has been passed on silently from generation to generation. Perhaps it still wraps us all in a bond of sympathy. Out of separate beings, trapped in their own concerns, it helps to mould one human race." Quantum Healing, Deepak Chopra, M.D., Bantam Book 1989, page 132.

Our psychological needs are the intrinsic means of strengthening the body-mind connection and heightening our awareness. Therefore, understanding and dealing with our inner needs is essential for creating a more sensitive and effective connection between our body and mind. But again, the trick is to initially realize and accept that we must come to terms with our psychological needs more often than we can expect to satisfy them fully and permanently. For achieving this kind of progressive mentality, which demands some type of graceful resignation, we must become more aware of our 'self.' Regardless of some psychological deprivations that we can never resolve, e.g., love or recognition, we must always strive to move up in the personal needs tree and approach self-actualization as the ultimate personal need and achievement. At this stage, one reaches the height of awareness and body-mind connection, which is the boundary of spirituality. At the same time, however, one recognizes, and also learns to live with, the possibility of not ever satisfying even some of the middle range personal (psychological) needs. So another purpose of learning about 'self' is to become more needless and thus cope with the high chance (and deprivations) of not ever finding love or fame or recognition, etc. This is a major requirement for building our spirits.

Recognizing Our Unconscious Needs

We usually refer to 'spirituality' as a special state of transcendence. In reality, spirituality is a need; a high form of psychological need. It is a need that extends from, goads, and reflects our highest level of psychological growth and aspiration. At this point, self-awareness and body-mind connection cease being an unconscious matter in the form of an idea. Rather, they manifest as a conscious affair and a way of life. Referring to Maslow's research, we can conclude that, at the highest level of the needs tree, i.e., self-actualization, the psychological needs approach and intermingle with the spiritual needs of the individual, most likely without him even recognizing it. While most of our psychological needs are felt at subconscious level (as subconscious needs), some of our psychological and most of our spiritual needs have submerged deeper and deeper to the unconscious level for the majority of us (unconscious needs). Dealing with our subconscious needs (e.g., love and belongingness) is already a difficult task despite the fact that at least we recognize them and somehow know how to go about satisfying them. Accordingly, we can appreciate the extreme difficultly of dealing with our unconscious needs that we can hardly even recognize. At the same time, the needs tree model shows that, as we grow, we finally realize that none of the other needs in the middle range (e.g., love, status, recognition) feel important or even an authentic need once we mature enough to look merely for self-actualization and spirituality. All our efforts and pains for satisfying our middle range needs feel so unnecessary and vain.

Our inability to recognize and attend to our unconscious needs (e.g., self-actualization and spirituality) causes constant surges of negative reactions and conditions in our lives, including anxiety, frustration, and psychological dysfunctions. Our hidden potentialities try to surface when we receive signals in the form of strong inner urges, aspirations, and restlessness. We feel a need to explore our potentialities, which seem to reside in our unconscious as precious, unexplored resources. They are available for satisfying our higher needs, including spirituality. In all, learning about our unconscious needs not only protects or relieves us from psychological dysfunctions, but also opens up the opportunity to access our hidden potentialities. It helps us grasp the futility of worrying about our middle-range needs and causing ourselves so much pain for nothing. In the process, we also gain new insights about the real world, which is ordinarily hidden from us. We learn about the world of illusions that has misguided us all along. To achieve these objectives, our challenge is to bring our highest psychological needs, including spirituality, from unconscious into conscious and develop it into a deep drive for self-awareness—a body-mind awareness.

The Spiritual Sensations of Self-actualizers

Maslow describes the characteristics and feelings of self-actualizers who were the subjects of his research in great depth. He stresses that the state of a self-actualizer or a person at a 'peak experience' resembles very much a person achieving some kind of spirituality. From his findings, one can gather that these individuals are not only satisfying their psychological needs, but rather transcending to a new height that is usually witnessed by, and ascribed to, spiritual persons and moods. These individuals overcome their Ego, become self-reliant, and find an extremely high level of consciousness and contentment from the basic things they do. They reach out and touch their spirits. These descriptions indicate that a self-actualizing person senses and explores his spirituality needs even when s/he is merely driven by his/her psychological needs (i.e. recognition and self-actualization). Maslow's findings and theories are good examples of the relationship between human's hidden potentialities and spirituality dimension. Many other scholars have reached similar conclusions based on scientific research. These findings clearly affirm that some intrinsic aspects of our psyches bring us to the threshold of our spirituality. Some of Maslow's findings with respect to the characteristics and feelings of self-actualization (peak) experiences are quoted in the next couple of pages.

"It is true that human beings strive perpetually toward ultimate humanness, which itself may be anyway a different kind of Becoming and growing. It's as if we were doomed forever to try to arrive at a state to which we could never attain. Fortunately we now know this not to be true, or at least it is not the only truth. There is another truth which integrates with it. We are again and again rewarded for good Becoming by transient states of absolute Being, by peak-experiences. Achieving basic-need gratification gives us many peak-experiences, each of which are absolute delights, perfect in themselves, and needing no more than themselves to validate life. This is like rejecting the notion that a Heaven lies some place beyond the end of the path of life. Heaven, so to speak, lies waiting for us through life, ready to step into for a time and to enjoy before we have to come back to our ordinary life of striving. And once we have been in it, we can remember it forever, and feed ourselves on this memory and be

sustained in time of stress." Toward a Psychology of Being, Abraham Maslow, Van Norstrand Reinhold, 1968, page 154.

Maslow's findings regarding his subjects' divine feelings during these peak experiences are in particular interesting and thus some of them are noted below:

"In some reports, particularly of the mystic experience or the religious experience or the philosophical experience, the whole of the world is seen as unity, as a single rich live entity. In other of the peak experiences, most particularly the love experience and aesthetic experience, one small part of the world is perceived as if it were for the moment all of the world. In both cases the perception is of unity." Ibid., page 88.

"...the experience or the object tends to be seen as a whole, as a complete unit, detached from relations, from possible usefulness, from expediency, and from purpose." Ibid., page 74.

"...the percept is exclusively and fully attended to. This may be called "total attention". What I am trying to describe here is very much akin to fascination or complete absorption. In such attention the figure becomes <u>all</u> figure and the ground, in effect disappears, or at least is not importantly perceived. It is as if the figure were isolated for the time being from all else, as if the world were forgotten, as if the percept had become for the moment the whole being." Ibid., page 74.

"...perception can be relatively ego-transcending, self-forgetful, egoless. It can be unmotivated, impersonal, desireless, unselfish, not needing, detached. It can be object-centred rather than ego-centred. That is to say, that the perceptual experience can be organized around the subject as a centering point rather than being based upon the ego." Ibid., page 79.

"In all the common peak experiences which I have studied, there is a very characteristics disorientation in time and space. It would be accurate to say that in these moments the person is outside of time and space subjectively. In the creative furor, the poet or artist becomes oblivious of his surroundings, and of the pas-

sage of time. It is impossible for him when he wakes up to judge how much time has passed. Frequently he has to shake his head as if emerging from a daze to rediscover where he is. But more than this is the frequent report, especially by lovers, of the complete loss of extension in time. Not only does time pass in their ecstasies with a frightening rapidity so that a day may pass as if it were a minute but also a minute so intensely lived may feel like a day or a year." Ibid., page 80.

"At the higher levels of human maturation, many dichotomies, polarities, and conflicts are fused, transcended or resolved. Self-actualizing people are simultaneously selfish and unselfish, Dionysian and Apollonian, individual and social, rational and irrational, fused with others and detached from others, and so on." Ibid., page 91.

"The person at the peak is godlike not only in senses that I have touched upon already but in certain other ways as well, particularly in the complete, loving, uncondemning, compassionate and perhaps amused acceptance of the world and of the person, however bad he may look at more normal moments." Ibid., page 92.

"...as the essential Being of the world is perceived by the person, so also does he concurrently come closer to his own Being (to his own perfection, of being more perfectly himself)." Ibid., page 95.

From the above characteristics of peak experiences of self-actualizers, it appears that spirituality needs are in fact a continuum of the psychological needs and very much interconnected. We strive to deal with our psychological needs to maintain our mental health and strengthen our body-mind connection. As a main step, we build our convictions, ethics, spirits, and certain beliefs to control our psychological defects and needs. Yet it is also interesting to note that while we habitually associate the knowledge of psychology with our mental defects and neediness, in reality, our psyche can bring purity and tranquility to our lives when it is groomed and grown properly. At this state, we approach the spirituality continuum of our psyches once we overcome personal hang-ups and move on beyond our futile middle-range needs and greed that agitate and taint our psyches in our customary living.

We have accepted various psychological theories and we practice them as a body of scientific knowledge with expected benefits and effects. We have come to believe in psychology as a valid scientific approach to deal with one's psyche and to treat the sick with special and sometimes drastic measures. We find these treatments necessary and effective. However, humans' psychic power in terms of spirituality has not yet been given enough attention. Our scepticism toward spirituality stems from the fact that all such ideas have come from gurus, prophets, old cultures, and ordinary people who have not offered a scientific methodology and proof for their claims. Even the assertions made by people with educational credentials and Ph.D.s are speculative and unsubstantiated by scientific evidence. Nevertheless, while proof in all respects is still lacking, it appears that the link between psychology and spirituality is becoming more established and better validated in our minds. Because of our presumptions about the value, and the judgments, of the Western science, we are now more flexible in accepting spirituality ideas as plausible realities.

Also, with the reduction of faith in religions, as partly caused by the disrepute of these organizations, as well as the contradictory themes of the religions themselves, the spirituality needs of individuals must, and seem to, become more active at a different level with a new perspective. Now, people are trying to find it themselves, which is the right way, compared with the traditional blind faith and dependence on others, such as clergies, explaining it to them. It is the right way because spirituality starts with an inward search to find one's self and then reach a higher level of consciousness to see beyond the realm of physical life. It is quite plausible that we intuitively seek spirituality by referring to psychological knowledge that we can find about ourselves. Carl Jung has reached the conclusion that:

"The public desire for more psychological knowledge is largely due to the suffering which results from the disuse of religion and from the lack of spiritual guidance." Psychology and the East, First published in 1978 by Art Paperback, page 125.

Nowadays, in fact, we seek psychological knowledge to penetrate our inner self and satisfy our innate need for spirituality. Let us hope we learn soon to replace religions with our personal spirituality and our proactive compassion.

The Unity of Psychology and Spirituality

The link between psychology and spirituality is obvious, with the individual's 'psyche' being the main common factor to study and heal. In spirituality, however, the psyche steps into the supernatural domain to seek a more fundamental remedy through a divine connection with the universe. In such an instance, the psyche supposedly becomes the same as, or joins, individuals' spirits (or souls) for the purpose of self-therapy and containing the perils of humans' wicked nature. Other disciplines, such as biology and physics, are also finding similar common denominators with spirituality and psychology, which makes future research and theories more intriguing, and perhaps provide a background for understanding our souls.

Spirituality has always been an intrinsic need of humans, except that it has been mostly suppressed and tainted by religions and superstitions and thus lost its potential for building our spirit. Nowadays, however, some evidences from the scientific world affirm the value of spirituality and attention to our souls for physical and mental health and perhaps for reaching a higher wisdom beyond our illusive perceptions of the world. The western world seems willing nowadays to give some benefit of the doubt to the teachings and thoughts of eastern philosophy, such as the Buddhism and the notions of karma and yoga. Modern psychologists, as well as new physicists and philosophers, are speaking similar ideologies offered by eastern philosophers for centuries. The fields of physics, medicine, psychology, philosophy, and many other disciplines are getting more integrated and coming to terms with the ideas that were considered illogical and whimsical a few decades ago. For example, Gary Zukov's scientific conclusions and thoughts as well as Deepak Chopra's assertions related to the field of medicine indicate the convergence of scientific notions into some kind of reconcilable spiritual observations. Some of their remarks have been quoted in several places in this book. The following couple of quotes from Gary Zukov have similar connotations:

"According to quantum mechanics there is no such thing as objectivity. We cannot eliminate ourselves from the picture. We are part of the nature, and when we study the nature there is no way around the fact that nature is studying itself. Physics has become a branch of psychology, or perhaps the other way round." The Dancing Wu Li Masters, Gary Zukov, Morrow 1979, 1st Edition, page 31.

"If the new physics has led us anywhere, it is back to ourselves, which, of course, is the only place that we could go." Ibid., page 114.

Without making a final judgment about the ultimate validity of these assertions, the main purpose here is to reflect scientists' efforts and eagerness to relate psychology and spirituality to hard scientific facts. Obviously, there is still a long way to go before all these speculations find real meaning and application. Nevertheless, we are moving into a new frontier where spirituality research and thoughts could become more objective instead of being dismissed quickly as shallow speculations. Spiritual senses and supernatural notions have always overwhelmed us at a personal level rather regularly, yet spirituality and our need for it is still not well explored and developed. We must redefine the meaning of spirituality and isolate it from superstitions and the rituals of the old era, as well as the new dogmatic presentations of spirituality. We must keep our scepticism, with an open mind, regarding the validity of so many hasty, subjective interpretations about the supernatural and spirituality nowadays. If not careful, the new approach could easily contaminate the foundation of our thoughts in a different way and damage our spirits even more. The only thing we can conclude with some degree of certainty is that our psychological needs extend into our spirituality needs and collectively they drive our existence. We are born with them and we need to satisfy them in order to survive physically and mentally.

The Main Personal Dilemmas

Our subconscious and unconscious needs, i.e., psychological urges and spirituality, drive us regularly to refine the foundation of our thoughts and our life philosophy. Studying and attending to these needs must be a personal habit as part of self-awareness for strengthening our psyche and spirit, and for remembering our day-to-day living purposes. During this study, we understand the nature of our higher needs beyond the basic needs of food and shelter. We should then honour only those needs that can enhance our personal effectiveness in daily life, self-actualization principles, selfless love, and inner happiness. All other superficial needs should be gradually abolished from our lives.

In particular, the following five dilemmas (objectives) are constantly boggling our subconscious mind and demanding our attention for building our spirit, a sensible foundation of thoughts, and our personal life philosophy:

A. Know (about) ourselves. This is the point of reference, focus, foundation, and structure for our thoughts and actions. We achieve a spiritual wisdom through self-awareness and by learning about the dimensions of 'self.' This topic will be covered in Chapter Two.

B. Reconcile facts, myths, and life challenges. This is an attempt to study the *presumed* facts of life in relation to myths and challenges. We like to understand why we are conditioned to believe in certain facts and myths, and how we should deal with them during our journey of life. This topic is explored in detail in Chapters Three and Four of Volume I.

C. Establish a list of basic ingredients of happiness (The 'Formula' in its crudest form). The objective is to study the possibilities of real happiness and decide, on an individual level and independently, how a personal Formula of happiness may be developed. We like to explore the traits of a hypothetical role model, and determine how s/he would behave and define happiness. Accordingly, this would be a definition of a desired self. This subject is discussed in detail in Chapter Seven of Volume I.

D. Establish a philosophy of life. With a grasp of the above objectives (A-C), we would like to establish an overall picture of a hypothetical lifestyle (life philosophy) that can contain, nurture, and direct an ideal personality. This life philosophy should also explain, and help us understand, external factors that have the highest impact on our lives and personality. It must help us judge the prevalent socioeconomic environment objectively. Accordingly, building a philosophy of life would lead us in the journey of life within a path of wisdom about self and the universe. This topic is covered in Chapter Eight in Volume I.

E. Apply the formula of happiness and life philosophy (our 'wisdom') to most common decisions in life. This is for keeping ourselves alert with respect to major life decisions and actions that influence our lives deeply and to be prepared to deal with significant life issues effectively. This is how we apply our foundation of thoughts and our free spirit to guide us in the journey of life. This topic is covered partially in Chapter Thirteen in this volume as a general framework and then expanded in Volume III.

We wrestle with the above five life objectives (dilemmas) routinely, but rather ineffectively, without realizing the process or distinguishing them as fundamental thoughts that affect the building of our spirits. In our minds, however, these objectives (and the ideas revolving around them) are passively and vainly linked, interrelated, and often perceived and pursued intrinsically as a unified path for survival and for finding happiness. Thus, a study of these five life dilemmas (objectives) separately has some value for clarifying this rather messy routine of processing life variables in one's subconscious mind. In particular, the first objective, i.e., knowing (about) ourselves, as discussed in Chapter Two, is quite important for boosting our spirits. The other four objectives are addressed in depth throughout this trilogy as specified above.

For resolving the above noted five life dilemmas and building our spirits, we should first develop the motivation and right mindset for following such huge challenge actively. We should know the factors that goad a person to ponder, grasp, and satisfy his psychological and spirituality needs. After all, not all of us have adequate incentive, interest, time, motivation, or desire to pursue the set of strenuous objectives proposed here. Without a proper incentive and readiness, our efforts would not be sincere and sufficient. Without a proper mindset and attitude even our most obvious and greatest potentialities would not come to fruit.

Preparing Our Minds and Attitude

Attending to our psychological and spirituality needs requires courage and motivation to resist the status quo and the life-conditioning rules containing us. We need personal conviction to explore our deepest feelings and unconscious mind for a preliminary level of self-awareness, which would then turn into an *awareness motion.* Every day a higher level of motivation and satisfaction would fuel the energy required to move ahead and keep pace with the expansion of our mind and spirit. Reading books of old gurus and philosophers helps in sustaining the required momentum for gradual development of a deep personal conviction and for pursuing self-awareness exercises steadily. This approach is quite different from positive thinking techniques that assume people can automatically, with a simple desire, maintain their level of enthusiasm and motivation to get over life obstacles and personal limitations to achieve what they wish.

Positive thinking techniques advocated in recent decades supposedly motivate and enable a person to understand his suppressed needs, take riskier actions, and find happiness. S/he is expected to change his/her mindset quickly while functioning smoothly within his/her normal routines. Yet, unfortunately, the implementation of our good intentions is usually hindered by both human limitations and life's persistent erratic challenges. Only if one has a highly flexible and adaptable mindset, s/he may possibly implement and benefit from some of those positive-thinking techniques. Preaching positive thinking and making people believe that it is easy to change quickly and painlessly are futile attempts. Actually, these efforts often result in further frustration and setback when people fail to fulfil such high expectations from their psyches. For example, videos and books on special diets and workouts, or the use of exercise machines, try to motivate people to change their lifestyles and get major results, but they are mostly marketing gimmicks. After spending their money and raising their hopes for quick results, most people realize that they do not have the right mindset to pursue a rigid and demanding workout program. This leads to further damage of individual's self-image. Overall, positive thinking principles become practical only to the extent they can realistically fit human nature, socioeconomic realities, and each individual's unique personality and potentialities.

Although positive thinking is intended to be an internal (mental) process to induce motivation, it is treated more like an external stimulus—a quick fix. It is supposed to force us believe in ourselves or 'reconsider' our internal feelings and perception of our abilities. It attempts to achieve all these goals without recognizing our deep dysfunctional traits that override all our positive thinking efforts. We get suddenly excited and pursue something for a while, and then lose our motivation and stamina. For changing our mindset, we must become fundamentally convinced of our needs and plans first through gradual self-awareness and by developing a deep conviction about a matter and our mission—and positive thinking per se cannot achieve this.

Contrary to the explicit or implied suggestions by some experts that people can easily change their attitude and personality, people's unique mindsets and life conditions at any specific time and stage of life depend on the environment they have been living in and thus cannot be modified rapidly. People's life conditions and intelligence constrict their ability to change quickly and maintain a new mindset. In order to take advantage of any technique to improve self-image and positive thinking, an internal stimulus is required for developing a tremendous level of motivation merely to understand and manipulate our existing mindset and life conditions. Therefore, the first level of any positive thinking should emphasize on finding the right inner stimuli that can motivate a particular individual. A strong, sustainable personal incentive is required according to each person's level of needs and aspirations. This goal can be achieved only personally through gradual self-awareness and mental adjustments. Only if these prerequisites have been fulfilled, and if s/he still finds it necessary to pursue whatever his/her new challenges are, s/he might utilize his/her gained wisdom and motivation toward the final objectives. S/he would then learn the techniques (including positive thinking) that are expected to help him/her.

Overall, mindset calibration is a long process that should be implemented successfully over time before we can apply any techniques to recondition our thinking and behaving. Never a technique can influence a person's mind to reverse its conditioning quickly and painlessly, and not before deep personal beliefs and convictions allow the use of a technique such as positive thinking. With this guideline, one may ask, 'Then what would be the learning value of any book and particularly this one?' The answer is that discussions in this book are only for the purpose of raising self-awareness. It is intended to provide only the stimulus that people need to ponder and manipulate their own mindsets for whatever purposes. Only personal conviction and perseverance, and mostly due to a real need deeply felt by an individual, can lead to success.

We can never be a positive thinker if we are not inherently a positive doer by the conviction of our inner urges, or if we are not strenuously trained to recondition our beliefs and convictions when necessary. Our thoughts and deeds are reinforced from the same source, i.e., our habits and conditioning forces registered in our brains. Thus, we cannot turn into a positive thinker or doer if our mind is not properly recalibrated and prepared to be one such person. Many years of reconditioning (self-awareness) may reverse our mentality to become a natural positive thinker and doer, but never as a result of reading a book or attending a few seminars. A *real* positive thinking can be achieved only through a rigid process of mindset transformation, which requires a great deal of patience, motivation, and hard work.

Delving into the questions of, 'Who we are and what we are here for,' can be a good scheme for stirring the initial motivation, however. This initiative would soon generate the inner power required to resolve all our life's dilemmas and build our spirit. As our self-awareness heightens, so does our power of self-commitment and energy to create a sensible life philosophy and make proper changes in our mentality and lifestyles.

CHAPTER TWO
Knowing (about) Ourselves

Knowing (about) ourselves is a sacred crusade to grasp our existence and its potential value. The goal is to access our essence as a bewildered human and to understand the motives behind our thoughts and deeds within the finer realms of the universe (and not society per se). Thus, a definition of 'self' has evolved, mostly as a symbol of our idealism and the perfection we seek in ourselves. We hope to find a sign of humility and contentment beneath the contaminated and convoluted minds pervading the society. Yet, our search for 'self' also shows our despair and lack of confidence in the purity of 'who we are.' Witnessing too much of our wickedness makes us wonder if God had really meant us to be this bad or whether we have become like this all on our own! Of course, there are also some evidences of divine abilities and sensitivities (including compassion) that some of us can behold and portray occasionally. These inherent abilities and sensitivities reveal the essence of 'self,' because they appear to be instinctual and in most cases noble. In this sense, 'self' is not merely a moral side, or internally focused characteristics, of human that loathes and defies the selfish humanity surrounding us. Rather, 'self' reflects mostly those innate aspects of a person that seeks a proper means of relating to the outside world and other humans, but also craves a natural connection to the supernatural dimensions of life.

Our genetics determines some aspects of the self. The roles that parents, teachers, and society play also have direct, deep impacts on how we observe the world containing us and the world we imagine is right for us. Another important aspect of 'self' manifests in one's dynamic mentality and determination to change things, to grow from an existing state to the next in order to remain content and healthy. Each one of these aspects of 'self' must be studied with scrutiny and an open mind.

'Self'-awareness starts with a study of humans' crooked perceptions of themselves and then delves into a process of recognizing and analysing our personal idiosyncrasies, needs, and potentialities. In particular, understanding the inherent relationship between humans' spirituality and potentiality, as divine dimensions of 'self,' is important for knowing who we are and for redeeming our spirits. We feel empty and dispirited if we cannot nurture our potentialities and gain our personal sense of spirituality.

The ambiguous usage of 'self' in different connotations and contexts could be annoying for many of us. Even trying to *explain* what 'self' constitutes or contains is quite cumbersome and subjective. Yet most people have some personal notion of 'self.' Chapter Five of Volume I discusses 'self,' along with 'ego' and 'model,' as individuals' three aspects of personality. In this Volume, however, we discuss the role and characteristics of this elusive 'self' for connecting us to the universe through our consciousness and spirit, but also guiding our daily endeavours according to our level of self-awareness and integrity. For this dual role of the self (i.e., our needs for spirituality and practical living), several aspects of 'self' collectively establish who we are and what we need from life. Using all these general knowledge as a platform, examining and understanding 'self' is nevertheless a personal, never-ending endeavour.

For our limited study, the main aspects (or essence) of 'self' are explored within the following seven dimensions:

1. Spirituality
2. Potentiality
3. Individualism (integrity, compassion)
4. Relationships
5. Contributions
6. Growth
7. Social responsibility

Spirituality

Spirituality is the main aspect of 'self.' As an inherent human urge, it evolves from our psyche along our psychological needs to offer a much deeper sense and purpose for our existence. It has the power to lift our spirit in general, but also soothe our melancholy naturally. 'Spirituality need' is, in fact, more instinctual than most other psychological needs that we have developed artificially, such as the need for love, power, recognition, or status. Yet, for many of us, this need remains in our subconscious, or unconscious, simply because we are unaware of its nature or role, although many people try to satisfy it through religions and superstitions.

Actually, the upbringing influence in many societies still deprives a large population from exploring their spirituality need independently. They get brainwashed quickly by some debilitating religious teachings and stories, which seem to fulfil (but actually only kill) their innate spiritual need. After all, it is easier and faster to accept a religion according to some naïve illusions and move on, instead of bothering their brains with an elusive idea of spirituality without any of the luring religious promises. Trusting some other people's stories and promises (nonsense) about the heaven and God's mercy or punishments relieve their natural urge for a self-assessed spirituality so conveniently too. In all, they are simply too lazy or unprepared to think independently and figure out the inherent purposes of spirituality outside the tempting teachings of the perceived world.

On the other hand, some people's ambitions, pragmatism, or apathy toward religious ideologies dampens their spirituality need. Especially when we are young, we usually have many aspirations and worries, so the last thing we have time to explore is our spirituality need. We normally have a tendency, due to our upbringing and education, to think of physical and material things rather than intangible and inconsequential concepts. Sometimes, we detach ourselves from spiritual ideas during our contemplations or communication with others, simply because we fear being associated with superstition and naïveté. We believe spirituality makes us look outmoded, soft, and vulnerable, which is contrary to what our culture and value system is propagating.

Nonetheless, for many reasons, including family beliefs, culture, and our wrong impression of spirituality and its purpose, we suppress our spirituality need unconsciously. Under these circumstances, we usually reach a point where only a big shock, crisis, insight, or enlightenment can trigger our spirituality senses. Of course, in desperate situations, we resort to our spirituality urges subconsciously to seek the extra energy that we need to face a major challenge or pull through a crisis. Somehow, we seem to know about this source of energy that lies within our spiritual and non-physical realms. But then we forget about it or ignore it when we do not have an immediate use for it. We forget that this spiritual energy manifests merely through an ongoing conscious acknowledgment of its existence. Carl Jung states:

"There is an undeniable psychological fact that the more one concentrates on one's unconscious contents, the more they become charged with energy; they become vitalized, as if illuminated from within. In fact they turn into something like a substi-

tute reality." Psychology and the East, Carl Jung, Published 1978 by Ark Paperback, page 124.

Whatever the source of spiritual energy, it is hard to prove it scientifically, although some scholars claim the evidence of some kind of psychological and medical nature.

"The possibility that each person is an infinite being is becoming more real now. Gifted with real flexibility in our nervous systems, we all have the choice to build boundaries or tear them down. Every person is continually manufacturing an infinite array of thoughts, memories, desires, objects, and so on. These impulses, rippling through the ocean of consciousness, become your reality. If you knew how to control the creation of impulses of intelligence, you would be able not only to grow new dendrites but anything else." Quantum Healing, Deepak Chopra, M.D., Bantam Books, 1989, page 225.

Other scientists and scholars have offered similar thoughts and personal experiences to confirm the existence of a mysterious source of energy hidden within humans. Yet, it is difficult for many of us to associate or even understand the true implications of claims similar to the above quotes by Deepak Chopra and Carl Jung. Only our own random encounters with divine feelings can motivate us to explore spirituality more deeply. In such moments, we feel relaxed, our spirits lift, and our mental capacity increases, all of which provides a clearer vision of reality for making better decisions effortlessly. We feel a mysterious power of insight, which is a new type of experience, like a divine source of wisdom coming to one's assistance when it is called upon selflessly and purposefully. Obviously, the conditions for asking and receiving the energy and insight should be right, including the sincerity and genuineness of our intentions.

For many of us, the 'need for spirituality' should be awakened and brought into our conscious thoughts. Some suggestions have been offered mainly in this book, but also other volumes of the trilogy, about achieving this objective. The most difficult part of it is, of course, to change our attitude and mentality beyond our conventional view of spirituality. We must stop seeing it as synonymous with superstition or abstract non-physical concepts. As Carl Jung says:

"... spiritual understanding ... is a capacity which no man is born with, but which he can only acquire through special training and special experience." Psychology and the East, Ark Paperback, 1978, page 76.

Jung's point about 'the capacity for *understanding* spirituality requires training and special personal experience' is important. However, more important is to remember that the seed of spirituality, as an inherent psychological human need, is already cultivated in 'self' when we are born, and we feel incomplete and lost forever until we learn to nourish it. In fact, through our sporadic divine experiences, we find the naturalness of our need for spirituality as an inherent link to Nature. Spirituality arises from our natural belief in a sacred dimension of being ('self'), which we readily feel within us.

Potentiality

The second dimension of 'self' contains our potentialities.

We have two types (levels) of potentialities—genetic and divine. The former consists of our unique capabilities, such as artistic, intellectual, or special talents according to our inherited properties and superiority. We are somewhat familiar with these potentialities and apply them rather routinely, though not completely, for our careers and creations. On the other hand, divine potentialities refer to the universal capacities of humans as soulful creatures. This inherent human quality, which links them to the universe, is less understood and often abused, although everybody feels it subconsciously, depending upon their level of self-awareness, of course. Our veritable insights and intuitions, which surface in *special circumstances* and lead to the feelings of spirituality and self-actualization, manifest our 'divine' potentiality. This abstract perspective about humans' divine potentialities indeed fits the findings of 'self-actualization' research, where peak experiences (and spiritual sensations) occur subsequent to some insight or discovery. The question then is, 'What those *special circumstances* are that make such moments of ecstasy achievable?' And, 'How one is moved to pursue a wisdom path that makes such special circumstances and moments of spirituality possible?'

Divine potentialities reflect humans' inherent capacity to feel and seek a connection to the universe. This capacity manifests through supreme intuitions and feelings of spirituality, which appear to be unique to humans (as privileged creatures of God). We also imagine that a particular purpose exists for this sacred capacity in humans. We seem lost and lack a real identity until we activate our divine potentialities and answer many questions about our existence. Definitely, some innate urges initiate the proccss of inquiry and curiosity in a person, perhaps a need for awareness about self or some matter related to human life or suffering. We may also say that our past peak experiences (however small on most occasions) along with new intuitions create a state of mind to focus on an idea exclusively and fully. This basic attention generates the energy needed to initiate and pursue the process of exploration. This energy, which goads us to recognize and delve into worthy endeavours, is by itself a spiritual energy (our spirit) because it expands our regular span of attention and intelligence. It represents the divine potentiality that exists in all humans, though we have to know how to honour and activate it at a higher capacity.

This energy (spirit or potentiality) would not only generate the insight and intuition that enrich us immediately, but also lead to still higher levels of sacred curiosity and discovery as a result of the new feelings of actualization and spirituality. Every time we go through this cycle, we reaffirm, revitalize, and intensify the level of spiritual feelings and the energy that stems from them.

Spirituality reflects humans' ultimate level of aspirations (and needs) at the highest spectrum of human potentiality. Thus, it induces a particularly high level of attention and awareness, and it increases our stamina and motivation to understand and pursue worthwhile objectives in life. Ideally, if we realize this potentiality early in our lives, we can better focus on the essential facets of life and grasp life's real opportunities and purposes. We would not waste our lives on trivia and materialistic values, while constantly doubting the purpose of our struggles, too. Spiritual energy helps us see beyond the obvious and rudimentary facts, and thus brings out the best in us.

The energy that stems from our divine potentiality is not an end in itself, as a sense of spirituality per se. Rather, it helps us penetrate our unconscious mind and explore the wisdom that resides beyond the primary boundaries of our intelligence. It allows us to envision those dimensions of ourselves that we have ignored and suppressed. The power of enlightenment in fact comes from the same source that induces insight when a person's new potentialities are excavated. Enlightenment and insight are parallel phenomena.

Both levels of our potentialities (i.e., genetic and divine) have several effects, each of which is a source of new energy and wisdom by itself. One aspect of these potentialities relates to higher awareness, insight, and creativity that emerge during our endeavours, such as the music that Mozart composed. As said about his music, it appears that it came to him directly from God. Apparently, he had made a comment about waking in the middle of the night and sensing music pouring in magically. He just wrote them down without a single correction. His creations are not directly attributed to a state of spirituality, as no clear evidence exists to show him as a devout spiritual (despite his religious music, remarks, and rearing influence). Nevertheless, most likely his sense of actualization and deep potentialities gave him a unique power and intuition to penetrate his unconscious mind and obtain the energy, the insight, and the genius that one finds in his music. In a way, we can say that his ingenuity was already his personal means of spirituality and enough in itself, since the main goal of spirituality is to give us the power and energy of creation and feeling. This is exactly the kind of property that all religions lack. They actually kill people's divine capacity and power of intuition and instead make people dogmatic and naive.

It is possible that the two types of potentialities converge at some stage of one's life (maybe even childhood) to create a genius. People like Mozart and Einstein have definitely benefited from both genetic and divine potentialities knowingly or inadvertently. The majority of us, however, at best apply a limited supply of our genetic potentialities for survival and personal growth. For accessing our divine potentiality, however, we can incite our spirituality energies (our beliefs) more consciously. Through self-awareness and by building inner beliefs, we can trigger our divine potentiality for insight and wisdom without additional efforts. Spiritual insight grows parallel with the level of self-awareness as we attain selflessness and enlightenment eventually.

One aspect of knowing 'who we are' is to explore and activate our potentialities, both genetic and divine, most realistically and perhaps professionally by the aid of an expert. Detecting our true potentialities has a lifelong implication, because it affects not only our routine and major life decisions, but also the level of energy we ignite for choosing the right path of life. Focusing on trivial life matters, pursuing a dull career, stagnation, and behaving contrary to our real potentialities cause personal suffering, because we are constantly trying to be the person we are not built to be. Our struggles to pretend being someone else—with a different personality and temperament—hurt us more than anybody else can harm us. Aside from these negative psychological effects, ignoring our real potentialities would be a complete waste of life and losing a chance to actualize our 'self.'

Our genetic and divine potentialities have the same root as one's personal characteristics—as an entity of 'self'—even though they are distinguished here for their opposing roles, i.e., for making money versus exploring our divinity. Our only relief from life's hardships comes from realizing our potentialities and working harder—an odd mystery of creation all by itself. We must work even harder and sacrifice even more if we seek real happiness. Thus, even for people denying the power of spirituality, excavating their real potentialities requires an understanding of 'self,' which is ultimately the only practical means of handling life's hardships, while exploring its beauties for possible happiness. Even if we do not believe in spirituality per se, our inner urges for self-actualization would eventually awaken our divine potentialities. Conversely, for reaching our unconscious mind and activating our divine potentialities, knowing our 'self' becomes an inevitable task, and a major step, for all intelligent people.

Individualism (Integrity, Compassion)

Individualism is the nucleus of 'self,' because it must ensure our survival and progress in society while fighting the evils of social living. Its goal is to strengthen our spirit, integrity, and compassion instead of becoming ruthless or losing our resilience. Individualism portrays the simple and pure characteristics of an evolved man with a transcended soul. His integrity and compassion lead him to deal with others fairly and avoid wickedness. More importantly, however, individualism reflects the traits of a man in peace with himself and the world despite the pervasive societal imperfections and weaknesses.

Defining 'individualism' as a transcended state of being rightly shows our mistrust in the inherent purity of human nature. It reflects our realistic view of human character and its influence on our cultures and lifestyles. It reveals our desperate struggle with humans' natural tendency toward immorality as their basic qualities. On the other hand, our societies hinder the advance of individualism as a common human attribute. Unfortunately, individualism and integrity often sound like some rare virtues found only in saints and highly evolved individuals—like some divine manifestations beyond most humans' capacity.

Humans' low integrity affects them mostly in their relationships, but also personally. One becomes what he practices as part of coping with all the hypocrisies and deceit in society. He is forced to become cruel like everybody else despite his potentials to be a better human being. We see people who have become so absorbed in their evilness that malice has become their real nature. They cannot do anything without some form of treachery even when it does not have a direct benefit to them. Their individuality has simply collapsed to a mere deceit-brain. Strangely enough, they actually fall for their own lies with such deep commitment they often sacrifice even their valuable assets in the process, including their families and friends. The world of deceit and hypocrisy that they choose to live in contradict even the raw social ethics, let alone a sense of humanness. They just float within a vastly crooked illusion of life and behave like the devil.

The Webster's dictionary defines individualism as, 'The conception that all values, rights, and duties originate in individuals.' Thus, individualism seems like an attempt to gain our independence and establish our identity, not merely in society, but mostly in our own heads. We like to 'know (about) ourselves' and the possibility of being a better person. Therefore, we strive to assess ourselves in terms of values, rights, and duties that we have adopted (created) in the process of earning and proving our identity.

We try to understand where our values come from, how authentic they are, and how they help humanity and us. In terms of our rights, we ensure they coincide with the rights of others, so that all individuals and society as a whole can move toward a peaceful harmony and relative relief from life hardships. The problem nowadays is that a person's rights often turn into self-serving demands on others for personal gains and interests. People have difficulty making this distinction when looking for their rights. They try to impose their misperceived rights on others deliberately or inadvertently by their egotistical attitude and unrelenting struggle for power and authority with little regard for the rights of other human beings.

With respect to our duties, individualism reiterates our personal obligations and social responsibilities. Some of them are instinctual, such as our duties toward our children and parents. Other duties, e.g., toward our spouses and friends, are expected to come natural to us, too, if genuine feelings exist. However, in reality, people are too self-absorbed nowadays to maintain their integrity and fulfil these types of duties naturally. Therefore, they must extend extra efforts more consciously to discharge their duties to some degree at least. Finally, some duties are mostly moral obligations, such as our duties at work and society. Our passivity in acknowledging and discharging our duties may be intentional or due to mere ignorance. Intentional passivity is hard to repair, as it mostly reflects our pomposity, deep psychological flaws, and the impact of social adaptation. Ignorance, on the other hand, can be remedied a bit easier through self-awareness and involvement.

Overall, individualism reflects the quality of our choices, decisions, and actions, as we determine and practice our rights, values, and duties for accomplishing notable purposes. While the objective of 'individualism' is to strengthen the inherent value of 'self' as a wise and humble person, it also stresses on personal integrity to adjust our values, rights, and duties in line with the needs of all humanity. Individualism is not merely an inner growth and satisfaction, but also an outer reflection of integrity and morality. The Webster's definition of 'individualism' does not quite reflect the need for the rightness of one's values, rights, duties. Yet, without integrity and compassion, we cannot set the right 'values,' as we cannot see their rightness. And we cannot comprehend the value of people's 'rights,' because our criteria of rightness is personal and selfish. Contrary to common view to interpret individualism as a means of self-absorption, its value lies mostly in a person's regard for other individuals' rights. In fact, individualism is an inner exploration instead of an outwardly ostentatious presentation of one's Ego, as it is mostly implied in our common pretensions of individualism.

Individualism evolves only through compassion and modesty while a person gauges the truthfulness of his connection to other individuals, things, and concepts with a genuine interest and care. Only then, s/he can see the rights of other individuals and the values of things and concepts in their purest sense in line with his/her own authentic life purposes. Without compassion and integrity, one lacks the sensitivity and sensibility required for perceiving things or people outside one's rigid and biased prejudgments. The lack of compassion and modesty reflects Ego domination, which is the main hindrance for knowing our 'self.'

Each one of the seven dimensions of 'self' is a source of energy with the same effects noted for the first two dimensions, i.e., spirituality and potentiality. The energy from 'individualism' stems from the integrity of our choices, decisions, and actions. A sense of 'self' realization lifts our spirit when we finally choose a modest option after contemplating many self-serving possibilities, make a compassionate decision, or take a worthy action. We strive to make the right choices with integrity and compassion for the betterment of humanity and for building our own spirit, despite our sour experiences and the normal distractions of social living. Perfecting every dimension of 'self' brings more energy and wisdom for living peacefully with contentment. This proactive mentality helps us build our integrity and spirit to go through life with minimal confusion and distress.

Relationships

The fourth dimension of 'self' manifests in our relationships, in terms of connecting to our surroundings (including other humans and things) for raising our spirit and energy. Other than our instinctual urge for socializing, we have an inherent sense of connection with the universe and Nature. Accordingly, compassion and integrity become equally important for this aspect of 'self' too.

Relationships enrich our lives when people, especially couples, share life experiences together. Furthermore, relationships motivate us to accept more risks and make more sacrifices than we would consider doing otherwise. We work harder and think deeper because of our urge to keep our relationships strong and healthy. Of course, relationships often bring us anxiety and frustration, and they increase our doubts about the true nature of human beings. In our relationships, we give and receive passion and compassion; we despise each other and feel deep animosity toward others; we help each other develop things and ideas and then turn around and kill one another. Sometimes we seem to get close and understand a person and the next day we feel so completely strange and hostile. We all seem to be saying the same things, but are unable to communicate. And while we feel our ever-increasing need for trust and sharing our thoughts with somebody, the whole society seems to have become robotic and passionless—unwilling to listen and cooperate. In all, our relationships raise our spirit on some occasions and deflate it quite frequently too. That is why managing them is a big challenge and responsibility for 'self.'

Our relationships also has the potential of raising our awareness about ourselves when, in some situations, people's hints can be a more objective judge of our character. Their viewpoints or even harsh reactions provide a good source of reflection for learning about ourselves. Without getting some input or a reason to think, we can hardly be objective about who we are. Our Egos and idiosyncrasies prevent us from judging ourselves honestly. Of course, we must trust those people who give us feedback directly or subtly. Their method of advising us must be effective, too, in order for us to at least think about their direct inputs or subtle hints. We normally have deep doubts about other individuals' intelligence, objectivity, and judgment. In fact, we often believe others are ignorant and biased, and that their judgment is malicious or at least not based on a realistic view of life and us. Our doubts about people's objectivity and character are often correct. Yet, relationships and people's inputs make us think about ourselves more than any other tool that is out there for knowing who we are—the 'self.'

Despite our supreme need for healthy relationships, it is getting harder to build constructive ones nowadays due to, (a) people's misperceptions about the nature of love and relationships, and (b) their inability (or unwillingness) to relate and communicate a bit less selfishly. They cannot portray a real image of themselves, so their partners are confused and misled. In this contaminated environment, relationships have become calculating, robotic and pretentious for the sake of coping and keeping the general appearances as long as possible. We portray a false image of ourselves for the sake of being accepted and popular in society. And we have become more confused about the nature of human beings due to the complexity and vanity of relationships. We are also becoming more sceptical about the purpose of our relationships—its healthiness, and partners' level of sincerity and genuineness. All these obstacles for building good relationships and connecting with people and the universe have dampened our sense of 'self' as well as our spirit, which is the essence of our being. As our 'self' is becoming weaker every year, we wonder who we really are and why we live.

The form, depth, and completeness of our relationships are major factors for 'knowing (about) our 'self.'' Partners' various personal needs and expectations constitute the form of a relationship. The extent and scope of partners' genuine feelings depict the depth of a relationship. And the accuracy of partners' perceptions about each other and their relationship determines the completeness of a relationship. Of course, our encounters with ourselves and Nature are other forms of relationships that are also important for knowing about ourselves.

Therefore, the exercise of 'knowing (about) oneself,' requires a study of our relationships with other human beings, Nature, and ourselves. Understanding the relationship with ourselves is extremely important, as it could reveal the level of our objectivity, integrity, wisdom, and a large host of other important information. First, we must have a capacity to assess this relationship honestly, however. If we notice a major discrepancy between what we think of the form, depth and completeness of this relationship compared with the feedback we receive from other people and our conscience, we may try to find the reasons a little less selfishly or ask an expert to help us with this process. It is also quite possible that what others think of us is due to their biases and perceptions of us based on their personal values, which we may no longer share with them. Therefore, in some instances, a rejection may in fact be an indication of us being on the right track for our divine purposes, although it may be making others uncomfortable. However, we must be careful when making judgments about others and ourselves from personal perceptions per se, or from the impressions we get from others. Often, it is difficult to comprehend the real intentions of others or depend on our perceptions of ourselves and of others.

We must know what we should reasonably expect to get out of our relationships, and usually keep our expectations modest or even low for longer lasting relationships with minimal frictions. Naturally, partners' expectations clash in relationships due to their unique needs and perceptions. In fact, their exaggerated needs often ruin the whole intention for any kind of relationship. Thus, it is crucial to know the real purposes of a successful relationship and its particular requirements instead of relying on our misleading personal whims and perceptions, which we apply to build a long list of ludicrous expectations. We should then decide what we are willing to give up to make a relationship more stable, and how comfortable we are in doing so. What do we need or expect to receive in return? Can the other party give us what we need? Can we keep this relationship without imposing our needs on the other party? And if not, how long do we think we can tolerate not having our needs satisfied? We should resist our ulterior motives or interests beyond what we express explicitly and expect to get from a particular relationship. Grasping and honouring the authentic needs of relationships is an integral attribute of 'self,' in addition to its importance for enriching our routine lives. The minute we lose our basic sense of integrity and individualism about our intention for a relationship, it is only reasonable to expect failure and major disappointment. For example, if one is seeking a partner for financial exploitation, the relationship is obviously doomed from the beginning.

The simplest, most gratifying type of relationship is when a person gives his/her love or attention to someone or something without an expectation for anything in return. The relationship is personal and its reward, i.e., the inner satisfaction, is the experience itself. When we learn to enjoy Nature, nothing in the world can substitute the purity and reverence of this relationship. One simply enjoys the beauty, power, and delicacy of every single aspect of this experience without expecting outer rewards or a lasting commitment. The love of our children is an experience in pure selflessness. This may, of course, change when kids grow up and the parent-child relationship creates a new atmosphere and form. A relationship between grownup kids and their parents would have a different requirement, although it usually continues to stay less selfish on parents' side. The nature of parent-child relationship changes anyway, because all the three aspects of form, depth, and completeness of their relationships change. On the other hand, the selfish love of something or somebody emerges out of love for self, and from the need for attention and dependence on others.

'Who we are' strongly dictates the type of relationships we can create and be comfortable in, including the option of choosing solitude. Our personal preference for the type of relationships we like to maintain changes according to our personal growth and the life philosophy we choose at any point in our lives. Overall, our perceptions and expectations from a relationship develop according to our personal needs, maturity, and the strength of the 'self.' The more superficial our needs, the more primitive and clashing our relationships would be. If we are still obsessed with our needs for power, money, social acceptance, or fame, we get stuck in relationships that may support those needs, but ruin our 'self' and cause interpersonal frictions too. If self-actualization need drives a person, s/he would search for more profound relationships that can help him/her achieve those higher goals and sustain his/her individuality.

In primitive relationships, we forget—and nobody reminds us either—that our real potentialities go much beyond the superficial goals that we try to satiate in our contacts with others. We merely endure those relationships and perhaps even consider them our happiest life experiences too. Meanwhile, our real potentialities and self-actualization needs often remain unfulfilled because our time and energy are consumed on the shallow needs of our relationships. Unfortunately, most relationships nowadays grow around partners' selfish needs that infect their relationship and prevent the growth of partners' potentialities too.

The topic of relationships can be studied from different perspectives to highlight the perplexing dimensions of 'self.' Overall, our relationships directly affect 'who we are' or want to be, especially considering the long-term effects of being in some relationships, like marriage. The level of partners' individualism, compassion, independence, and integrity determines the format and strength of their relationship. Accordingly, our social conundrums and chaos are very much due to the loss of integrity of our relationships—because friendships, marriages, family, and organization relationships have mostly become calculating and uncompassionate. We waste almost all our lives in a large variety of long-term relationships and quarrel about various selfish needs and demands of others and our own. Therefore, we hardly get a chance to explore our 'self.'

Overall, 'relationships' is an important dimension of 'self' because it can either boost or threaten a person's attitude toward 'self,' as well as the other elements of 'self' such as spirituality, individualism, etc. The integrity of 'self' is often threatened when partners feel obliged to compromise their standards in order to maintain a primitive relationship.

Volume III of this trilogy explores relationships and marriage in detail as major life decisions. Organization relationships are studied in Volume III too.

Contributions

The fifth dimension of 'self' evolves when we selflessly devote our thoughts and deeds outwardly—for the objectives that are not self-serving by any means.

'Contributions' reflect one's ultimate life purposes. 'Who we are' is also measured by our modest accomplishments—the marks we leave behind as a trace of our existence. In essence, a person's life purposes direct him/her toward certain goals and possible accomplishments that comprise his/her contributions to other human beings' welfare, though 'self' obtains a sense of actualization and magnificence too.

Studying the research findings of Maslow, it appears that the concept of self-actualization coincides very closely with the philosophy of 'self' and 'being.' He explains the characteristics of peak experiences within which one senses the most significant and pleasant aspect of humanness. These findings show that any significant contribution not only causes self-actualization, but also authenticates 'self' as an inherent element of humanness.

Self-actualization is certainly a valuable personal experience in the way it induces sacred feelings and moments beyond the common experiences of the perceived world. Yet its higher significance lies in the mere *contributions* that result from a person's endeavours. Most often, the feelings of a self-actualizer result directly from the anticipation of the value of one's work as a contribution to others and society, rather than a selfish gratification of personal success. This is true because actualization and peak experiences happen only in pursuit of worthwhile purposes and projects. The main goal is to make a significant contribution. Even a personal capacity to think in these terms is precious all in itself. Maslow has referred to the self-validating aspect of peak experiences as an end in itself without explicitly raising the sense of contribution that a self-actualizer feels automatically as part of his endeavours.

"The peak experience is felt as a self-validating, self-justifying moment which carries its own intrinsic value with it. That is to say it is an end in itself, what we may call an end-experience rather than a means-experience. It is felt to be so valuable an experience, so great a revelation, that even to attempt to justify it takes away its dignity and worth." Toward the Psychology of Being, Abraham Maslow, Van Nostrand Reinhold, 2nd Edition, 1968, page 79.

The self-validating aspect of peak experiences can, of course, be justified as an end in itself (*which carries its own intrinsic value*). But an even more intrinsic value is evident in the initial purpose of a researcher or explorer who begins his/her journey with the idea of making a contribution. That inherent intention is always present as the main intrinsic value behind all the feelings of self-actualization. We can say that, on the one hand, peak experiences depend on the significance of the purpose and its impact on humanity. On the other hand, we know that these peak experiences happen when a self-actualizer attains a high level of humanness, and perhaps lives in a state of spirituality. Together, the state of humanness and the significance of his experience (and the results of his/her work) reflect a person's egoless attempt to make a worthwhile contribution to society. In brief, if we consider a self-actualizer's product a true reflection of his compassion and humanness, we can easily agree that his/her contributions surge from pure devotion and conviction rather than a mechanical motion or ambitions induced by shallow personal needs and greed. Only these kinds of selfless contributions reveal the essence of 'who we are.'

A person receives substantial inner rewards instantaneously when s/he contributes to society, although receiving a reward has never been the intention or motivation for him/her as a scientist, a writer, an inventor, or an explorer. S/he is only following his/her instincts and talents for unselfish purposes with no expectation. But this very natural urge that drives him/her to spend his/her life and energy to achieve something activates the inherent 'self' surging within him/her, which then automatically brings him/her unparallel joy and ecstasy. That is the 'spirit' of the 'self.'

It is hard to imagine the feelings of a self-actualizer and the way his/her spirit ascends beyond the realms of physical existence. Yet, the lack of imagination is exactly what prevents us from actualizing our 'self.' Our limited perceptions of life, and our obscure definition of success, do not allow us grow psychologically to seek self-actualization and aesthetic values found only in a meaningful path of life. We cannot imagine a life outside the perceived world. Therefore, we remain ignorant about this vital dimension of 'who we are,' and how our contributions may develop and signify it.

Growth

The sixth dimension of 'self' is its inner urge to grow and attain the highest level of awareness and wisdom.

We are bound by nature to grow biologically and psychologically. The physical growth, from childhood to adolescence, to middle and old ages, has been accepted as a fact that extends from birth to death in a steady manner with little control by us. We refer to the physical aspect of growth as aging, although the increase in the size and strength of body are implied as well. The body reaches an optimal growth regardless of its size and strength, perhaps around the age of 30, before starting to decline. Overall, bodily growth may be viewed mainly in terms of aging. After certain age, we resent the growth as one feels the loss of attraction and vitality that have high social appeals. With aging, lethargy and body shrinkage or fat replace our vigour and youth, and thus the growth after certain age becomes undesirable. We are aware of this aging process, we anticipate it, and become more concerned and conscious about it when we reach probably 30 or 40 and see the signs of old age, grey hair, wrinkles, loss of energy, etc. We try in many ways to stop this undesirable aspect of biological growth at all costs, to no avail. The point is that while we accept the desirable portion of this growth gracefully, we find the second stage saddening. This unflattering growth affects our behaviour, spirit, and outlook on life. Mid-age crisis that we often tease one another with has in fact a major influence on people's level of doubts and decisions about themselves, their lives, and their options.

We strive to develop methods of reducing the negative aspects of growth in the second stage, or at least make ourselves look younger. We do more physical exercise, take vitamins, are careful about our diet, dye our hair, and avoid strenuous bodily activities, cigarettes, and liquor, etc. We try to feel good about our body and about ourselves. Feeling good about our bodies—even though we often only pretend it—minimizes the negative psychological effects of being in the second stage of our physical growth. In addition to these impotent methods of alleviating our psychological depression because of aging, another major factor helps us overcome, forget, or ignore the effects of aging. This factor is maturity—the individual's psychological growth.

The process of 'knowing about ourselves' definitely involves a thorough knowledge of our bodily needs. We should learn about the things we ought to do with our body, not only to reduce the negative effects of aging on body, but also to support our psyche in dealing with the negative thoughts of aging and death. Also, 'knowing about ourselves' has a lot to do with the way we can grow psychologically, become mature in the way we actualize our self, use our potentialities to make more valuable contributions and to develop more integrity, compassion, individualism, and meaningful relationships with ourselves and others. People lose their motivation for living when they have no knowledge and control of their bodies and do not think or act in terms of their mental growth, especially if they are in the second stage of their aging process, i.e., negative body growth.

Contrary to physical growth that goes through two stages of positive and negative bodily experiences, psychological growth is a natural and continuous progression, subject to individuals' awareness, participation, and conscious efforts to achieve it. Everybody, with relative physical and mental health, has the capacity to nurture his psychological growth throughout his/her life by understanding the meaning and methods of heightening mental growth. In fact, the whole process of 'knowing about self,' and doing the right things—to transcend 'self' beyond the boundaries of a normal person to a spiritual being—is for goading our psychological growth and keeping our spirits high.

There is a kind of risk associated with growth, though: Growth demands the risk of breaking away from our existing dependencies in order to break into new boundaries and to experience new concepts and thoughts. Our reaction and aversion to this risk hinder our psychological growth. To grow psychologically, we must attempt new (meaningful) things and this is sometimes too daunting or hurtful for some of us. We may be willing or even attempting to reinforce our psychological growth, but some of our psychological defects prevent it. We are addicted to our stagnant way of living and thinking. In order to grow, we should let go of the past, but this involves losing the security we have in the existing value systems, or losing the support or respect of others. As we do not have the insight of living in the present, we cling to our pasts and its conditioning forces. We wish to experience and search new meanings for our lives, but they all sound threatening to us. We do not want to give up our attachments to many established forms of whatever(!)—family, love, status, lifestyle, thoughts, attitude, sex, etc. The safety of our existing habits, values, thoughts, defence mechanisms, inhibits the possibility of a new outlook and a fresh thought process.

Unless we overcome most of our psychological defects, we have no chance for growth; and without psychological growth, we intensify the level of suffering and stress all our lives, as we are not maturing or satisfying our higher needs. We do not build an antidote for aging. It is not easy to get rid of psychological flaws that hinder our growth, of course. This is because we often have difficulty recognizing and acknowledging the sources and depth of our defects, which is the first phase in overcoming them. Psychological growth ultimately requires the growth and awakening of one's spirituality too. Yet, most of us have difficulty finding an authentic sense of spirituality for all the reasons noted in the previous chapter.

While we cannot control physical growth—the aging process—, we can have good control over our psychological health and growth. This control of psychological growth, along with a conscious care of the body, to the extent possible, would assist us in minimizing the agony of old age and the inevitable sufferings of life. In order to know 'who we are,' we ought to measure the extent of psychological growth that we have allowed ourselves, what we know about this growth, and how it can be achieved and perhaps maximized.

Social Responsibility

The seventh dimension of 'self' is its ability to acknowledge and fulfil certain responsibilities.

Whether we realize it or not, like it or not, or practice it enough or not, we all have a responsibility toward one another individually and collectively. We all share a planet, a country, a society, a family, and are members of some organizations. Social living creates social responsibility. We cannot only take from a society and not give back adequately to maintain it. The equilibrium has already been lost when a large majority only takes with little enthusiasm to give back something worthwhile in return. A very small minority now owns the world, whereas over 99% of people live in either destitute or agony like some kind of modern slaves. Social responsibility is not restricted to monetary issues only, although most of our social problems are caused somewhat and somehow by our greed and economic mechanisms. We can look around ourselves and observe how we engage in various unethical activities to increase our wealth, the simplest kind being to lure people into buying things they really do not need, by brainwashing them through sales gimmicks and advertising, which we so proudly call creative marketing. Instead of feeling responsible for the hardship and chaos they are causing in society, this selfish group just keeps exploiting the helpless public more every day. Their goal is to find better ways of keeping the public in ignorance and sell them more stuff at outrageous prices. Hardly anybody thinks twice when an opportunity arises to manipulate or rob others. Our so-called democratic governments let that happen too—actually support it.

A wide range of social responsibilities covers all facets of human life in the new era. It includes, especially, the morality of activities and decisions of individuals and businesses that have an impact on the overall welfare of the society and Nature. Polluting the environment, destroying the forests and wild life, and political and business corruptions are only a few examples of unethical and irresponsible ways of thinking and acting. We are all responsible for the drastic repercussions of our thinking and acting on our lives and the future of this planet.

Having a sense of social and family responsibility is a natural extension of one's level of individualism and integrity. And for 'knowing about ourselves,' we should evaluate our understanding of what these responsibilities are, and how we are discharging them.

The Integral 'Self'

The discussion of the seven main elements of 'self' has been quite brief and only to provide a basic framework for self-evaluation. To embrace the integral 'self' and 'know about ourselves,' these seven dimensions can be defined in a universal phrase. That is, we can say that:

Man is intrinsically built of spirituality and potentiality, which he can explore within himself in order to develop his individualism, compassion, and integrity, make meaningful relationships, make contributions to himself, to Nature, and humanity as a whole, and perform his social responsibilities selflessly. Only through this holistic process, a person maintains a constant growth of 'self' toward enlightenment.

The basic objective of 'learning about ourselves' is to find a midway compromise between devoting our lives to spirituality in search of 'self' and the option of living in the perceived world totally. Most of us are unable, and have no desire or courage, to withdraw from the luring social life completely. However, while attending to the demands of social living, we may wish to find a life path that could help us refocus our thoughts and build our psychological strength, to actualize our 'self,' and satisfy our most profound inner needs. This approach would give us a chance to make our living tolerable and meaningful, but also have a better control over our psychological and spiritual growth.

An integral 'self' emerges when its seven main elements are nurtured and work harmoniously. Especially, the 'individualism' dimension plays a guiding role regularly to ensure all other elements are functional and in balance.

The fact that 'self' emphasizes highly on personal choices and actions may again appear contradictory to the idea of giving fate at least a modest weight in the foundation of our thoughts. This is a major dilemma, especially since nurturing 'self' demands so much work and initiative on our side. That is, if one's destiny is preordained for an ultimate (perhaps divine) purpose, then why should anybody care about building 'self' or working so hard to grasp individualism? Maybe doing nothing and waiting for things to happen by themselves is the best approach and least tiresome. The answer is that while we cannot change or fight our fate, we have a priori role or choice in directing our lives. In fact, individualism is the best means of maintaining our cool and composure when destiny imposes life's hardships on us and we need to depend on our inner strength to survive the ongoing turmoil. We always face options and choices, and we must learn how to make those decisions properly according to the rules of individualism for a 'self'-driven person. If we were to do nothing or not use our basic instincts, we would simply perish. A simple 'doing nothing' is to not go to the fridge to pick up a loaf of bread or a glass of water, or perhaps even not swallow what is in our mouth. The destiny stirs our instincts to eat, but we must get the bread and swallow it as well. We can expand on this simple example and notice that we should show initiative in doing so many 'right things' with integrity and compassion in a timely manner.

Without determination, we would lose life opportunities and perish quickly. This could be a simple task of walking to the refrigerator to get food, to eat, to have strength, to work, to make money, to buy food, to store it in the refrigerator, and up the scale we go. Perhaps one of these times when we swallow a piece of bread, it goes the wrong way and we choke and die, which would be our destiny, but still our job was to swallow it, because it was the right thing to do with the right purpose when we initiated that step. In particular, we should show initiative to satisfy all our instinctive needs—starting with the needs for food and shelter all the way up to self-actualization. This is a prominent demand on humans, to prevent the deterioration of our physical and psychological health.

The idea of the inevitability of fate in fact demands that we always stay highly alert for unpredictable developments in our lives and react accordingly. In fact, we must be proactive and plan for avoiding the hardships of life. The need for this high degree of consciousness reinforces our responsibility for playing an active role in making 'proper' and 'purposeful' choices and decisions regularly. Now, someone may even ask, 'Why should our choices be proper and purposeful?' The answer is that, they do not really have to be, but why do things in a wrong way intentionally if our intelligence could guide us? Why would one prefer to shove his food up his nose if he is no longer a baby or a retard? Doing the wrong things intentionally or ignorantly, such as crimes and drugs, is going against individualism and our instincts that we so desperately wish to support. By acting against humans' instincts and moral values, we have brought so much suffering and pain upon ourselves. To reverse the process, and as part of knowing what 'I' or 'self' is all about, we should recognize our nature and instincts and abide by some moral rules too. For example, sex is a basic need and necessary, but becoming slave to it is beyond the dignity of a 'self' driven person. We must eventually learn to do the right things as human beings, individually and collectively, let us hope!

The numerous properties of 'self' direct us in choosing the right options by using a proper value system and recognizing everybody's rights, all for the purpose of performing our righteous duties. While 'self' may contain the principles of morality, it is not bound by it. It contains many higher principles for 'self'-imposed thinking and doing things independently, regardless of the narrow morality that society publicizes naively. We can and should aim for our highest sense of humanness beyond what society can ever support.

Since we are not saints and do not work hard on establishing our 'self' and understanding its implications, we all engage in doing both the right and wrong things knowingly. Thus, as a major step in knowing who we are, we should *consciously* assess the intensity and frequency of those things that we do right or wrong. We should build and maintain a conscious knowledge of our deeds and ask ourselves why we prefer to do them in that manner. Some very small urges, as well as deep habits, make us do the right or wrong things. We must distinguish and keep them in our higher conscious. Of course, we first need valid standards to measure our deeds against and gauge their aptness. We can apply our instincts, conscience, and objective judgments as a preliminary yardstick. The wrong deeds we have been justifying all along should now be reassessed with a fresh attitude outside of our prejudices, neediness, and Ego. Measuring the rightness of an action is not easy, since we need practical techniques to stay objective. Mainly, we must believe that assessing our integrity is the right thing to do, and that it is for the purpose of healing our own sick psyches. To save our spirit.

Doing the right or wrong things *knowingly* occurs when our conscience is at least partly aware of its rightness or evilness. Correcting our deeds and thoughts is still a difficult task, even though for this case at least our conscience plays a direct role in acknowledging them privately and tentatively. We are also responsible for two other types of deeds, which are much more difficult to handle: The ones we engage in unknowingly or out of ignorance, and the ones we do habitually because we are conditioned to believe in their rightness or enjoy acting in certain ways. Obviously, the process of activating one's conscience and 'self'-awakening requires even more professional techniques and therapy if a person is totally incognizant of his behaviour.

What makes us do the right or wrong things? How have we come to make a habit of it? These questions must be reviewed for each of the three groups who do wrong things, a) knowingly, b) out of ignorance, and c) due to their rearing and social conditioning, and believing in the appropriateness of their actions.

Our motives for doing wrong intentionally or innocently are quite different. When no direct or obvious motivation exists, some underlying causal force (or conditioning), including ignorance and naivety, is driving us. Psychological idiosyncrasies, their roots, and who or what is responsible for our bad deeds, and 'how and if' they can be corrected, require a lengthy discussion—although many aspect of these issues are hinted throughout this trilogy. A more urgent question is, 'How should one assess his individualism, integrity, and compassion, and how can he improve himself once he agrees that some self-awareness can help him?' Fortunately, if we ever get serious about knowing our 'self,' we notice our weaknesses in terms of individualism, integrity, and compassion readily. Whether a person quits justifying his errors in his mind at this point—when he stands on the wisdom path —and whether he stops his old habits, would become a personal challenge. If this challenge is accepted, he would get the opportunity to review the seven elements of 'self' and decide to help himself through self-awareness. He would learn to make objective judgments and decisions. Yet, choosing this rather divine path of life to reach a higher stance of 'self' requires personal initiative and commitment.

Our wrongdoings are the result of social order, disorders, and pressures. And it is obvious that unless we redefine and correct the foundation of social values, the remedies for reconditioning the elements of this social system, i.e., individuals, would not succeed. On the other hand, how do we go about changing the superstructure when the operators, i.e., individuals, do not believe in a need to modify their mentality and refuse to participate in changing social values? Thus, we must do both simultaneously. We need to appreciate our role in both making a global change in social order and building a fresh personal mentality. While revamping our perspective of life and our deeds, we must participate in the development of support systems to reverse the process of manipulating and conditioning people in society. We need to propagate social conscience and a more compassionate foundation of human thoughts. We must learn to respect the sanctity of our spirit instead of destroying it with our misguided shows of individualism.

We have a long way to go to attain a relative sense of human integrity as well as building social systems that would support and allow such qualities prevail. Meanwhile, we should still deal with imperfect characters and personalities, especially our own. We must help ourselves a little at least, while we wait and hope for a bit of universal morality too.

We inherit a great deal of defects and acquire a lot more through our relationships and encounters within society. Together, our genetic and acquired defects overwhelm our perceptions of the world, others, and ourselves. Naturally, we do not conceive our defects, or quickly justify them. Yet, we have little patience and compassion toward the defects that we immediately detect in others. We are usually great experts in criticizing social structure, political systems, and even God sometimes, yet unable to see our own flaws. As a result, we lose our chance of becoming better human beings with some notion of 'self' driving us. Furthermore, the effects of our biases and misjudgments scatter the seeds of suspicion and distrust in other individuals and society as a whole. In general, it seems that neither our basic personal traits, nor the outcome of our relationships in particular, can help us achieve a level of nobility and purity that we hope to find in human beings.

If we are seeking, or believing in, an inherent purity of human nature, we may be setting ourselves up for major disappointments. We would suffer due to our unreasonableness and stubbornness in placing the emphasis on the wrong faith. Instead of expecting integrity and morality in others, we must simply seek and develop them in ourselves and then stay content with the reality of social living. If the purity of human nature is achievable at all, it can evolve in particular ways and by special individuals only. We cannot expect it universally as an inherent human property.

PART II
Science and Divinity

CHAPTER THREE
The Spirit in Human Spirituality

Previous discussions propose that humans' unrelenting urge for spirituality is ingrained in their deepest unconscious as a primary personal need. In fact, spirituality is so instinctual we can arrive at some fundamental principles and conclusions: First, our drive for spirituality provides a plausible clue about the existence of spirit as a distinct feature of humans aside from their body and mind. Second, human spirit feels real and evolves faster when we stir our divine potentiality (spirituality) to understand 'who we are.' Third, while human urge for spirituality is responsible for finding and strengthening our spirit, the spirit within us is the force that drives our desire for spirituality. Fourth, our spirit's craving for spirituality is simply for liberating itself and us. Fifth, the most natural and direct function of our divine potentiality is to induce inner peace, which we believe comes only from empowering and freeing our spirit through an authentic sense of spirituality.

Most of us agree with these basic principles behind humans' urge for spirituality, as we attempt to find it by exploring our 'self.' Spirituality feels like the most natural way of reaching and redeeming our spirit, cleansing our mind, and connecting to the universe. It also appears to offer a simpler perspective of life for building the foundation of our thoughts and drawing a functional structure of life to face our major life challenges, decisions, doubts, and limitations. In reality, however, we are killing both our spirits and the spirit of spirituality with our shoddy lifestyles or naïve faiths and religions. Thus, the chaotic world we live in. With our sullen spirits, we wander aimlessly in life and never learn how to handle its hardships or show compassion. We have no idea how to draw on our divine potentialities to redeem our shattered spirits.

Volume I of this trilogy raises many unsettling questions about life and the dilemmas of living. We humans (our spirits in fact) seem determined to resolve all those mysteries like a sacred mission embedded in our psyche—as if our spirits' salvation depended on the accuracy of our answers. Obviously, the main question is about the creation of this incredibly complex, yet orderly universe. We like to rely on logic and mathematics to explain this amazing phenomenon, but more crucially, understand humans' *imaginary importance* in the midst of this colossal creation. To do so, we apply common sense, philosophy, psychology, physics, theology, and other disciplines to come to terms with ourselves and possibly find peace and happiness too. We think too highly of our status at the centre of this grandeur, as if no amount of science and knowledge could convince us of our mere infinitesimal existence. Mainly, we like to satisfy our curiosity about 'who we are,' which most of us (including many scientists) believe to be inherently linked to Nature and a universal existence. The essence of 'who we are,' the 'self,' our spirit, is the entity that supposedly connects us to the real world and our creator.

All humans, in the last ten thousand years at least, seem to have encountered similar questions and dilemmas according to their intelligence and teachings. In recent centuries, however, we have become even more curious and scientific about our ways of thinking and living. We have delved into detail research within a wide spectrum of subjects and disciplines. We now need more facts and proofs about the issues we discuss among ourselves and apply to our daily lives. At the same time, we have also become too philosophical about the nature of our existence and the role that some form of spirituality can play in answering the fundamental questions of living. The role that religions used to play for centuries to guide people is gradually fading away, too. No longer can those simplistic, untenable assertions withstand the test of science or even our growing common sense. Thus, a new question is how a common person with average intelligence and patience can go about building his/her convictions, foundation of thoughts, and spirit. What would be the main platform for justifying our conclusions, setting our mindsets, and choosing a proper path of life? Can we depend on science, religion, philosophy, spirituality, or a combination of them to get a relatively reliable point of view about our existence and purpose of living?

The Role of Religion

Fortunately, the role of religion is diminishing in line with the rise of people's education and intelligence in recent decades. In modern societies, in particular, only a small percentage of the population believes in religion and practices it seriously. This is amazing as the percentage of people believing in God is still high. This seeming contrast is interesting in many ways. **First,** it reiterates the fact that people's need for divinity is an intrinsic need that almost everybody feels sincerely and seeks urgently. **Second,** it emphasizes the depth of people's disappointment with religions to satisfy their divinity need rather intelligently. **Third,** it shows that people are getting smart and, thus, no longer willing to put their faith in any shallow type of divinity despite their extreme and urgent need for a means of reaching their gods. **Fourth,** it reveals the fact that people can somehow feel and try to contact their gods outside the religions, although not everybody is quite certain about the method of doing it. **Fifth,** although science can answer many questions about the creation and the origin of the universe, people still need a more intimate way of connecting with a creator beyond the narrow connectivity that the scientific world offers and everybody accepts as facts too. **Sixth,** people are looking for a more practical, reliable, intelligent, and honest means of fulfilling their spirituality urges. **Seventh,** people are severely distracted by phony social values and sexuality, which hamper their natural sense about spirituality and for building their spirits. **Eight,** people's attempts to understand other sources of spirituality feel equally phony and superficial to them, like all other features of modern living. **Ninth,** they still hope to satiate their niggling spiritual urges fast by adopting some shallow concepts instead of devoting enough time and effort to learn about themselves and explore the means of spirituality personally and objectively.

Nevertheless, a basic (**tenth**) conclusion at this point is that we are all beginning to at least realize that no religion can fulfil our inherent spirituality need, and no amount of science can disconnect us from our inner need for a symbolic god, beliefs, spiritual thoughts and feelings.

The Role of Science

The supersonic progress in science in the last few decades does not need any explanation here. The volume and depth of scientific discoveries in thousands of fields can make us all proud, although only a small fraction of us plays a significant role in all these amazing achievements. While the majority of us struggle with our Egos and pleasure-seeking endeavours, a small group of geniuses are devoting their brains and lives to the betterment of human knowledge and living condition. We all owe them a heartfelt salute, although they are the ones getting the ultimate rewards of existence through self-actualization and reaching the height of elation with every one of their accomplishments. At least they have found a way to answer many existential questions and dilemmas for themselves, while the rest of us must struggle with our doubts and decisions forever. They rather find their spirits and means of spirituality during their search for the truth. What are the rest of us supposed to do?

With all its power to enlighten us regarding our origin and organism and to help us live longer, healthier, and more comfortable, still science cannot answer our quest for the truth that appears too deeply seated in our psyches. We are still not impressed by all these scientific explanations. We still want a god and we still need to feed our souls. Actually, it is doubtful that science can even play a role in terms of humans' general wellbeing and easier life structure, despite all the new gadgets and tools that have become available to us. Certainly, more astonishing discoveries will come in the future decades if that very same science and knowledge do not bring us to the verge of idiocy and extinction. Anyhow, no matter how amazingly successful we humans (our scientists) become in the future in terms of new discoveries, or how stupidly we humans (our politicians) destroy our existence and spirits with those technologies and profit motives, science would never satiate our need for the truth. Neither religion nor science has the capacity to save us from the evil within and without us. They are both exploited by business pressures and agendas and they are tainted by dirty politics more than they serve the pure, intrinsic needs of people.

The Role of Personal Life Philosophy

Eventually, all our knowledge, scepticism, beliefs, and needs should come together and make sense within a sustainable, 'self'-satisfying philosophy of life. We grasp the misleading role of religions in the history of humanity and its negative role in the growth of human spirit and true freedom. We expand our knowledgebase and learn all the secrets that science keeps unravelling. We measure both our authentic and artificial needs and appreciate the ultimate objective of fulfilling our spirituality need. We ascertain our general beliefs and convictions. We attempt to know 'who we are' and exploit the strength of 'self.' We understand our doubts, apprehensions, and scepticism. We try to learn from the scattered ideas regarding spirituality. And then finally, we turn all these fundamental thoughts and deep feelings into a dynamic life philosophy. We keep building our future and peace of mind on this platform. We design a sensible life structure and choose a lifestyle suitable for an independent, humble, and confident person. We strengthen our life philosophy with actual experiences and compassion, and we follow some form of spirituality toward transcendence.

Our life philosophy, saturated with juices of spirituality and self-determination, might give us the best opportunity to maintain our sanity in this chaotic world, while keeping our practical contact with normal life conditions and deteriorating environments. Yet, we must find many plausible answers and the truth about existence to develop our life philosophy and a sense of spirituality.

The Role of Spirituality

In recent decades, many concepts and terms like self, truth, reality, meditation, consciousness, enlightenment, and transcendence have evolved under the heading of spirituality. Whether borrowed from ancient cultures or invented in-house, we have felt the need for a new discipline to satisfy people's thirst for spirituality now that religions have failed to do so. We all seek a means of connection with a higher reality to boost our spirits, raise our hopes, and get at least some temporary relief from our superficial reality. Thus, we try to at least understand some of the spirituality concepts that many of us, including this author, would like to explain and propagate. Yet, so far, this promising innovation has not borne fruit, but in fact caused some confusion about the purpose and process of spirituality. We are getting familiar with the jargons and expected benefits of enlightenment, but very few of us start the journey on a path of spirituality, as its purpose and process are obscure. Yet, we believe that some form of spirituality is our only hope for saving our souls and regaining our confidence about the purpose of living. Furthermore, spirituality is a main vehicle for building our spirits and the foundation of our thoughts, and for developing a practical life philosophy. Our ultimate goal is to use at least the therapeutic property of spirituality intelligently, without getting carried away with another bunch of naïve assumptions about humans' immortality or the intentions of a supreme creator. In order to develop a practical sense of spirituality in line with our rising intelligence, yet limited humanistic logic, we should first review some of the weaknesses of our present approach to spirituality.

Shortfalls of Present Spirituality Approach

1. Too many types of spirituality

First, the types of spirituality prescribed by known religions are not included in the definition of spirituality in this book. The reason is that all those religions have risen from naïve speculations about God and His direct words in holy books. Those principles and approaches have only caused more animosity and wars, instead of fulfilling people's basic need for compassion and divinity. They have caused more segregation than integration of humans' life and mentality. No real God would destine all these atrocities on its privileged creatures if our logic about God's ultimate wisdom and compassion should withstand a test of validity.

Besides religions, we have many new spirituality ideologies that have come from eastern cultures, mainly China, India, and Persia. Advocates of these spiritual and philosophical thoughts have tried to formulate a path of transcendence in books and lectures with no common ground or purpose. Most of these devotees seem to have the good intention of helping us find our serenity and a path of wisdom. Yet, the fact that these ideas are not focused and uniform creates the same misunderstanding and confusion that religions have caused for centuries. Now, an intelligent description and mechanism for spirituality is required for drawing people's attention and trust. Otherwise, spirituality would never be understood and accepted as a reliable vision of 'self' and a process for addressing our spiritual needs. It would lose its value and impact the same way religions did, most likely even worse and faster.

2. Abstractness

The terminologies and teachings of spirituality, such as 'self', consciousness, truth, reality, are too abstract to absorb easily or even explain adequately to people. For example, a big difference of opinion exists between scientists and spiritualists regarding the nature of consciousness. Some scientists are working hard and have succeeded in small measures to prove that consciousness is a functionality of the brain itself. Yet, spiritualists insist that consciousness is a holy phenomenon outside the brain that embraces the whole universe. They believe that humans' consciousness is an extension of the universal consciousness. Most of us cannot even get a good grasp of this abstract interpretation regarding consciousness, let alone putting our trust into it. We like to know the meaning of this 'consciousness' in a more tangible manner, instead of the vague notion that this word creates for us. These types of ambiguity in spirituality terminologies and concepts are the cause of our frustration and an obstacle for taking the need for spirituality more seriously. Sometimes, the emptiness of words and concepts, e.g., about consciousness, is surprising and worrisome in terms of not only its meaning, but also the means of reaching that proposed level of consciousness. Even worse, how can we trust those spiritualists who insist on pushing these abstract notions so emotionally and expecting people to accept those ambiguous concepts without having had a chance to experience spirituality personally?

3. Lack of proof and credibility

Like religions, the new spirituality teachings insist on humans' immortality and the existence of some supernatural power running the universe. Obviously, without any kind of attractive incentives to offer, spiritualists would have a much harder time to draw people's attention if they do not promise immortality at least. Thus, they make outrageous claims and offer convoluted assertions without providing any solid proof. They also remain adamantly unconcerned about building a basic credibility for themselves, other than drawing on people's emotions to have faith in some unseeable, unimaginable, unexplainable truth and reality. They simply want us to accept their words and agree with their flawed logic as proofs and evidences. Just have faith, they say.

Deepak Chopra quotes a 'startling idea,' according to him, from the Indian source *Yoga Vasistha,* for describing the ultimate reality as,

"It is that which we cannot imagine, but from which imagination springs, It is that which is inconceivable, but from which all thinking springs."

Deepak Chopra then adds his conclusion,

"To me, this statement is so close to quantum reality that I keep wondering when my scientific friends will jump into the water—and discover that not only it is safe, it's familiar." The War of Worldviews, Deepak Chopra and Leonard Mlodinow, Harmony Books, 2011, page 291.

To most of us with sufficient intelligence, the above *Yoga Vasistha's* quote appears only like some naive playing with words that proves nothing, nor even clarifies anything about reality. In fact, it only induces more scepticism and mistrust about any kind of spirituality claim that is built on similar grounds. The whole description sounds, at best, only another abstract presentation of an imaginary phenomenon beyond our comprehension. The vagueness and wordiness of a sentence is supposed to raise our faith, because it might soothe our inherent need for spirituality and immortality! Because it feels like a great scapegoat for our laziness to figure out spirituality on our own with some efforts and hardships! This does not sound like a productive manner of drawing people's attention to spirituality and enlightenment, but in fact causes more confusion and apprehension. Deepak Chopra's both comments, regarding the similarity of *Vasistha's* quote to quantum reality, and his astonishment about scientist not yet jumping in the water (*which is safe and familiar*) after reading the *Vasistha's* quote, cannot convince many of us.

Spiritualists refer to their own or other people's personal experiences or interpretations as a reliable proof of spiritual facts, e.g., human's consciousness as their guiding light and means of connection to a higher power beyond their normal potential. Again, expecting people to blindly accept these examples and assertions, even if the wordings of those claims were honest and clear, is a doomed expectation. The problem is not merely the lack of proof and credibility, but rather the spiritualists' pushy, irrational approach to explain their points. Instead of offering random magical experiences as evidences, which may be explainable by scientific facts someday, spiritualists should admit the inherent limitation of human logic to ever understand even the simpler mysteries of the universe. This would not deprive us, including spiritualists, from having a full appreciation of the natural (and supernatural) phenomena and the complex creation that we are all a part of. In fact, these basic privileges should be sufficient clues for us to build our spirituality beliefs without needing miracles, supernatural evidences, or wordy sentences.

Even if there have been saints with miraculous connections to God, it does not mean the rest of us can reach the same level of enlightenment no matter how hard we try. Yet, this human limitation, due to the weakness of our souls or life's routine burdens, does not mean that we should deprive ourselves from finding spirituality in a simpler way without putting our blind faith in the possibility of a mysterious reality that some gurus have felt, or the fact that they have contacted this certain god or another. These people's experiences or words cannot offer a ground for a blind faith. Spirituality should stick to the basics, instead of trying to offer crooked, shallow proofs. There could be an intelligent, but simple, language within humans' limited logic for building our personal beliefs and philosophy about living. That language and understanding would fulfil our spirituality need too.

4. Lack of a clear methodology

If people attempt to follow a path of wisdom, especially such a long one typical for spiritual enlightenment, they must understand the steps and expectations for doing so at the outset. They must believe that it is a reasonable and feasible process for a normal person to follow within his/her heavy daily duties and struggle for survival. Not only such a methodology for practical application is not available to people, spiritualists have not yet created even a uniform set of guideline to share among themselves at least as a reliable platform for spreading the simple objectives of spirituality.

5. Lack of organization

Big organizations, especially religions, have failed to offer a means of reaching basic tranquility that we expect from life. They have in fact brought us more disappointments and bigger proofs of human evilness and potential for deceit and manipulation. Thus, we have developed a deep apprehension toward big organizations, as they somehow strive to influence and exploit our naivety. Yet, without some form of organization, spirituality thoughts and methods would remain sporadic, unreliable, and random. In order to make a kind of true spirituality accessible to a larger group and gather credibility, too, some form of organization of our thoughts and methods is necessary. The dilemma is how to get some plausible spirituality thoughts organized without creating another big self-serving organization to exploit the naivety of people.

6. Lack of discipline and easy guidelines

Following a path of spirituality is difficult for people with average intelligence, patience, and social responsibilities. We hardly have the personal discipline to develop and believe in a path of enlightenment to satisfy our important need for spirituality. On the other hand, following the guidelines and routines of our contemporary lifestyles feel natural to people even though they must bear all the hardships associated with their values and implausible aspirations, e.g., the way they pursue love or the way they impose such high expectations on relationships. It feels easier, straightforward, and valid to most people to follow the normal life routines instead of investing time and effort to invent a new untested method of living, e.g., a path of wisdom that could lead to enlightenment. Obviously, whatever lifestyle we choose should come natural to us instead of demanding extreme devotion, hard work, and clear thinking. We should not feel weird or struggle with some ambiguous ideas and processes in pursuit of some imaginary divine goals. Therefore, any spirituality effort must somehow consider and respect people's overall shortcoming to focus and think regularly. Moreover, people need enough self-assurance about the value of pursuing a new lifestyle contrary to what they are used to. They need tangible clues and incentives before giving up all or a good portion of the symbolic pleasures of their current lifestyles. This new lifestyle and discipline should bring them real results, too, in terms of a higher spirit and peace of mind.

7. Lack of incentives

On the one hand, it is almost impossible to disregard our habits and pleasure-seeking motives in hopes of finding spirituality and happiness. It is hard to remain satisfied only with peace of mind and set aside our ambitious goals and adventures. Presently, no direct incentive exists for common people to define and pursue spirituality, especially when getting tangible results requires long-term commitment and perseverance. Therefore, people's efforts and knowledge about spirituality remain half-hearted at best.

On the other hand, spirituality is an inherent need of humans that unless satisfied in some manner, we keep hurting ourselves and others. We are often not quite aware of this need prickling our spirit, because we are distracted by life's hardships and daily struggles for survival. But a good part of social stress and our rising feeling of emptiness are the symptoms of our spirituality needs being ignored.

As noted in other parts of this trilogy, this author believes that some of our higher needs on Maslow's personal needs tree must indeed be taken and treated as basic needs. For example, our need for a companion is so strong it must be considered a basic need in modern societies at least. The same thing can be said for our need for spirituality, which is at the highest level of the needs hierarchy in Maslow's model in line with self-actualization. It sure makes more sense to treat spirituality as a basic need, because it is such a deep and urgent need of humans.

Anyway, considering the importance of spirituality for our health, satisfying this need should by itself be our most reliable incentive in life. Our urge for peace and happiness should be incentive enough for us to design a lifestyle that can support our need for spirituality as an ultimate personal victory in life. Spirituality discussions should emphasize this understanding and respond to this natural drive (incentive) in people.

8. Incompleteness

Spirituality thoughts and processes are extremely incomplete and sporadic the way they are offered to the public now. A large amount of abstract ideas are communicated to people in bits and pieces, which appear disorderly and incomplete at best, if not dishonest or deceitful on some occasions. A more complete picture of spirituality should be developed to explain the reasonable purposes, processes, assumptions, and limitations of spirituality, while avoiding any abstract ideas and intangible promises, such as immortality. To talk about 'the truth' of existence, we must first speak the truth (and nothing but the truth that we know) to the public and still give them cautionary hints about the level of doubtfulness that should be placed even on our most seemingly honest truths.

A structured presentation of spirituality should establish some form of uniformity in its methodology, processes, and ideologies, with continuous development, very much the same way science emerges, grows, and assists us.

9. Scepticism and apprehension in general

The present approach for spreading spirituality ideas are disregarding people's high intelligence and need for at least some sensible understanding of the purpose and limitations of spirituality. Instead, spiritualists give them all kinds of unattainable hopes and promises again, almost like the way religions tried to build their cases based on people's passion and gullibility in the past. People have doubts about any kind of spirituality that its purposes and limitations are not clear and logically presented.

10. Spiritualists' naïve insistence about the truth

The biggest hurdle for developing and spreading a sensible spirituality discipline is that some imaginary ideas about supernatural, truth, reality, consciousness, etc. are presented to people with absolute certainty. Instead of understanding and admitting to the speculative nature of their 'truth,' spiritualists insist to have all the answers to all human questions and dilemmas. They simply disregard the fact that nobody, not even science, can ever answer the fundamental questions about the creation, human existence, god, etc. Just imagine ants trying to figure out human life and thoughts and then swear with absolute certainty about the accuracy of their discovery too. Spiritualists' mentality to insist on the certitude of their truth merely reflects their arrogance and naivety and it contributes directly to all the other nine shortfalls numerated above.

Both the scientific and spirituality evidences are still speculations within the limited parameters of human logic and intelligence. Science stands on a more solid ground considering the mathematical and methodical supports they can offer for their theories and the way the overall design of the universe is explained by some scientific rules. However, in the final analysis, neither science nor spirituality can answer all our fundamental questions and dilemmas yet—and most likely they would never do. In this environment, spiritualists' persistence about knowing the truth sounds merely immature and perhaps even deceitful to people who are now depending more on their intelligence than passion to build their beliefs. Spiritualists' current approach merely restricts the limited use that spirituality could have for people.

As a rule, any sensible spiritualist would never insist on his/her presentation of the truth even if it were not pure speculation. S/he would only offer it as a mere plausible perception and not certainty, because at the end whatever we humans see and think would remain a perception. We can always hope those plausible perceptions carry enough methodology and logic behind them, similar to science, so that we eventually end up with one set of spirituality principles instead of a bunch of scattered opinions and dogmatic cults. This is the main premise and the most basic principle. We can only perceive things—and merely based on the strength of our spirits and the validity of our foundation of thoughts. In particular, we can never know anything about the mysteries that stand in a domain totally outside of human range of logic and even basic perceptions. In fact, if by any unconceivable fluke a person ever reaches that ultimate transcendence beyond perceptions, s/he would never find it necessary to discuss the divine truth that s/he has found, let alone insist on it with such prejudice and absoluteness. S/he would be transformed into a being outside the realms and needs of humanity. Persistence and doubtlessness are in fact the signs of prejudice, which immediately ruins any inclination for truth. Instead, certitude reflects personal attachment, which is more a symbol of arrogance and a desire for acceptance, or hiding one's gullibility, than a sign of transcendence.

In all, if we are going to build a reliable foundation of thoughts and include spirituality as a main building block of it, the first assumption must be that we humans would never find the whole truth about the nature of the universe, our limited role and importance within this superstructure, and the very miniscule possibility of our immortality. We must build our spirits and foundation of thoughts and make major life decisions within an environment akin to endless doubts about existence and a large host of other related mysteries.

If the present shortcomings of spirituality can be remedied, it can definitely become a main platform for building our personal life philosophy. Somebody would eventually put together a comprehensive book and suggest a practical approach for the public to grasp and experience spirituality in their own ways, but according to a tested process, without going overboard and making outrageous claims about some imaginary truth and reality. Meanwhile, we can try to achieve at least a certain degree of self-awareness by adhering to some sort of a guideline, as stepping-stones for building the foundation of our thoughts and some minimal form of spirituality. We can build our own spirituality beliefs according to certain facts like the ones suggested in Table 3.1.

Table 3.1: The Main Characteristics of Spirituality

1. Spirituality is a personal journey and experience.
2. It demands self-discipline and true commitment for enhancing self-awareness and reaching basic tranquility.
3. It requires a certain level of understanding about its purpose (as briefly outlined in this chapter) before one starts the journey. Especially, spirituality's main purpose must be to eliminate human gullibility and instead help them depend on their intelligence and intuition to build their beliefs independently.
4. It should not advocate the existence of a particular god or another life for humans beyond their present being. Nobody is in a position to understand or claim any fact about the deep aspects of the universe with certainty, especially about its creator, even if such a phenomenon exists.
5. Spirituality is built on basic beliefs, not faith. Beliefs do not imply as much certitude the way faith demands. In fact, one objective of spirituality is to avoid and eradicate dogmatism and fanaticism that comes with faith.
6. Spirituality is for building a simple belief system, calming our urge for divinity, satisfying our curiosity, and raising our spirit.
7. Spirituality is also for propagating compassion and comradeships among humans instead of arrogance and hostility that result from certitude and persistence.
8. Even though humans are built from same molecules and energy that the universe is, the existence of human soul, consciousness, or its connection to a unique overall consciousness is at best an idea. Therefore, any other claim beyond this

preliminary notion is absurd. Even the basic meaning of consciousness is still vague and arbitrary.

9. The universe does not seem to have a specific purpose for itself, let alone for the life of human beings, which are a minute element of this colossal system. Yet, human life can have a purpose if a person gets smart enough to set it properly for him/herself without trying to relate it to the purpose of the universe or human existence.
10. Spirituality is merely one dimension of human life and thoughts. It helps us build our spirits, but it should serve only as another philosophical notion for building the overall foundation of our thoughts and pursuing a simple life. Spirituality must not dominate our life philosophy, because it is as speculative and instable as all other kinds of beliefs we include in the foundation of our thoughts.

CHAPTER FOUR
Spirituality and Philosophy

Philosophy's main goal is to challenge our naivety, desires, ideas, and ideals, such as heaven and immortality. Philosophy also fulfils humans' inherent curiosity about existence, God, creation, and other social subjects to find better means of living in peace. Accordingly, our goal for mastering spirituality emerges mostly as another philosophical notion, too. Of course, humans' sacred urge for spirituality, as an inherent virtue, is important for stirring our divine potentialities and enriching our lives. However, viewing spirituality realistically and honestly, like a philosophical principle, within the overall foundation of human thoughts, can serve people better. It can also help humans' long-term goal of eradicating social gullibility by mixing enlightenment and self-development.

Unfortunately, we have not still applied either philosophy or spirituality to help people after such a long history of struggles and research. Especially it feels strange that not even scholars and spiritualists have found a common ground for their speculations. They have not succeeded to play a useful role toward the ultimate purpose of eliminating superstitions, naivety, dogmatism, and arrogance. In fact, they often attempt to prey on people's gullibility and emotional vulnerabilities to push their shoddy ideas about spirituality.

Besides scholars' failure to relate to people in a simple and honest language, our social structure is too dysfunctional to worry even about people's gullibility, let alone fighting the sources and motives behind the rising social credulity and chaos. The list of shortfalls regarding spirituality in the previous chapter shows the ineffectiveness of scholars' approach for helping people with their spirituality needs in a natural and honest manner. At best, they are only offering many tentative ideas about spirituality with no ultimate goal in mind. They merely intend to evoke people's deprived emotions now in a different way, which has the same effect and outcome as religions. Nevertheless, they have failed to help people develop their own spirituality and foundation of thoughts, based on our limited science and logic, for a productive marriage of social life and divinity.

The foundation of human thoughts includes both spirituality and philosophy for the ultimate purpose of helping us with our daily lives and fulfilling our authentic personal needs, including self-actualization and divinity. As the main feature of this platform, all our ideologies, including the foundation of human thoughts and spirituality, always entail some level of doubtfulness and scepticism. They never imply certitude based on some perceived facts and myths, because 'certitude' merely stops our thinking ability and drive. It merely diminishes the validity of our arguments and defeats the purpose of enlightenment. The same is true for human logic as a tool for building philosophical and spiritual notions. It must be built and applied with an eye on other fundamentals beyond our perceptions and dogmatism that presently form the main pillars of our reasoning.

The success of science is in the use of methodology, design, conceptualization, experimentation, validation against natural laws, and many other factors. Yet, one main factor for its success is doubtfulness and scepticism, even about its latest findings, as someone always tries to retest and challenge those theories. They find vaster knowledge and more details in this process, simply because science is built around continuous scepticism, experimentation, and evolution. This plausible approach is exactly what spiritualists need, too, to achieve tangible results and help humanity. Instead, they insist on forcing certain ideas with their arrogant certitude and expect people to form their faith around those ideas too. They push for extreme, i.e., building faith, rather than staying satisfied with the task of helping people develop merely some practical and intelligent beliefs. This approach sabotages the possibility of building even some tangible beliefs and a healthier structure of life. Instead of wasting time and effort to explain unsolvable mysteries and playing with people's emotional vulnerabilities, we could propagate an atmosphere for personal contemplation so that people can develop their own beliefs based on their own plausible conclusions and inherent sense of spirituality.

Thus, the goal in this chapter is to suggest some tentative philosophical notions about the truth of existence, while we wait for a more sensible spirituality to guide us more profoundly. Nowadays, we need spirituality more than ever to cope with life's hardships and to replace the outmoded religious practices. However, it will take a long time before an intelligent and reliable spiritual method and purpose is offered for our use. Meanwhile, we must build our own mode of spirituality based on the list of facts outlined in Table 3.1 at the end of the last chapter. That would be the best way for now to use some spirituality notions actively, along with philosophy, to build our spirit and a solid foundation of thoughts. A platform for building our philosophical spirituality is offered in the following pages.

Most importantly, however, the goal is to emphasize the dangers of pursuing the present spirituality methods and ideas. We must know the risks of any form of spirituality outside a plausible philosophical format, and the danger of not changing our approach. The question is whether the existing mentality about spirituality has any value for giving the public an honest and realistic view of the truth about the universe and human life. Unfortunately, many clues, including a review of the arguments between scientists and spiritualists, reveal the urgency of reformatting spirituality ideas in a philosophical framework to engage the public in a more sensible manner. For example, the following two quotes by Deepak Chopra in *The War of Worldviews* demonstrate the narrow approach of spirituality nowadays, without any apparent support from either scientific or philosophical principles. Thus, you wonder about the basis of these perceptions or prophesies!

"I equate the future of belief with the future of God." Ibid., page 260.

"Since God is intimately tied into who we are and what life means, there is no separate future for God and for the individual. You and I will make decisions that determine if God has a viable tomorrow." Ibid., page 260.

These statements are perplexing and vague for most of us, because it is hard to believe that *the future of God* (as emphasized in the above quotes) would have anything to do with how intelligent we ever become about the nature of an absolute God. Are not we talking about the same God, by the way, who is supposedly responsible for the creation of everything, including our existence and thoughts? How could the future of God, such an almighty creator of all things and humans, reside in the hands (actually, beliefs and imaginations) of His minute creatures? Or, are we talking about the God that is merely a figment of our imagination to begin with? Deepak Chopra is also making a major assumption that, 'God is intimately tied into who we are and what life means,' which again is not a valid base for building a case, anyway.

In all, it is best that neither scientists nor spiritualists insist on their viewpoints about the nature of God, though scientists do it much less frequently due to the requirements of their research processes and the need for practical applications of their theories.

The disagreements between scientists and spiritualists are usually the result of one or both sides' persistence on the truthfulness of their thoughts and their certitude. For example, Leonard Mlodinow says,

"The issue that separates Deepak and me is not whether the universe has design, but whether something designed it, and whether it was designed for a purpose. Creationists and adherents of "intelligent design" believe, as Deepak does, that the intricacies of living creatures could not be the result of natural law." Ibid., page 108

At least scientists admit the undeniable depth of the mystery regarding the universe even after all their vast scientific discoveries, as Leonard says,

"Why nature follows laws is a mystery. Why the specific laws we have observed exist is also a mystery. But what is clear is that the laws of nature are sufficient to enable us to show how life arose without the necessity of there being any immortal hand or eye executing the design." Ibid., page 108

Overall, science takes a more compromising position along with their continuous research and scepticism, but also admitting to the mystical nature of the universe and humans' need for spirituality and appreciating life. Leonard says,

"I would be dishonest to dispute it when Deepak says science sees human beings as 'isolated specks in the cosmos, accidental outcroppings of mind in a mindless creation.' There is much in humanity to be thankful for, but to deny that we are isolated specks in the cosmos is to avoid the truth rather than embracing it. Deepak said it takes courage to see ourselves as he suggests we should, but he paints a rosy picture, one that, as in the quote above, he likes to contrast with the worldview of science. What

takes real bravery is to embrace the reality we actually observe, without regard to whether it is a bleak or a rosy picture. To grow old, to see friends die and planes crash, and to experience love and loss without the comforting illusion of a living, thinking universe imbued with a divine essence takes courage.

"At the same time. I do choose a less bleak outlook. To me, though humans might be isolated specks with accidental outcroppings of mind, what is important is that we do have the capacity to experience art and beauty and joy." Ibid., Page 240-241.

"Understanding my essence doesn't diminish my appreciation for the gift of being alive; it makes me appreciate it even more. That's not a scientific principle. It's just the way I feel." Ibid., page 133.

That is the way any intelligent person would normally feel—according to a truth that embraces everything we have found out so far about the universe and ourselves, while also appreciating all the mysteries about the grandeur we happen to be the specks within it.

Obviously, scientists feel the beauty, passion, joy, and compassion that all humans feel and embrace. They even seem eager to include some form of spirituality within their logical minds. Despite his opposition to the methods and certitude of present spirituality, Leonard says,

"A scientific and spiritual life can exist side by side." Ibid., page 236.

This is, of course, an ideal possibility and necessity, and in fact not too difficult to achieve either. The only requirement is to stop being so arrogant and persistent about views that are merely tentative suggestions and cannot provide a definite answer to our life dilemmas. All we need is some honesty and modesty in our views as we try so hard to unravel the mysterious truth about existence. We must offer spirituality as another source of thoughts useful for building our beliefs, but never for proving our faith and getting more dogmatic. We desperately need honest thoughts, beliefs, and feelings based on personal convictions, but not blind faith and fanaticism.

Many mysteries remain that science would never be able to solve. Only a combination of philosophy and spirituality can fill this gap with some plausible models and arguments, without showing prejudice and persistence, while welcoming scepticism. We all crave an intelligent method and description of spirituality to satiate our urge for divinity and to replace the controversial ideologies propagated by religions for so long. Spiritualists have so far failed to see and accept these basic points. They have no platform for their arguments and models other than persistence and depending on humans' naive sentimentality. They are not serious in building human intelligence and revoking the need for religions altogether.

The Ultimate Truth

We all search for a more meaningful life and a purpose for living, because our experiences and ambitions seldom feel fulfilling enough. Intuitively, we believe that there must be a more viable truth in this complex universe behind all this chaos we call life. We realize that our narrow logic and huge Ego obscure our perceptions of the world. Therefore, we seek a higher truth within some realm of divinity, which actually feels like an inherent aspect of our being.

The purpose of spirituality is to help us get a sense of this ultimate truth in hopes of bringing tranquility into our lives and spreading the seeds of a more harmonious life structure. However, we are discouraged and disheartened by the way our search for this eluding truth remains too sporadic and unproductive. Our search and wonderment have caused us only more confusion and reduced our chance of ever grasping anything tangible about this truth. Yet, we seem obsessed to learn at least about the fundamentals of this mysterious truth and its connection to a divine reality. To make our job a bit simpler, we can review the question about the ultimate truth at three levels as follows:

1. The truth about the universe
2. The truth about humanity
3. The truth about our personal lives

The Truth about the Universe

While science, spirituality, and philosophy help us speculate about the origin and destiny of the universe and humans' inherent connection to this enigmatic scheme, we should eventually get serious and admit that we can never unravel the mystery of the universe. Scientists and philosophers seem more inclined to accept this fact while they continue with their research and contemplation for further insight. Only spiritualists and religions still insist on knowing the answer to the ultimate truth, which they also insist lies in people's blind faith in certain ideologies they put forward with no intrinsic support and value. Obviously, their persistent certitude about knowing the ultimate truth only reflects humans' gullibility or self-serving agendas. Unfortunately, this mentality and approach hinder the chance of preparing people's mind for even an elementary perception of the truth. At the end, we all suffer individually and collectively as long as societies promote gullibility and exploitation.

For building our personal beliefs about the universe and the humans' role within it, nowadays we merely have two options: (1) Blindly accept the shallow claims of religions or spiritualists to build our faith and feed our gullibility. (2) Use some degree of intelligence and accept, once and for all, that no evidence indicates the possibility of human logic ever (or at least for many more millenniums) reaching a capacity to understand and explain the truth about the universe. It does not matter how much science we muster and how much spirituality and philosophy we wish to adopt for building our belief systems, the ultimate truth about the universe is beyond humans' grasp. Now it is up to us to decide which of the above two options we like to choose and build our life philosophy around. We can entertain the possibility of learning the grand truth about the universe and the secrets of creation in more detail *someday*, but we accept that knowing this truth at this point with even small degree of certainty is only a sign of our immense immaturity and stubbornness. We can go even one step further and include in our beliefs some plausible notions about this truth (regarding the universe) as long as we remain doubtful about our interpretations. It is only when we lose our doubtfulness about our own or other people's ideologies, and keep insisting on their truthfulness with certainty, that we emerge as fools.

The Truth about Humanity

This level of truth plays a more significant and direct role for the welfare of humans in the long run than finding the truth about the universe. Although our curiosity about the universe is important for satisfying our spirituality need, the survival of human race in itself depends on how we interpret and tackle the truth about humanity urgently. Furthermore, while the truth about the universe remains forever hidden from us, the truth about humanity is much easier to grasp and measure if we become sincere and objective about it. This trilogy, including the scholars' opinions quoted in it, has been mostly for drawing a relatively reliable picture of the fast deteriorating state of humanity at the present time. We can all see the hardships we have brought upon ourselves and the way we have ruined our planet with our greed and arrogance, yet have gotten less tangible results from all that knowledge, efforts, and egotism. George Carlin's view of the state of humanity in the 21st century is quite to the point:

"The paradox of our time in history is that we have taller buildings but shorter tempers, wider freeways, but narrower viewpoints. We spend more, but have less, we buy more, but enjoy less. We have bigger houses and smaller families, more conveniences, but less time. We have more degrees but less sense, more knowledge, but less judgment, more experts, yet more problems, more medicine, but less wellness.

We drink too much, smoke too much, spend too recklessly, laugh too little, drive too fast, get too angry, stay up too late, get up too tired, read too little, watch TV too much, and pray too seldom.

We have multiplied our possessions, but reduced our values. We talk too much, love too seldom, and hate too often.

We've learned how to make a living, but not a life. We've added years to life not life to years. We've been all the way to the moon and back, but have trouble crossing the street to meet a new neighbour. We conquered outer space but not inner space. We've done larger things, but not better things.

We've cleaned up the air, but polluted the soul. We've conquered the atom, but not our prejudice. We write more, but learn less. We plan more, but accomplish less. We've learned to rush, but not to wait. We build more computers to hold more information, to produce more copies than ever, but we communicate less and less.

These are the times of fast foods and slow digestion, big men and small character, steep profits and shallow relationships. These are the days of two incomes but more divorce, fancier houses, but broken homes. These are days of quick trips, disposable diapers, throwaway morality, one night stands, overweight bodies, and pills that do everything from cheer, to quiet, to kill. It is a time when there is much in the showroom window and nothing in the stockroom. A time when technology can bring this let-

ter to you, and a time when you can choose either to share this insight, or to just hit delete..." Online communication by ingenious George Carlin.

We know a lot about the truth of humanity and we can do something about it too, if we ever happen to become smarter beings. Spiritualists blame this sad state of affair on science for its soulless approach to the truth (about life and the universe) and scientists blame it on spiritualists for their triumphant spread of gullibility and unfounded ideologies. Regardless of all these arguments, the ultimate truth about humanity indicates that it is at the verge of total collapse and we do not have a solution for our looming demise, nor do we seem to care. Some religions and fanatics actually look forward to, and some even strive to force, the end of humanity in hopes of reaching the judgment day sooner and going to heaven. Do we really need any further proof about the depth of human gullibility?

The fact of the matter is that the technologies that science offer and the ideologies that spiritualist and philosophers propagate are only tools at our disposal for proper interpretation and application. It is all a matter of human intelligence and goodwill as to how we use those tools for people's welfare. When we use technology to destroy one another, it shows humans' wicked nature and not science's mistakes in its calculations and revealing the laws of nature. It is our own fault when we abuse science for evil purposes, not the science itself. We must also blame our own naivety for the prevalent social chaos when we become fanatics and put our faith in some shallow ideologies of religions or spiritualism. It is not the fault of science and not even the fault of simple-minded or phony spiritualists. It is our own persistence to stay naïve that spreads gullibility and allows another group of humans to exploit us and the situation. It is our own lack of conscience and rising greed that goad us promote many unfounded assertions to become famous and sell more books.

A few other quotes from Chris Hedges show the scope of our naivety and the depth of human tragedy in early 21st century.

"We are a culture that has been denied, or has passively given up, the linguistic and intellectual tools to cope with complexity, to separate illusion from reality. We have traded the printed word for the gleaming image. Public rhetoric is designed to be comprehensible to a ten-year-old child or an adult with a sixth-grade reading level. Most of us speak at this level, are entertained and think at this level. We have transformed our culture into a vast replica pf Pinocchio's Pleasure Island. Where boys are lured with the promise of no school and endless fun. They were all, however, turned into donkeys—a symbol, in Italian culture, of ignorance and stupidity." ***Empire of Illusion,*** Chris Hedges, Alfred A. Knopf, Canada, 2009, page 44.

"The America we celebrate is an illusion. America, the country of my birth, the country that formed and shaped me, the country of my father, and his father's father, ..., is so diminished as to be unrecognizable. I do not know if this America will return, even as I pray and work and strive for its return.

Our nation has been hijacked by oligarchs, corporations, and a narrow, selfish, political, and economic elite, a small and privileged group that governs, and often steals, on behalf of moneyed interests. This elite, in the name of patriotism and democracy, in the name of all the values that were once part of the American system and defined Protestant work ethics, has systematically destroyed our manufacturing sector, looted the treasury, corrupted our democracy, and trashed the financial system." Ibid., page 142.

"America has become a façade. It has become the greatest illusion in a culture of illusions. It represents a power and a democratic ethic it does not possess. It seeks to perpetuate prosperity by borrowing trillions of dollars it can never repay.

The corporate power that holds the government hostage has appropriated for itself the potent symbols, language, and patriotic traditions of the state. It purports to defend freedom, which it defines as the free market, and liberty, which it defines as the liberty to exploit. It sold us on the illusion that the free market was the natural outgrowth of democracy and a force of nature, at lest until the house of cards collapsed and these corporations needed to fleece the taxpayers to survive. Making that process even more insidious, the real sources of power remain hidden. Those who run our largest corporations are largely anonymous to the mass of the citizens." Ibid., page 143.

"We have been steadily impoverished by our own power elites—legally, economically, spiritually, and politically. And unless we radically reverse this tide, unless we wrest the state away from corporate hands, we will be dragged down by the dark and turbulent undertow of globalization. In this world there are only asters and serfs. We are entering an era in which works may become serfs, no longer able to earn a living wage to sustain themselves or their families, whether in sweatshops in China or in the industrial wasteland of Ohio." Ibid., page 144.

"We embrace the dangerous delusion that we are on a providential mission to save the rest of the world from itself, to impose our virtues—which we see as superior to all other virtues—on others, and that we have a right to do this by force." Ibid., page 145.

In all, in terms of the ultimate truth about humanity, we have almost all the facts, as noted above, especially regarding the truth about humans' inherent impurity, which is expanding fast due to the extreme social corruption, greed, gullibility, egotism, illusions, and fake ideologies, including spirituality. It is this very ultimate truth that is destroying us and our planet.

The Truth about Our Personal Lives

We have some power to understand the truth about our personal lives, too, and deal with it in some effective manner according to our priorities and intelligence. Again, the whole purpose of this trilogy is for making the job of understanding the truth about our lives and choices somewhat clearer and easier. However, our psychological defects, passion, gullibility, vulnerability, needs, and social pressures make our job of dealing with this essential truth rather difficult too. Our illusions, as symptoms of living in the perceived world, would never allow us to see the truth and find our identity and integrity.

In the final analysis, we still have some sense about the ultimate truths about humanity and our personal lives, but remain incapable of handling these truths and bringing them in line with our authentic needs individually and collectively. Instead, we fight among ourselves about some mysterious truths and realities in imaginary realms beyond our apprehension. We prefer to feed our illusions and gullibility or fool others, instead of saving the humanity or facing the sad truth about our personal lives and integrity.

The book, *The War of the Worldviews,* mentioned before, provides more clues about both the state of humanity and personal lives of people driven by enormously complex and often weird thought processes. Discussions in that book can be helpful for understanding the ultimate truths. Reading at least the epilogue of that book would supplement the discussions in this chapter. Some important points raised by the authors in the book's epilogue are quoted here, starting with a comment from Leonard Mlodinow.

"When philosophizing, one can talk freely about unseen realms, invisible realities, and organizing forces that guide evolution. One can illustrate the ideas with stories and anecdotes, and

argue by analogy. One can use everyday language with its pitfalls of vagueness, and terms with multiple meanings. One can pepper one's prose with satisfying terms like 'love' and 'purpose.' One can even appeal to ancient sages and texts. These arguments may seem attractive. But science answers to a higher authority—the way Nature actually works." The War of Worldviews, Deepak Chopra and Leonard Mlodinow, Harmony Books, 2011, page 297.

Leonard's summary about the role of science compared with the sloppy language that spiritualists use in describing divinity is totally understandable to many of us, especially when spiritualists keep insisting on the truthfulness and certitude of their assertions. At the same time, it is still plausible, as perhaps Leonard agrees too, that a real reality exists beyond the perceived reality that we are capable of witnessing and measuring remotely according to our limited knowledge and logic. There is no harm in having this type of beliefs with adequate scepticism about the nature of those beliefs. The problem begins when some spiritualists insist on turning those ideas into blind faith.

The following quotes are from Deepak Chopra's counter-argument:

"I'd suggest that the war doesn't need to be fought anymore, because it's already over. Hidebound science is ready to topple, making way for a new paradigm where consciousness takes center stage." Ibid., page 300.

"If our life has meaning, it must have come from somewhere." Ibid., page 301.

These assertions, again, seem too definite and final to most of us with average intelligence, let alone in the ears of emotionally vulnerable people thirsty for any kind of easy conclusions and fanaticism. Science being toppled by *a new paradigm where consciousness takes center stage* is a major claim that is hard to swallow easily and not wonder. And in the second comment, again Deepak has already concluded that not only life has a meaning because of the mundane activities we do (what kind of meaning is that for life?), but is also assuming that this 'meaning' comes from an external source (*somewhere,* according to him) rather than being a creation of humans, and according to their personal erratic tastes actually. It makes absolute sense for humans with some intelligence to set logical purposes for their activities and lives. However, their urges or habits for setting purposes for their activities (for being efficient and proactive) do not prove that the universe does the same or that humans' habits are a derivative of a universal purpose or direction. Any type of spirituality built on these types of raw assumptions is only a waste of time to discuss, let alone practice. Using humanly logic to set a meaning for the universe and define its characteristics is a futile effort, especially when those ideas come from people who insist on the certitude of their conclusions.

In another example, Deepak asserts,

> *"When a professor of medicine smirked at the notion of the mind affecting the body, I would blurt out, 'How do you wiggle your toes? Isn't your mind sending an order to your feet?'"* Ibid., page 301.

Obviously, brain's neurological system has the power to order and move all parts of the body including our toes. This is science and proves the complexity of the brain. However, this type of connectivity (or the human logic explaining it) does not prove the absoluteness or the spiritual aspects of the body-mind connection, which could then also be used as a ground for making many other unproven claims. For example, wiggling our toes cannot help us think better thoughts simply because we like to insist on the power of body-mind connectivity. For one thing, this connectivity is not a two-way, clear, concise relationship. Wiggling our toes may at best give us weird (speculative) ideas about the extent of body-mind connection. So far, the evidences offered by spiritualists in their spectacular assertions are equally speculative and flimsy. They are often based on some form of nicely packaged, attractive fallacy.

Deepak continues to say:

"Ordinary people aren't going to give up emotions and inspiration just because science sniffs at subjectivity. Science shouldn't be so edgy and defensive." Ibid., page 303.

"One must be decisive here: a world ruled completely by science would be hell on earth. Being wedded to rational thought is acceptable inside the lab, but once science ventures to dismantle faith, striving, love, free will, imagination, emotion, and the higher self as so many illusions cooked up in our fallible brain, a rescue effort must be mounted, and quickly." Ibid., page 303.

The above quotes also appear like some kind of effort to spread faith in some unclear form of spirituality only by discrediting science. It also depends on *ordinary people* (according to Deepak) and their gullibility to propagate spirituality. Is not this approach itself the nucleus of all our problems? It sounds like making a case against science to not only cover up one's pure subjectivity, but also invent a *novel* kind of subjectivity that strives to push absolute certitude! This weird notion and logic merely indicates either the pure naivety of some spiritualists or their ambitious agendas (maybe even similar to the exploiters of science). Some spiritualists merely laugh at the naivety and suggestibility of people, who accept any attractive idea to validate their own laziness, love, illusions, hallow sentiments, and lousy imaginations. Spiritualists' attempts to mix subjectivity and certitude so readily are just amazing. Their ideas may have good value and benefit, but, at the very least, their mode of presentation and deep certitude about their subjective points of view cause most of the problems.

Analysing some spiritualists' statements in a variety of books reveals the vanity of their approach and the enormity of inconsistencies in their ideologies. Hiding behind words and exploiting people's emotional vulnerability and confusion cannot serve humanity. We should know by now to keep subjectivity within the domain of myths and doubtfulness and leave any hint of certitude (if at all) only to cases where some form of objectivity is evident. Spiritualists should also remember that exploiting people's emotions and vulnerabilities has been the cause of enough religious wars and human ignorance already. Following the same path again with new spirituality themes, but within the same frame of mind, would not have a better outcome.

As an elementary step for building a progressive and more useful kind of spirituality, spiritualists should clarify a few hundred points initially before even speculating about narrower topics or fighting with science. Among those few hundred points, they should first answer to some basic questions, such as the following:

1. Do they believe in the Big Bang or not?
2. What do they think was there before that split second of the Big Bang? How can they prove it?
3. What they believe the nature of Creation is?
4. What they believe the purpose of Creation is?
5. What aspects of Creation and its purpose(s) they are absolutely sure about? On what grounds?
6. What issues they still have some doubts about?
7. What do spiritualists expect from scientists?
8. What do spiritualists want scientists do beyond following their existing methodology?
9. Are spiritualists offering a better method for handling the known truths about human nature and the doomed destiny of

humanity? Or they believe that mere faith can solve all these problems? How?

10. Can spiritualists offer a better mechanism for revamping humans' gullibility, perhaps through a more intelligent means of spirituality? What are the main characteristics of such a spirituality model?

At the same time, it would be a great service to humanity if some scientists, preferably Leonard Mlodinow too, write a few books about the kind of spirituality that might be applicable to the 21st century, with objective scepticism about the truths and realities, to cover the following objectives:

1. Humans' need for spirituality.
2. Humans' need for science.
3. How to handle the ultimate truth about humanity.
4. How to face the ultimate truth about our personal lives and integrity.
5. Exploring our inner self.
6. Use of spirituality for soothing the burdens of living and social stress.
7. Eradicating gullibility in society.
8. Abolishing the need for naïve forms of spirituality.
9. Raising people's intelligence to find their own truths and spirituality.
10. Controlling the side effects of science on human life.

The bottom line about the 'ultimate truth' is that we will never know some aspects of it. However, we have a capacity to understand a great deal of the truths that actually affect our wellbeing directly and immediately, as were briefly discussed above. The only condition is to get smarter and less self-serving with our ideologies and plans.

Unfortunately, the mere ultimate truth is that 'we cannot handle the truth,' as Jack Nicholson said in the movie, *A Few Good Men*. What is the point of knowing the ultimate truths when we are unwilling or incapable of doing anything about them? We know the ultimate truth regarding the doomed future of humanity and we know how we are causing our own stress and sufferings, due to our lifestyles, mentality, and egoism, but simply do not wish to do anything about them.

What is the point of fussing and fighting over the ultimate truth when we humans are so adamant to ignore the obvious truths right before our eyes? We simply cannot handle the truth. Period.

PART III
Potentialities and Limitations

CHAPTER FIVE
The Spirit in Human Potentialities

The enigmatic spirit that drives humans' need for spirituality (as discussed in Chapter Three), propels our potentialities as well. On the other hand, our thriving potentialities and insights both reveal and revitalize our neglected spirit. Chapter Two's discussions of genetic and divine potentialities, and quotes in Chapter One about self-actualizers' idyllic experiences, reflect this integrated, two-way connection between our potentialities and our spirit.

Everybody has some talents (potentialities) and a great deal of quirks (limitations). We try to pinpoint these talents and quirks intuitively, through self-awareness, or by people's suggestions, mostly for career planning, but also for boosting our spirit and feeling positive. We believe that our success and happiness in life depend on our *timely* assessment of our potentialities and limitations, mostly for career decisions. We wish to create our identity and individualism, get a chance to choose our purpose of living, and make our major life decisions rationally, but we also have a hunch that we can touch our 'self' and fulfil our spiritual urge through our potentialities. Thus, resolving our limitations and exploiting our potentialities become major life decisions by themselves.

Exploring our potentialities is a daunting task, however, as it demands initiative, learning, social adaptation, sacrifice, and serious decisions. It would be a big challenge, considering the pressures to adapt ourselves quickly to job market, handle many tough demands of social life, face many doubts (including self-doubt), and try to curb our debilitating idiosyncrasies too. Therefore, we normally neither realize our potentialities (to get a sense of self-actualization), nor eliminate our bad habits and flaws (to revive our spirits). We do not find the time, willpower, or courage to do these kinds of 'self' explorations and cleansing. Accordingly, we lose the chance of grasping our identity and spirituality attributes to live happier on a rather independent path of life.

Many reasons exist for neglecting our potentialities, while we eagerly pamper our flaws, such as egoism and aggression. **First**, societies have not yet explored the boundaries of human potentialities other than measuring people's general aptitude and intelligence for performing some tasks. The outer limit of our potentialities (e.g., creativity, spirituality, or our possible connection to the universe) is still a mystery for us. Throughout human history, only gurus and odd spiritualists have delved into higher limits of consciousness. The rest of us either do not bother with these seeming supernatural stuff or at best adopt a religion to get the matter over with, hoping that we have done an adequate job of satiating our spirituality need. **Second**, our aspirations, greed, and social norms often encourage us to either exaggerate or misuse our potentialities. Our misperceptions of our potentialities in fact often mislead us, thus we lose the chance of tapping this source of energy and wisdom. **Third**, we tend to ignore humans' deep limitations, especially our needy personalities and crooked perceptions of life. Instead, we believe we can achieve everything we put our minds into, simply because the positive thinking slogans say so. **Fourth**, our need for 'practicality' goads us to pursue only good-paying jobs and wealth accumulation, which consume all our physical energy and mental capacity.

Even when we are fortunate enough to notice the streaks of our genius and innate potentialities, we have a hard time utilizing them. Sometimes, they are wasted on trivia. Sometimes, they appear useless in the context of our social standards and the criteria of success. And sometimes, they are wasted on evil thoughts and deeds. Thus, many of us feel incomplete and depressed when our potentialities are not appreciated or used properly. Our spirit sinks when not even our seemingly marketable potentialities can help our subsistence or bring us peace of mind. This epidemic is saddening many of us, though our negligence about our 'self' and our divine potentialities dampens our spirit the most, as explained in Chapter Two under the heading of 'knowing (about) ourselves.'

Nonetheless, we must know that our unique potentialities are hidden treasures bestowed upon us, perhaps for some divine purpose, which we have not figured out yet due to personal and social limitations. We must remember that self-cleansing (by overcoming our limitations) and self-realization (through our potentialities) remain the main objectives of our lifelong self-awareness regimen, past the urgent need for an initial, timely self-assessment during youth.

The Makeup of Our Potentialities

A person's 'potentialities' comprises the outer limits of his inherent capacity—'cognition'—, which is not fully explored and developed. It entails his higher mental, physical, and spiritual abilities to perceive, feel, think, reason, act, react, and connect with others and his surroundings at a high degree of consciousness. Awareness is the amount of cognition (or potentialities) that we have learned to master at a conscious level rather systematically and routinely.

We have unique potentialities to do some tasks better than others. We also have an intrinsic capacity to feel life's beauties, moments, and values in our own special, imaginative ways. And we have divine potentialities that can provide the wisdom and mental energy we need to deal with major doubts and decisions of life more effectively. Potentialities include our general intelligence, but intelligence per se does not reflect our potentialities. While intelligence is a common criteria and measure of our mental ability, it does not pinpoint those creative areas we can apply for finding our 'self,' and it does not produce the wisdom and energy that stem from the magical experiences of self-fulfilment and spirituality. Only through exploring our innate potentialities, we can attain self-fulfilment, spirituality, tranquility, and capture the essence of life.

We usually think of our potentialities as those abilities in which we seem to excel, mainly for adaptation and success according to social norms and values. We are drawn to those fields of expertise and activities that offer the highest financial rewards. Therefore, we choose a particular profession and become an expert in that field. Meanwhile, we find little time or incentive to explore other aspects of our potentialities that incite our creativity and insight, especially for grasping who we really are. In our materialistic societies, we have no serious motives to search for our essence and potentialities, while we follow a deceptive path of success obsessively.

We cannot sense or measure our potentialities objectively according to humans' real needs, because we are distracted by either our struggle for survival or our ambitions for superficial needs. Applying even those abilities that we muster consciously is a tough task in our dynamic and demanding societies, let alone the huge amount of our potentialities that remain unchallenged at unconscious level. In this kind of environment, achieving self-fulfilment and tranquillity becomes a matter of accident for many of us, rather than a conscious pursuit.

We have an inherent potential (or nature) to seek a 'self' controlled and 'self' dominated life, but do not receive the family and social support to recognize and accomplish this basic instinct of humans. In this context, our personalities and attitudes toward life and relationships actually reflect how little humans' overall logic and potentialities have so far been developed. Our haughty personalities and phony social values are obstacles for discovering our potentialities, including our spirituality potentials for guiding us toward a more harmonious humanity. How can we ignore the simple fact that the world's incredible poverty and misery is an irrefutable proof of our miniscule use of intelligence and human potentialities? Sometimes we feel our needs for divinity in the latter stages of our lives when our lifelong depressing experiences shake our belief systems. Ideally, though, we should not limit ourselves to this possible late discovery with a much lower chance of helping us at that point. By understanding all aspects of our potentialities, including spirituality, we can increase the quality of our lives and inhibit our agonies significantly.

The Functions of Our Potentialities

Our life path is set according to the type of potentialities we nurture for, 1) exploring our divinity and 'self,' and 2) building our careers and satisfying our artistic passion. Let us refer to these dual purposes (functions) as divine and career potentialities respectively. The main purpose of *career* potentialities is to incite our creativity and attain self-actualization, which provides inner satisfaction and fulfils our need for achievement. On the other hand, our *divine* potentialities are for connecting us to our spirit and Creation. We find our 'self' and attain 'self'-actualization as we see ourselves a part of humanity, feel global sufferings, and show everlasting compassion. Thus, the terms self (for career) and 'self' (for divine) are used as two distinct actualizing virtues of our potentialities. In this context, 'self'-actualization is the ultimate stage of self-actualization, where one attains selflessness and connection to his soul and the universe. In a sense, our creativity can link us to Creation.

Of course, our potentialities fulfil other purposes, too, other than building our careers and satisfying our sense of spirituality. Actually, exploring our potentialities is the main process for activating every one of the seven elements of 'self', as discussed in Chapter Two. We like to contribute to society by offering our potentialities (maybe our simple thoughts). We like to be a little genius in some respect if we could. Even in the absence of this ultimate capacity, we believe we have some creativity and ideas to offer to others or ourselves as a symbol of who we really are and what we have done with our lives. As bare minimum, we like to ascertain our identity for our own sake, and for an honest self-presentation to others. Therefore, our efforts for realizing our potentialities could ideally address the question of, 'What am I here for?' in line with the question of, 'Who am I?' While our socioeconomic motives for using our potentialities are deep and urgent, our instinctual motive to grasp 'who we are,' and 'what we are supposed to achieve' always prickle our subconscious too. This strong urge reflects the unique essence of our being—our spirit.

In our conventional thinking, we ignore the main functions of our potentialities quickly and move on to explore only those skills that we enjoy doing or appear practical for making more money. We attempt to measure our potentialities merely in terms of tangible outcomes and a perception of success, which are usually gauged by monetary rewards. This narrow perspective is warranted in most situations as a practical means of living in our tough societies. However, this prevalent view of our potentialities undermines the depth of who we are or can be. It shows our tendency to bypass all the clues about our inherent need to know who we are. It shows our one-dimensionality. We forget that the ultimate purpose of exploring our potentialities is to emphasize on our humanistic needs properly, much more than we waste on satiating our artificial needs.

The *ideal* option would be to find and nurture our innate potentialities regardless of their financial and social appeal. Some rewards may flow in as well, but taken only as fringe benefits, rather than the goal. This may not be wise or practical nowadays for most people, however. Thus, the implications of career and 'self' potentialities are discussed in some detail in the next two chapters respectively. The objective is to get a better grasp of our approach toward our potentialities. We should know which aspects of our potentialities might benefit from our higher scrutiny for creating some balance in our lives. Maybe it is time at last, in the 21st century, to invent a better criteria and structure for living, by emphasizing on more important aspect of 'self,' instead of continuing with the same old habits of thinking about money and success to define ourselves, for God knows how many more centuries. One thing is clear, though: We are not compelled to follow the crowd like a fool!

CHAPTER SIX
Genetic (Career) Potentialities

Career potentialities refer to a person's genetic abilities to think and act for creating a valuable product while enjoying both the work process and output passionately. But how many of us get a chance to explore at least this basic level of our potentialities and apply them in our careers? What are the consequences and value of any career that does not use our potentialities?

At home and school, children are asked what they want to become when they grow up. They are trained to envision a particular life structure they must follow rather blindly merely for getting rich and powerful. They also sense an urgency to imagine a profession and guess the level of skills needed for it. Furthermore, they feel obliged to guess their capabilities, passion, and potentialities for doing those kinds of jobs. But who can do all these assessments and decide realistically, especially as a child or teenager? Therefore, they get confused, instead of learning about the role of human potentialities more logically and naturally. They just attempt to pinpoint a profession that appeals to them for some reason. If they cannot think of a smart answer, they simply make up an ambitious one, anyway, because they do not wish to appear like fools with no clue about who they want to be. If they are shy with deep doubts about this whole shenanigan and the presumed urgency, they may even depend on the feedbacks from their teachers, parents, and classmates about their intelligence and temper. Children's answers often reflect their brainwashed minds to appear ambitious for choosing a fancy career, anyway—unless it ends up to be a silly or funny answer that surprises the parents and teachers. In all, children only imitate what they have learned from TV or adults' conversations. They just want to become as rich and famous as all those celebrities out there. This is the general mentality that everybody builds at childhood and follows for the rest of his/her life.

Both society and parents play a major, and often misleading, role in directing kids' perceptions about the purpose of life and the role of a profession based on some common social norms. The emphasis is placed on the highest paying profession they can handle, and sometimes regardless of how good they can handle it, if they can learn to fake it. This is the closest everybody comes to understanding the purpose of, and applying, his/ her innate potentialities. That is also how most people learn to supposedly assess and develop their potentialities, mainly by some rudimentary perceptions about the means of satisfying their professional needs and serving their Egos.

Besides the fact that a majority of us never gets a chance to explore our potentialities, we do not even grasp the main role of our innate potentialities for personal growth. There is not even much concern about how our services can benefit others, but how much it can serve our greedy needs and ambitions. The whole society, including most parents, cherishes this shoddy mentality. We merely focus on our professional success, while ignoring our need for 'self' realization that requires a deep excavation of our innate potentialities.

Another obstacle for exploring our career potentialities relates to our opportunity for college or university education. Financial or social limitations may hinder this development. Our marks may not be sufficient for admission to some particular fields according to our passion or potentialities. We may be misled by job markets for planning our profession and field of study. Or, the job market changes by the time we graduate, and thus we feel obliged to adjust our career plans.

The Reality of Job Markets

The urgency and pressures of 'career planning,' adjusting to market demands, and job insecurities, throw the idea of search for our potentialities out of whack. Facing all these constraints and expectations, we hardly get a chance to *choose* a profession compatible with our primary talents and education, let alone in line with our real potentialities. We simply follow any means of training ourselves for the available jobs. Accordingly, we have learned to produce an acceptable level of product or service. Jobs get done, mostly inefficiently and ineffectively, and our efforts at best support our subsistence. Nowadays, most jobs are becoming routine and automated, anyway, and often performed by incompetent, egotistical people who occupy those jobs not based on their potentialities (qualifications), but rather due to their power games and socio-political affiliations.

Nowadays professions and professionalism are hardly compatible. We bring enough intelligence and shrewdness to work environment to keep our jobs with limited efforts and expertise just to make as much money as possible. This type of lazy mentality and lousy work ethics give people little motivation to worry about their potentialities. We feel lucky to find a job and a source of income. Thus, all other factors, such as social responsibility and the development of innate potentialities, feel quite irrelevant.

Giving 'job security' precedence is a realistic attitude and approach. After all, we must somehow pay our bills. Survival takes precedence over self-fulfilment and many other personal expectations that socioeconomic systems cannot necessarily offer to everybody. This becomes particularly truer as our societies face all kinds of restrictive socioeconomic challenges in the years ahead.

Some of us might learn to *create* our own professions according to our potentialities and psychological needs. And some of us may have the willpower or resources to *pursue* only those professions that match our passions and potentialities. However, these groups would always be in a minority. They should have special talents, intelligence, and patience to sustain themselves throughout their lives and stay sane. Thus, most of us must learn to cope with the rising mismatch of our potentialities and job markets. Yet, we must at least beware of the effects of the social disorder and deteriorating job markets on our personal welfare and plans.

The Implications of Unfulfilling Professions

On the one hand, even if we can determine the kind of profession that matches our potentialities and temperament, we still face a tough decision to pursue it if it causes financial insecurity, inadequate income, or social isolation.

On the other hand, life gets boring and aimless when our inherent potentialities and needs are not explored and activated. Especially, our work feels laborious, frustrating, and stressful if not driven by our passion and potentialities. We may feel or pretend to be happy and purposeful with our routine pleasures and moneymaking schemes. However, most intelligent people cannot stand the vanity of their lives without doing some meaningful work. When motivated only negatively by financial needs and a sense of job insecurity, the chances are high that we resent the work, the environment, and often even our colleagues. Fortunately, some superficial factors compensate for the lack of more genuine motivating factors. For example, we get trapped in the games of promotions, affluence, rivalry, recognition, work incentives, and other management tools to keep our Egos amused and happy. Nonetheless, deep down we feel unfulfilled and hopeless. We feel deep stress, but cannot pinpoint the real cause of it. Thus, we blame our boss's attitude, colleagues' lack of cooperation, or even family and personal problems, etc. Most people try to concentrate at least on wealth accumulation to replicate the sense of true achievements and amuse their brains.

Our lifelong struggle with our jobs remains a deep source of stress, as we seem to have limited choices for both subsistence and success. This social reality in the new era would always cause a major life dilemma for most people, because we have been conditioned to believe in a life structure that evolves around money, a career, a family, etc. Many people must accept this harsh reality at the end, no matter how much their spirits object. But, initially, when we assess our potentialities and professional choices, and then throughout our lives, we should remember why we made those major decisions as we did. We should always remember that our fulfilment in life merely depends on the realization of our potentialities and not necessarily finding a high paying profession, raising a family, etc. We should remember that as long as our innate potentialities are ignored, we remain doubtful about every work and challenge we undertake. We lose our work motivation and a chance to grow psychologically. We remain doubtful about our identity, self-worth, family values, means of self-fulfilment, and even the purpose of living. Unless, of course, we conclude that we have no potentialities and are largely useless, even despite all the wealth we have gathered. At the same time, not building a basic career, because we cannot figure out our potentialities and niche is a bigger risk for our Ego, self-image, identity, and psychological health. Social needs, including need for a companion, are also important factors for our decision. We must somehow resolve this big life dilemma for ourselves. We must gauge the risks of making a wrong decision when we are young and inexperienced. How we then convince ourselves to live in the atmosphere of our choosing forever is our business.

Ultimately, the criterion for solving this major life dilemma and making such a critical decision is our own sense of judgment about the prospect *(final outcome)* of what we would do, now and many decades in the future. Naturally, making a right decision at young age is tough for many reasons. For one thing, grasping the merits of self-actualizing jobs and imagining the feelings of self-fulfilment are impossible unless a person has had an opportunity for those special experiences. These personal (and often scarce) experiences do not occur to everybody equally and easily. Yet, if we are lucky to imagine or experience these deep and authentic feelings, they provide the right clues about our true potentialities. No amount of money and social recognition can replace those sacred feelings. Accordingly, our decision about our path of life becomes easier. Conversely, egoistical feelings and satisfactions usually reflect our deviation from our innate potentialities.

The outcome of people's choices for career is that seldom anybody works effectively and feels fulfilled nowadays, because life structure and options are limited with little regard for people's true potentialities and spirits. Acknowledging this social deficiency, however, may at least help us learn to make our overall life plans more realistically, and to mitigate the repercussions and stress of our unfulfilling profession. We may admit the need to do something about the effect of this universal deficiency on our lives. We may at least look for extracurricular activities or thoughts that activate a bit of our potentialities and lift our spirits. Some of us may think of a side business or profession. Some may concentrate on hobbies, etc. The point is to stay vigilant of our need for some means of self-fulfilment, because our professions can hardly do that. As a rule, our professions cannot constitute (or be viewed as) a meaningful purpose of life. No matter how hard we work, how much money we make, and how successful our Ego makes us feel, we remain unfulfilled and shallow if our real potentialities are not challenged. Of course, most people do not realize their shallowness or lack of fulfillment, which is probably a way of living!

Sometimes, a person is attracted to several self-actualizing activities. In this case, s/he is one of those luckier individuals blessed with a chance for a lifetime of enjoyments and fulfilment.

Yet, at the same time, s/he is more likely to get into trouble, because s/he is more susceptible to losing both his/her focus and sense of practicality, which most of us need for adapting to socioeconomic environment.

Judging the viability of our potentialities is a difficult task by itself, of course, especially when we have the added responsibility of finding only one (or at best a few of them) that appears exceptional and most fulfilling. Usually some seemingly justifiable areas of potentiality or professions mislead us to assume we are good at them. For example, we may think and decide that we can be a good politician. However, in reality, this might have been only a premature judgment or wishful thinking behind our sneaky ambitions for power and manipulating others.

Aptitude tests such as SAT can help us understand our basic potentialities, at least as preliminary information. However, only our own judgment and decision, based on our true feelings of fulfilment and satisfaction, count. We should find our niche (potentialities) by testing and feeling them. We do this in line with our efforts to learn about our personality, stamina, values, life philosophy, spirituality needs, etc., maybe with the aid of some experts. Realistically, finding a fulfilling profession, or even a hobby, entails the gruesome task of knowing our innate potentialities first.

CHAPTER SEVEN
Divine Potentialities

Our innate potentialities stir creativity that soothes our spirit and brings us peaceful contentment. In return, peace, contentment, and creative energy induce a deep sense of spirituality beyond the initial feelings of self-actualization. Therefore, we can draw the following conclusions:

1. Search for our innate potentialities is a natural drive.
2. Spirituality is merely a manifestation of the finer, divine power of our potentialities.
3. Spirituality is not an external connection but rather an inner exploration.

We can actually set apart this divine aspect of our potentialities as a means of 'self' development and spirituality beyond their application for work and social purposes. We could choose the perspective that while our potentialities help us make a living, no amount of affluence reflects human essence and potentialities. In that sense, 'divine potentialities' (our spirit) become the force for exploring 'self' and withstanding the imposing social hardships that we cannot avoid. This type of mentality offers some radical life options (questions) to ponder when we face the philosophical dilemmas about, 'Who we are and what we are here for.' Can we justify our existence without nurturing our potentialities? Can we imagine, for a day, that our success in life is not measured by the wealth or products we create? Can we think, for one day, only in terms of the authenticity of our character and the quality of our lives, aside from the identity that society affords us?

If we care to dig out our divine potentialities, the first step is to pause and think about the question of, 'Who am I or have become?' In this context, the concepts of 'potentialities' and 'self' coincide. In fact, 'self,' cognition, and potentialities are related concepts for explaining the properties of a thinking human according to his/her level of consciousness and feelings. Therefore, the discussions in Chapter Two regarding 'self' equally relate to the topic of potentialities. We can consider our potentialities the essence of the divine 'self.' Therefore, we can explore the characteristics of 'self' and find our divine potentialities in the process automatically, clear from socioeconomic demands and obligations. Conversely, if we explore our potentialities mostly for reaching enlightenment (and not merely for work and social adaptation), we approach our real identity—the 'self.' While career potentialities emphasizes on self-actualizing virtues of our work and thoughts, divine potentialities reflect the endogenous feelings of selflessness, humility, compassion, passion, transcendence, and connection to the universe and humanity that our work and thoughts generate. Our *career* potentialities might satisfy our needs for achievement and actualization, but our *divine* potentialities have the power to soar our spirit to the thresholds of spirituality.

We could choose to view our potentialities as a hidden treasure requiring a deep excavation of our minds and souls, leading to a core of personal awareness and a tranquil path of life. Unfortunately, however, we usually remain doubtful about the role of our potentialities for either divine or career purposes since we are often forced to *supposedly* think and act pragmatically in this chaotic world. We undermine our basic urges due to self-doubt, sense of practicality, or our quest for social acceptance. Instead, we often depend on people's flashy feedback or rewards to gauge the sensibility of our deeds and achievements—the kind of success we then naively attribute to our genius and potentialities.

Obviously, our divine potentialities, including spirituality, cannot be tapped in the course of mundane social life and relationships. Once we get trapped in the mainstream, we abandon life's natural path and forget our search for divine potentialities. We get hung up on the trivialities of our lifestyles, and thus miss the chance of exploring the basic but profound options of living. Most of our natural senses have become desensitized and imperceptive during our efforts for social adaptation. Thus, while our spirit strives to know 'who we are,' our sense of financial and emotional practicality keeps us faithful to our fake identity and social rules, and we merely wander on a shaky path of life. We feel dependent upon other people's opinions and acceptance, even when we overestimate our talents and get too arrogant about our self-deceiving sense of ingenuity. All along, we get mixed messages from people and our conscience about our potentialities. We struggle with our doubts regarding the possibility of ever exploring our potentialities and never get a chance to grasp the meaning of living free. We feel trapped, unappreciated, merely meandering aimlessly, and only worrying about our day-to-day emotional and financial survival. We simply seem stuck to any work available instead of pursuing what we are passionate about.

Ideally, our career and divine potentialities must coincide to maximize both our social and spiritual needs. They can become complementary when the sense of self-actualization from our work and thoughts soars beyond normal life experiences toward divinity, like the examples that Maslow has provided about the subjects of his studies. In such cases, no inner conflict exists about who we are.

Actually, however, hardly anybody gets an opportunity to nurture either his/her divine or career potentialities in our modern culture, since even his/her basic survival always seems in jeopardy. Despite the rising depression in modern societies, we are forced to ignore the main causes of our stress and instead get absorbed deeper in our depressing jobs and relationships. Realistically, we have no other choice, while hoping upon hopes that things would improve somehow eventually. Sometimes, we run away from one employer or profession to a similar or worse situation. We try to relieve ourselves from the agonies of some career or marriage deficiency and then turn around and get into an equally unfulfilling profession or relationship. Until we recognize the necessity of fostering our divine potentialities, we merely keep searching for different professions and lifestyles unsuccessfully. All along, our spirit gets more suppressed. 'Self' exploration remains an idle ideal when our need for social adaptation occupies all our time and energy. We suffer for ignoring our 'self' that could fuel our mental energy and induce our sense of fulfilment and divinity.

Nevertheless, figuring out and applying our innate potentialities remain an ominous challenge and a major life decision. We must eventually make this major decision and choose a path of life that could at least fulfil a bit of our spirituality need. Some people may acquire the willpower to overhaul their life philosophy for a chance to explore their divine potentialities. After all, it is up to us to choose the right balance among practicality, social survival, and nurturing our divine potentialities. We must know that our divine potentialities can at least make up for our failure to develop our career potentialities properly due to socioeconomic hurdles. No matter what we do for subsistence, we can nurture our divine potentialities along with our normal routines. At least, we have a plausible personal remedy for the agony of our unfulfilled career potentialities. Our divine potentialities can enrich our lives even when we are stuck in our dead-end jobs. In the end, we are responsible for resolving our inner conflicts, stress, and 'self' dilemmas.

'Self' Dilemmas

'Who we are' consists of three complementary attributes. That is, in general, we are a sloppy fusion of what we: i) feel, ii) think, and iii) do. These philosophical dimensions of 'self' coincide exactly with the nature of our potentialities. A person with pure thoughts, proper attitude (actions), and authentic feelings has a much better chance for both self-fulfilment and spirituality experiences. Feeling, thinking, and doing are our sources of energy and intuition to pursue and satisfy the full range of human needs. The more completely these humanistic dimensions are developed in societies, the higher would be the level of personal needs that people would be capable of satisfying. The more authentic and purposeful our feeling, thinking, and doing, the more 'self' grows and solves the dilemmas of living within our complex and callous societies. And the more selflessly these three attributes pervade personally and socially, the closer we get to a definition of a complete and pure human being.

The same attributes of 'self' (thinking, doing, feeling) affect our professional lives too, although mostly in the form of compromised thoughts, activities, and feelings. We have failed to implement a humanistic value system in work environments. At work, we do some ineffective (and often crooked) thinking, perform our jobs rather inefficiently (often out of spite or incompetence), and ignore the feeling dimension regularly (save for all those tactful pretences, sucking up gestures, rivalries, and manipulations). The main problem at work environments is that the 'feeling' dimension is hard to implement due to humans' egotistical and greedy nature. With all the science in the fields of management and human behaviour, we are still too helpless in utilizing the 'feeling' dimension of our potentialities in the work place. For staying competitive, organizations have become very practical with respect to manpower management. The feelings and compassion have been sacrificed for productivity and higher profits, or simply for surviving in economic markets. Unfortunately, the impact of organization work and mentality evolves from individuals' personalities, and thus both our personal lives and careers are infected harshly. This fundamental problem is discussed in detail in Volume III of this trilogy.

Together, our divine and career potentialities define 'who we are' and shape our character. Meanwhile, the three aspects of our personality manifest who we have become. Our behaviour reflects our ideologies, logic, idiosyncrasies, preferences, knowledge, wisdom and so many other traits. We can study our thoughts and beliefs in terms of their origins, backgrounds, purposes, and logic. We can then try to justify or modify these thoughts and beliefs according to a particular life philosophy that makes sense for us. Next, we study the incentives and forces behind our thoughts and beliefs. We like to know which of the 'model,' 'ego,' or 'self' aspect of our personality drives our thoughts, actions, and feelings, how, and why. If our thoughts, actions, and feelings are driven solely by Ego, we are less natural than we could be. If we have a Model personality and needs, but deep down have authentic feelings and humanitarian thoughts, we have a better chance than an egoist to become a more reliable and conscientious individual by thinking deeper while evaluating 'who we are.'

Nevertheless, we all have the potential for being a better, more natural, and happier person if we really want to become one and are willing to do some soul-searching and revamping of our beliefs and Ego. Our potentialities and limitations characterize 'who we are' and 'what we are here for.' However, we are mostly characterized in terms of how we handle our opportunities and limitations for being a better human being within the context of our general life philosophy.

Understanding the essence of 'who we really are, what we can do in this world, and for what end,' imposes major dilemmas for people in search of fulfilment and freedom. In particular, these dilemmas haunt us on two specific occasions: When we strive to choose the right (fulfilling) career, and when our spirit feels low and we seek some spiritual guidance. However, most of us dismiss this instinctual urge for self-analysis outright, often due to a lack of foresight or laziness. Another group finds these 'self' dilemmas too philosophical to tackle and thus remains reluctant to spend time on them. They feel overwhelmed already figuring out their daily routines, needs, and potentials. Besides, how can they make a decision about their identity (self) when they know so little about themselves? "Who cares anyway?" they decide and move on. Only a few of us eventually find enough time and motivation to explore these basic 'self' questions. Even so, we often get to this point in a late stage of our lives when so many opportunities have passed us by and it is impossible to exploit our potentials. By then, it is often too late to rear the essence of our being.

Who Cares 'Who We Are?'

Our regular feelings of emptiness and the lack of purpose in our lives reflect the depletion of our spirit. This happens because we focus only on the world outside us and how best to exploit it. We become conscious of our existence mainly when we feel sad, anxious, and lonely; otherwise, we follow a routine life structure and certain habits in search of an occasional sense of pleasure. We are conditioned to seek happiness outside ourselves and get sad when we are alone. This crooked perception of life is exactly contrary to reality, as external sources always cause hardship and gloom, whereas happiness comes only from inner exploration and self-realization—a lone experience. We can think valuable thoughts in line with our interests and potentialities, do the right things regularly after determining what those right things are, and most importantly, we must learn about our authentic needs and feelings. With our feelings, we can create the most delicate and beautiful experiences, and at the same time become acquainted with our potentialities and need for spirituality. With an objective assessment of 'who we are,' we can find our identity, modify our personality, and become a more conscious and conscientious person.

Therefore, we are (or must be) the main person who cares 'who we are' or can be. Other people benefit from our efforts to grasp the neglected 'self' within us. However, ultimately, we are the one benefiting from evoking our spirit and the potentialities hidden inside us, so that we can change our outlook on life and means of living.

Undertaking a self-awareness regimen is a major life decision, however, as it requires self-sacrifice and commitment. Nothing results from a short and shallow self-analysis, since we must focus not only on our own lives, attitudes, and potentialities, but also study our relationships with the universe and other human beings. Learning 'who we are'—self-awareness—requires a thorough understanding of the seven elements of 'self,' which were explained in Chapter Two. We must question the validity of our routine actions over a long period and grasp their sources, purposes, etc. And we must assess and understand the rationality of our urges behind our feelings. Self-awareness exercises performed in reference to our personality aspects can reveal the mechanisms, causes, and motives of our thoughts, actions, and feelings. In all, with major determination and patience, we can learn the art of self-awareness and make it a permanent habit as an integral part of our daily routines. Then we learn more about 'who we are' *every day* and witness our transformation. In this process, our potentialities surge and blossom, too. Naturally, this is a tough challenge for most people. After all, it is not easy for most of us to create a right balance between 'life' (our worldly desires) and 'self' (our spiritual aspirations). However, the outcome would prove quite worth our efforts.

Self-awareness makes us a more insightful and intelligent person, while it raises our personal sensitivity, too, in terms of our actions, thoughts, and feelings. We also become more sensitive about other people and the world as we learn more tolerance and compassion. We acquire added power in seeing and sensing our surroundings, and sometimes even the things beyond our normal senses. As we become receptive and critical of our deeds and feelings, our Self grows while the influence of Ego and Model diminishes. With awareness, we step beyond the obvious facts we observe on the surface and see the urges, motives, and natural defects behind our own and other people's behaviour and reactions. In particular, we learn not to judge others or react quickly. First, we try not to taint our own mood and personality just to deal with other people's attitudes and defects in their ways. Second, we gain a tendency to attribute people's shortfalls to some type of psychological and personality flaws beyond their control. Third, we understand that people's expressions and our impression of them are not necessarily a reflection of their true personalities or intentions. We realize that the negative reflections of an individual's personality are largely a self-defence mechanism, developed due to their ignorance and uncontrollable idiosyncrasies, of course. Therefore, we accept them more patiently and compassionately. Accordingly, our knowledge of 'who we are' also helps us understand, or at least sympathize with, 'who they are.'

All these exercises lead to a wiser cognition and a deeper comprehension of human potentialities, including their types of thoughts, feelings, and actions. Our potentialities are not restricted to those things that we *do* best. Our thoughts and ways of thinking (e.g., logic, common sense, and analytical ability) are definitely intrinsic potentialities that support everything we do and excel in. This should be obvious. However, the fact that our feelings are also an important part of our potentialities is not quite appreciated.

The 'feeling' dimension of our potentialities ('self') has been suppressed and sometimes purposefully misguided to the point where we have lost our sense of basic compassion and morality while getting radically oversensitive and demanding. We expect a lot from others but have no pure feelings ourselves. We need and expect a lot of love from others, but lack passion and patience ourselves. At the same time, occasionally we get surprised when, in some special moments, our soft feelings suddenly surface and we do not know how to control or deal with them. We are shocked by these unexpected surges of sentimentality and try to hide them because they may be seen as signs of weakness and vulnerability. In all, we do not know or care how our feelings establish our thought processes, as well as our relationships with the public and the universe. We do not care about analysing our feelings nor consider the possibility of adjusting them for our own sake and also improving our relationships with the outside world. Not merely the physical aspect of this relationship, but mostly our overall mental connection with those outside elements affects the characteristics of the 'self.' Grasping and nurturing our relationship with 'self' has its own tremendous effect on our psychological growth and enjoyment of life. With our refined feelings, we attain a higher standard of being and relating. Our sensitized outlook on life and our relationships enrich other people's lives too.

Without feelings and passion, we cannot excavate our potentialities. Our thoughts and actions remain crude if they do not flow through our feelings and passion. Our highest levels of creativity also surge when an emotional connection develops between us and other objects and beings. The 'feeling' dimension of our potentialities connects us to our souls, with the truth of life, and with the secrets of the real world. Our sincere feelings, passion, and compassion guide us to develop and express our selfless thoughts and actions.

What Are We Here for, Really?

Most of the discussions in this volume suggest our options, purposes, and basic steps for understanding 'who we are.' The related question, 'What are we here for?' needs a brief conclusion now, too, before closing this chapter.

The creation of the universe several billions years ago started a series of precise chain reactions and evolutions (within absolute chaos and randomness!) leading to the manifestation of man as we know it today. Only God knows what man would look like even a few millenniums from now, if humans survive that long. As we stand in awe about this meticulous creation and strive to detect how every step of the evolution has taken place, we are simply incapable of imagining and grasping what all these seeming facts mean. Except that, we might eventually admit our absolute insignificance within the scope of this amazing phenomenon. Our limited knowledge about millions of species gives us some clues about their instincts, defence mechanisms, living habits and urges. All these life dimensions within the expansive universe on the one hand, and the energy and formation of even a single DNA or atom on the other hand, the measurement of facts and factors related to us humans becomes pale in scope. Thinking of our existence and gauging the question of 'who we are' within these huge orderly dimensions should only make us feel most humble and also lucky to be part of it.

Despite our vast science, we still do not know *why* and *how* of so many things, including those matters related to the theories of the Big Bang and the creation of the universe. Yet we continue to ask ourselves 'why and how' about all these phenomena, while we admit the infancy of human logic and brain to find suitable answers. Although we are not sure about the creation, the universe, and God, we can notice that all creatures are directed by the question of 'why' intuitively. We ask 'why' constantly as if we intuitively need a 'purpose' for everything. In fact, this intuition seems to emanate in all the living things, including animals and plants. All their actions and reactions are for specific purposes too.

As an alert human, we are ordained to live with a strong intuition that constantly nags in our minds when we attempt to do something, or question the purpose of our living: 'Why?' Even our sense of boredom is related to this inner nagging voice. We often attempt to suppress this intuition temporarily by artificial methods, such as the use of drugs, but we can never get rid of it permanently. Is our curiosity a good or a bad thing and how does it affect our lives?

Our observations and research confirm that doing things for a purpose is a natural and valid process that all living things, and even the simplest steps in evolution, behold intuitively for the betterment of their existence. In addition, this intuition has forced us to develop a 'logical process' for solving our problems, e.g., rigid scientific methodologies. Not surprisingly, all scientific researches and methodologies start with the question of 'why?' 'Why' is the objective of every scientific research and it provides the rationale for every intelligent decision or action. Every hypothesis is an attempt to answer 'why' a particular phenomenon behaves in a particular manner. Therefore, both intuitively and logically we have come to believe that a purpose is required for everything we do.

The matter appears even more amazing since many of us, including this author, believe that life and the universe have no specific purpose beyond their mere existence. They simply are, as a state of being. We cannot say, 'Why the universe exists, why the Big Bang happened, why there was nothing before it, or why humans were created?' In this context, the universe or 'life' has no purpose, or at least any purpose that we humans can decipher; they are mere facts per se (for the time being at least). This sounds terribly odd to us because we believe that every aspect of 'living' must have a purpose. We have this inherent need to justify our existence, in the sense of knowing the purpose of living, every single day and every minute of it. Besides, the evolution has followed amazingly sophisticated steps for specific purposes, too. On the other hand, it is plausible that even the most fundamental notions applied in our perceived world, as building blocks of human logic, such as 'fact,' 'purpose,' and 'why,' have no sense or relevance within the boundaries of the real world.

Often we imagine that since we need a reason to do things, the universe must have a purpose too. We are too eager to impose the idea of 'purposefulness' or 'consciousness' on the universe for our benefit. Some people insist that humans' sense of purpose is actually a reflection of the universe's general purposefulness. Both our purpose and conscious, they believe, derive from the universe's. But there is no way we can ever prove, or even find a rational ground for claiming, these types of naïve observations or conclusions.

Of course, it seems logical to ask that when every simple action or decision should have a purpose, how can the universe or the life of a person (his living, not his accidental existence per se) be left undefined in terms of purpose. We can safely assume that the overall purpose of living is not supposed to be the sum of all the simple and single purposes that we set for our random, rudimentary actions and decisions. Could we say that the whole purpose of living is the objective of 'being' per se? And, of course, right away we may question the 'objective of being per se.' In which case, we may even demand that there should be a purpose for the universe and 'life' per se, too. Why not? But that would be a totally crazy cycle of thoughts much deeper beyond any humanistic logic or even basic speculations, something in line with the old dilemma of who created the God. For the sake of our sanity and making even some basic levels of speculation possible, we need to assume that the universe and 'life' are mere facts (for our purpose at least) with no ulterior purposes. Since we can never prove otherwise, it makes more sense to believe that the existence of the universe (even the mere existence of a person) has no purpose.

Yet, within this purposeless dimension of existence, humans, and the evolution as a whole, need a sense of purpose to grow. There is no harm in that and actually no way to avoid our instinctual need for purpose and reason. The old cliché that, 'Everybody should have a purpose in life,' merely reflects a basic human instinct. Nevertheless, the important point here is that, regardless of the purposefulness of the universe in general, now the whole material existence (including humans) seems to be driven by a basic urge to constantly ask 'why,' as a justification for survival.

While our routine actions and decisions are often for specific purposes, the ongoing process of human life in itself (living) has a much more fundamental objective, so much so we refer to it as the 'philosophy' of life. The word 'philosophy' has a much broader connotation and meaning than 'purpose' as it includes not only the objectives (whys) we must define for living, but also the processes (hows) we offer for achieving them. It does not really matter which word we use, 'purpose' or 'philosophy.' However, the latter is preferred and used only to emphasize the importance and wholeness of the 'purpose' of living in relation to all other singles purposes we set for our actions and decisions. In fact, once we have a whole, encompassing life purpose or philosophy, all other purposes that we set for our actions and decisions should stay subordinate to the main philosophy. Every simple purpose has to pass the test of validity within the general framework and guidelines of one's life philosophy—our convictions and beliefs. This shows the importance of a life philosophy to guide us through life. A life philosophy gives us a point of reference for all our decisions and for assessing our doubts. Maybe even we all share one unified life philosophy someday to minimize human conflicts and disharmony. Whether that is possible or desirable is another philosophical dilemma in itself, of course!

The question of 'what are we here for?' is thus only another attempt to refine our personal life philosophy. By this question, we set out to establish a fundamental (but personal) purpose for staying alive (beyond our purposeless accidental existence), for doing the things that would empower our spirits, and for achieving peace and self-fulfilment. Thus, although we are not here on this planet for any specific purpose, we must define one for our personal use for many reasons, but mainly for keeping our spirits intact. A whole chapter in Volume I is devoted to the topic of life philosophy as a tool for synthesizing our thoughts.

'What we are here for' promptly imposes many related questions such as, 'Why would I do certain things, follow a doomed structure of life, or even live, and for what end?' These questions demand some major purposes for living. And of course it is implied that life objectives (or purposes) should be worthy of some values for self and others. The answer to these questions should, however, come from personal research and contemplation rather than only following the norms and imitating others. We must figure out life personally. Religions and cults have made people see things their ways. However, submission to other people's prophecies or philosophies is not the way to answer the question of, 'What we are here for' even if their messages sound profound and spiritual. One has to arrive at the answer personally the hard way, though reading and listening to others may be helpful if one learns to be objective and free from false sentiments and influence.

A counter-argument against having a life philosophy and a real purpose for living is that life is much easier, and perhaps happier, without all these disciplines and thinking. Why waste so much of our precious life worrying about these intangible issues even though they feel like instinctual dilemmas always haunting us? Why set life objectives or justify our actions and decisions, and even existence as a whole? This group may argue that since human life feels random and outside of our control, we should stop fussing so much and instead leave everything to destiny. Many other arguments may be offered for or against this viewpoint. However, we must eventually agree that the answer depends merely on people's character, personal outlook on life, and preferences. We could blame our crooked outlook on life and priorities (leading to our deep naivety and doomed choice of lifestyles) for our purposeless pursuits day after day. Alternatively, we could blame our naïve obsession for dwelling too much on the nagging voice in our heads about the need for knowing the purpose of living and working so hard. Chapter Ten will elaborate on this point some more.

Any of the above options define a type of personal life philosophy, though often people adopt a path of life passively, merely based on their personality and habits, without assessing their life options quite carefully. Yet, developing a personal life philosophy is so important it should be considered a major life decision for any intelligent person, instead of living randomly and imitating others. Having a life philosophy is essential regardless of our lifestyle and the life path we choose to follow. Most importantly, however, our life philosophy should establish 'what we are here for.'

'What we are here for' also implies our contributions and accomplishments. However, the question is, 'What are the meaningful and worthwhile things that one can accomplish?' The general criterion is that it should affect and enhance self and other individual(s) in a positive way. Many life purposes might fit this criterion depending on a person's talent, vision, and mood. Ordinarily, the public opinion is considered the main criterion for worthwhile achievements, like when 90-95% of people believe in those contributions to society. For example, a doctor practising abortion definitely assumes that s/he is doing a worthwhile service for his/her community and so many people agree with him/her. However, many people consider abortion a crime instead of a contribution. *Ordinarily,* this service might not quite pass the test, as long as we have this kind of controversy about its value. Yet, the judgment of a majority should neither justify a purpose, nor affect us in choosing the worthwhile things that we can do. At the end, we have to make the judgment personally merely based on our life philosophy.

The main test of achievement lies in individual's deep conviction about the value of her/his contributions today or in the future even though people may or may not appreciate them right away. As long as the purpose is pursued selflessly, and s/he is not insane, fanatic, greedy, or criminal in relation to the thing(s) s/he is doing, those purposes and contributions can be considered worthwhile. Making a living along the way would not annul the purpose as long as greed or recognition is not the main purpose.

Many things we do regularly have some value and affect us and perhaps others. However, they most likely do not qualify as life achievements. The difference is in the nature of our accomplishments, of course, but more importantly in terms of their 'purpose.' Only those achievements resulting from one's conscious decision, in line with some divine purpose and philosophy, followed by conscience actions, qualify as indications of 'who we are' and 'what we are here for.'

The two questions of, 'Who are we?' and 'What are we here for?' are the cause and effect of each other. We can view 'who we are' as the *cause* and 'what we are here for' as the *effect*, and vice versa. It makes sense that our existence should have a cause and an effect. Yet, this clear relationship is not the whole essence of the two questions. Who we are cannot be justified by what we do, nor does the mere purpose of our actions determine who we are. Rather, we must initially attempt to find out about many detail characteristics of our 'self' by objective thinking, free from parental and societal influences. During this process, we establish the REASONS for our living, the purposes of our actions and decisions in life, and the integrity of a value system that we choose. Conversely, the causes (motives) and effects (outcomes) of our decisions should validate our life philosophy and existence. All along, only the *legitimate* purposes (causes and effects) of our deeds, thoughts, and feelings polish our spirits and the essence of 'who we are.'

CHAPTER EIGHT
Insight and Foresight

Many natural, social, and personal limitations prevent us from nurturing our potentialities and enriching our lives. Fighting off these many obstacles for reaching enlightenment is difficult as discussed in this chapter. Yet, we can mitigate their effects, by drawing on the power of personal insight and foresight that our spirits provide most naturally. Meanwhile, we hope patiently that fate would also support our efforts to attain our dignity and the high spirit that we deserve.

Potentialities and Opportunities

For success in society, one's potentialities and opportunities must coincide to produce some marketable output. Furthermore, we need the right type of personality (often a pushy or haughty one) to sell our services or products to others. Overall, new societies place a great deal of demands and barriers on people in terms of the type of potentialities they get a chance to nourish. Thus, our social values and opportunities often induce personal deprivation, suffering, and depression, because not only our innate potentialities often remain untapped, but also we judge our success and self-worth based on the perceived world's approvals and standards.

Nevertheless, social opportunities and setbacks remain inevitable facts of modern life infrastructure, because we prefer social life to solitude. The more we embrace these rules and values, the more raw opportunities are made available to us too. Most of us cannot easily bypass the temptations and privileges of living in this perceived world in hopes of pursuing a rather stoic life. Accordingly, 'who we become' (compared to 'who we are' capable of being) reflects our 'adopted' personality (Model). It shows our (dis)ability to recognize and exploit life's real opportunities, and also deal with both our personal and social limitations. This personal dilemma was addressed in Chapters Six and Seven in some length, so it is not discussed further here. The main point here is that we have a choice in the way we perceive and grasp social opportunities and setbacks.

It sounds cynical and bizarre to say that the more social opportunities we embrace, the more self-development opportunities we lose. Yet that is the sad reality of modern societies. Following social norms often causes the big risk of losing more of our spirit and freedom, despite the seeming rewards and deemed security in the perceived world. Most socioeconomic opportunities restrict our chances of finding 'self', as they only encourage us to concentrate on, and worry about, irrelevant life purposes. They mislead us because they prevent any normal person to build the right values necessary for living in the real world. We get entangled in life's traps, which are often disguised as certain formulas for success and happiness. Particularly, our obsessions for wealth and pleasures prevent us from pursuing a more natural life, and exploring our potentialities. We cannot see the merits of a simpler lifestyle and nurturing a modest personality. In the final analysis, social opportunities often sabotage personal opportunities and dilute the content and integrity of 'who we are.' They cause vast psychological limitations and dampen our spirits.

An opposite argument prevails about life's seeming limitations, when our failures and disappointments finally force us to think and act outside the box. Social setbacks, such as unemployment or failed marriages, sometimes make us find our innate potentialities and peace, away from the hectic socioeconomic environment that intends to control us more every day. Social limitations and pressures sometimes compel us to dig deeper within our inner self and redeem our divine potentialities and spirit.

The bottom line is we are bound by socioeconomic rules and restrictions. Thus, choosing a right balance between adaptation pressures and personal growth is the basis for building our life purposes and philosophy. We should disallow our own narrow perceptions of life opportunities and success affect our chance of exploring our essence in our careers and through our divine potentialities. Recognizing life's real opportunities for personal growth is a major life challenge and decision for every intelligent person. Accordingly, developing a lifestyle, based on our authentic needs and philosophy in line with a finer perception of life's essentialities, is a serious personal responsibility. Our decision delineates 'who we are.'

Potentialities and Interests

Many activities and adventures feel interesting and challenging. They satisfy our curiosity and sometimes earn us money too. Yet, these *activities* are often unrelated to one's real potentialities when they do not encompass all three dimensions of potentiality, i.e., thinking, doing, and feeling, simultaneously and consistently. Therefore, some deeper life purposes must always support our sporadic interests.

In particular, at younger ages, we are drawn to many jobs or activities that appear 'interesting' or earn us a living. Of course, testing our aspirations is justified while we are exploring our career potentialities. This approach feels natural, especially when job markets and demands cannot match the vast supply of potentialities that youths can offer. However, pursuing our interests without a general plan can mislead us in the end and waste many precious years of our lives. While the learning aspects of our youthful experiences are useful, pursuing different interests or activities randomly over an extended period may damage both our sense of self and our chance of developing a career. These types of pursuits usually lead to more confusion, self-doubt, stress, and disappointments, not to mention the risk of losing the main direction of our lives. It also may hinder our chance of exploring our potentialities and opportunities.

The point is to not lose sight of one's real responsibilities and needs in the midst of the rising social chaos and cause further depletion of our spirits. Our mission is to explore and pinpoint both our careers and innate potentialities regardless of our fleeting interests or the money attached to them. We may decide (or feel obliged) to pursue certain activities, careers, or interests, but we should also focus on our ultimate plans. Our sporadic interests and erratic ambitions (e.g., being a singer) per se should not hinder the development of one's long-term plans based on a mature life philosophy.

Potentialities and Confidence

Despite our high Egos and exaggeration about our capabilities, we usually have nagging doubts about our potentialities and 'who we are.' Even geniuses often suffer from this condition. Many renowned composers, including Tchaikovsky and Rachmaninov, had doubts about their masterpieces. Some artists have suffered psychologically when they did not get the recognition they believed they deserved. Many geniuses have destroyed their artistic and scholarly works, because they appeared inadequate to them. However, usually, all these sufferings and destructions are the result of our self-doubts, or our severe neediness to look externally for recognition and approval. We might suffocate our potentialities when we *doubt* the ultimate value of our self-fulfilments due to a lack of social acceptance or valid criteria for measuring our self-worth. We sabotage our identity, confidence, and a chance for spiritual experiences, when we let the crooked values of the perceived world ruin even our feelings of self-actualization.

Normal people can never be fully confident about the value of their creations, feelings, or thoughts. Our feelings, in particular, are often misunderstood even if we expressed them with the most powerful lyrics and sincere intentions. Sometimes, somebody may truly appreciate the essence of what we create or say. But, in general, understanding other people's sentiments and intentions is difficult. Nevertheless, the main purpose of developing at least a bare minimum of our divine potentialities (a basic sense of spirituality) is to curb our endless craving for external appreciation. Confidence must derive naturally only from one's authentic self-fulfilments and spiritual energy. As long as one satisfies one's artistic and spirituality needs, other external factors would not distract the process of exploring one's potentialities. At the same time, in many cases, a person's negative sentiment about his/her work is proper, as it might rightly relate to the vanity of the work and the need for more insight and practice.

The opposite is even more prevalent, nowadays, when so many people have become haughty through self-hypnosis or due to commercialized publicity of their substandard creations. Accordingly, they sabotage their chances to explore their innate potentialities realistically and find who they really are. They prefer to hide behind their phony overconfidence, shoddy creations, and crooked self-image.

Both overconfidence and over-doubts obstruct the natural flow of our potentialities. Our superfluous societies reward even false confidence more than actual performance and thus misguide the pursuit of one's real potentials. People mostly judge one another based on their phony appearances and assertions rather than honesty and modesty. So, we are forced to produce a false personality to adapt and prosper, while hiding our self-doubt. We draw on Model to reflect a phony confidence merely for social purposes.

Of course, even if others could or cared to support us, we would always fear that they might withdraw it any time and leave us helpless and needy again. In fact, people do this quite often intentionally for controlling or manipulating one another. Sometimes, it appears that we have to break someone else's confidence or put him down in order to feel superior ourselves. This happens in work environments in particular, but also in families and friendships. We undermine others deliberately or inadvertently only in hopes of boosting our own Ego and confidence. We would continue to hurt one another relentlessly as long as we cherish these rules of social adaptation and quarrels for testing, pressing, and proving our superiority and potentialities.

Inner confidence evolves from needlessness contrary to norms in the perceived world where external acceptance and approvals must always feed one's Ego to maintain an outer show of confidence. Ironically, even if others were smart, or cared, enough to provide the kind of feedback required for building our confidence, it would always remain shaky as long as we do not know how to internalize confidence naturally. We would always doubt even other people's feedback and judgments if we were not genuinely convinced of our authentic potentialities—if our confidence lacks divinity and our spirit's backing. At the same time, rational doubtfulness is always a sign of wisdom and humility, and quite precious if not leading to chronic self-doubt.

For building our confidence, we need integrity and self-reliance to cultivate our potentialities and mitigate self-doubt. We need inner power and high spirits to dig deeper into the hidden treasure of our potentialities with perseverance when some sparks of ingenious or inspiration strike us. We need strong convictions to gradually build our self-awareness for realizing 'who we are' while sympathizing with 'who they are.' Accordingly, we develop inner confidence about our thoughts, emotions, and deeds. We grow enough confidence to respect other opinions, too, even those from people with a different perspective of life, whose values we no longer share or care for. Despite other people's wicked view of us, we remain objective about their feedbacks, while stay clear from their manipulations. We internalize our potentialities and who we really are. At the end, we are the only one who must care 'who we are,' as noted in the last chapter.

On the one hand, only through our divine potentialities we can build our inner, stable confidence, which supports self-awareness and further exploration of our potentialities. On the other hand, authentic, internalized confidence manifests through a genuine sense of selflessness and needlessness, as a reflection of our divine potentialities blossoming. That genuine self-confidence shows that the process of self-awareness has been productive. This feeling is unlike the ostentatious overconfidence (arrogance) that many people exude nowadays to hide their shallowness, egoism, and low potentialities. True confidence comes from a sacred feeling of humbleness driven by our high spirit.

Potentialities and Fairness

We firmly believe that life owes us the best of everything. We are convinced that we not only have huge potentialities to offer to society, but also deserve substantial rewards for what we do and who we are. We strive to demonstrate our potentialities so that people can discover and respect us. We change jobs, invent things and ideas, and pursue all sorts of business ventures in order to prove ourselves.

However, many forces prevent our dreams from coming true. Most of us realize gradually that our potentialities would never be recognized or rewarded, and thus we attribute this atrocity to the world's unfairness. It feels as though people deliberately refuse to acknowledge us for what we can do, think, and feel—our unique potentialities. They refuse to provide honest feedback, encouragement, respect, or compensation, which we seriously believe we deserve. Thus, we get frustrated and convinced that both life and people are unfair.

We often feel this way. Actually, our frustrations about life's unfairness and people's malice are warranted often too. The fact is that while everybody is self-centred and mostly concerned about his/her our own needs, desires, and Ego, fairness becomes an illusion automatically. We are not unfair necessarily out of spite, but mainly because we are self-serving individuals and must be fairer and nicer to ourselves first. We need the most and best of everything for ourselves and those whose friendship and loyalty we need. If any charity is still left in us to share, only then we might be less prejudiced occasionally. These are real facts and we must recognize that we cannot do anything about the matter. The rule is that we do not have enough compassion toward others, especially strangers—the primitive law of survival and success!

Another point is that we are often personally responsible for stirring the feelings of unfairness by exaggerating our potentialities and setting unreasonable expectations. It is in fact a sign of our unreasonableness (unfairness) when we expect people to appreciate 'who we are' while we persistently overstate our capabilities and remain arrogant. Even if we were honest with our presentation of who we are, still it is not usually possible for others to appreciate who we are. Thus, ultimately, either our perceived unfairness or actual social prejudices cause us stress and confusion. Yet, we must somehow learn to come to terms with this *unfairness* too.

'Feeling unfairness and inducing it ourselves' is a human shortfall. This awareness provides a basic consolation, as we can blame humans' nature for feeling and acting this way. Yet, some people can deal with unfairness better. They disallow the feeling of self-pity or aggression overwhelm them when they face unfairness. While they do not measure their potentialities and self-worth in terms of external rewards and recognition, the feeling of unfairness occurs to them less frequently too. Also, when a person develops his/her inner confidence and actualizes his/her potentialities, the question of unfairness hardly surfaces.

We have two choices on this matter. One option is to accept unfairness as an irreversible reality, like so many other limitations of social living. This mentality is hard to adopt, but it can save us a lot of agony and energy. The other more prevalent option is to let self-pity aggravate our stress and aggression toward others. Taking fairness less seriously helps us make better choices in life, however. Instead of self-pity or aggression, we could contemplate the chance of creating a life of needlessness or independence, while we dream about the possibility of humans becoming less self-serving and selfish eventually.

Indeed, we deserve to be understood and appreciated, but it is somewhat unreasonable to expect others to care enough, or be able, to perceive our feelings and thoughts accurately. People have too many problems and personal agendas to care about the depth of other people's personality, potentialities, and thoughts. Their judgments are at best hasty if not malicious. This is the rule and sentiments of the perceived world. This is human nature, because we have not built our spirits, especially the spirit of fairness. We must accept the reality of unfairness, despite the pervasive discriminations and prejudices at work and family life. As another step for exploring our divine potentialities, we must adjust our perspective of unfairness and our expectations from people in this regard.

Potentialities and Perseverance

It seems redundant to talk about the importance of perseverance in materializing our potentialities. On the other hand, not mentioning such an important factor would be negligence. The simple fact is that real potentialities are like hidden treasures buried in the depth of our unconscious and depleted spirits. The only tool for excavating these treasures is perseverance. In order to reach the depth of our thoughts and unconscious, we must believe in our ability and the strength of our convictions to pursue our goals without self-doubt or procrastination. We need resilience and a high spirit to conquer the depth of our unconscious and redeem our potentialities. We must break the normal living barriers and build our confidence, so that the stream of potentialities flows fluently. Once we whisper the right tunes in our unconscious, the process of self-awareness becomes automatic and natural, and our divine potentialities resonate musically. Perseverance requires an initial determination and a lengthy search for an opening to our treasure of potentialities. Perseverance is another manifestation of our spirit.

The Integrated Treasures of Potentialities

The purpose of understanding social limitations, unfairness, and cruelties is not for getting cynical or seeking seclusion. Rather, the purpose is to redirect our efforts toward the more productive feelings, thoughts, and actions. The objective is to step outside of social limitations and create a more meaningful life for ourselves from simple thoughts and feelings. At the end, the only way to redeem our souls is to discard our erratic thoughts and struggles. Only by exploring our 'self' and divine potentialities, we may heal our troubled souls and discover the beauty of the world inside and around us. That is the way to build our spirits. The most exciting aspect of our potentialities manifests in our ability to establish our connection with Nature.

Our personalities, logic, psyches, spirits, and other attributes stir our feelings, thoughts, and actions, which in turn manifest our abilities and potentialities. Our divine potentialities also determine our view of the universe and outlook on life. Influenced by external information and knowledge, our potentialities make us view our world as a beautiful place with all kinds of joyful and sensational experiences; or we let our limitations lead us to view life as a horrible journey filled with suffering and misery. We recognize the bad and sad sides of our personalities and all the social limitations and injustice. However, instead of giving up on life, we can create a life of our own by drawing on our potentialities to connect with Nature and the simpler stuff of existence. Life is not bound by social rules or our naive perceptions of people and the world. Outside those stressful boundaries, life can actually be quite fulfilling and peaceful.

We can discover our potentialities during our exploration of the infinite offerings of the universe as well as elite human beings. It is true that all the valuable things in life are free! Not gold or diamond, but rather the creations of Mozart, Beethoven, Monet, Van Gogh, and many other masters can stir our imaginations and creativity. This collective treasure of potentialities is not private. We can all enjoy them, get inspired, and supplement our personal potentialities to the extent we can observe and absorb the world's treasures privately. We would always have more potentialities of our own and others to explore and enjoy in a day. We would never have enough time to feel all these pleasures. Time constraint is in fact the only joyful *limitation* in life. We always look forward to our next day's discovery and self-fulfilment. And of course, in no way this time shortage is comparable with the kind that workaholics and people in search of wealth have.

The unfortunate reality is that even when we recognize the true purpose of life, we have difficulty to think straight or reduce our mundane activities to use our time more wisely. We still must sustain a family and struggle to pay the bills. Therefore, we continue working in an environment we do not care much about and do a lousy job that seems like a total waste of our potentialities. We still have to deal with sales people who try hard to convince us buy more useless stuff. We must deal with unending family quarrels and demands. And we must fight the traffic and waste time in line-ups in supermarkets, for social services, etc. It gets hard to find a few minutes for ourselves, to do the things we like, and to explore our potentialities. Even for those few minutes that we need to spend in solitude, we may be accused by our family of being selfish and uncaring. The struggles continue... Nonetheless, along the way, we continue our search for, and enjoy, the universal treasure of potentialities offered by geniuses, including our own and, of course, we bask in the vast treasures offered by Nature.

CHAPTER NINE
Life Limitations

Aside from the factors discussed in the last chapter, many other social and personal limitations obstruct our struggles to find 'self' and unravel the power of our spirit and potentialities. They also affect our doubts, decisions, and path of life, as discussed in this chapter. Overall, four types of life limitations make both our jobs of adaptation and personal development difficult. They are:

1. Social and Economical Limitations
2. Natural Limitations (Physical and Mental)
3. Personality Limitations
4. Self-imposed Limitations

Social and Economical Limitations

It is sad that we are becoming more susceptible every day to erratic forces beyond our control. We are not talking about fate or natural forces in the universe, but rather the manmade social and economic systems that dictate our way of thinking and living. Our social structure has become too complex to understand and cope with. We no longer know how to live naturally while our attitude and mentality shape around many superficial social norms. Ironically, we have lost, at the same time, our faith in the systems and mechanisms that build the social structure, including our political and judicial institutes. Family values have deteriorated drastically, too, due to social and economic pressures. The nature and purpose of family relationships have changed immensely in the last few decades. Partners have extreme difficulty to relate or understand each other's expectations. Everybody dreams and demands erratically in their relationships because no moral standards exist to apply as an objective, basic guideline. We have discarded our traditional family values, but have no new guidelines to curb our wild imaginations and rising idiosyncrasies. We are living in fantasy with our naïve life outlook and relationship expectations. We adopt fake identities to adapt and prosper, thus lose a chance to explore who we really are and what the objectives of our being and socializing are. All these routine pressures impose immense limitations for building a simple life.

In particular, our children are seriously confused about social values and ways. They lack some reliable criteria to gauge and build their life structure and define their companionships, which have become quite chaotic and frustrating for them. Many of them desire to free themselves from the anxiety of living in this environment, but do not know how or often end up choosing another lousy alternative for living and thinking. All we need to do is to look around ourselves and see how senseless the crimes of the recent decades have become and how unhealthy our environment and living conditions are becoming. The other day, on Friday August 16, 2013, three teenagers in Oklahoma City gunned down and murdered an Australian student, Christopher Lane, because, as one of them said, "We were bored."

The other night, a documentary on TV highlighted the life of a bunch of university graduates turned prostitutes in order to pay back their student loans. It is hard not to wonder about the deep demise of our social structure and values. It is hard not to wonder about the youth's mentality and our teachings to them. It is hard not to doubt the value of university education when job markets cannot help university graduates. All that education does not even teach people anything about basic human integrity, self-worth, and ethics. What are all these efforts good for then?

Random shootings, families kidnapping or killing own members, teenagers becoming murderers for a few dollars or out of boredom, police shooting innocent people unnecessarily only out of arrogance, unemployment and the absence of an economic infrastructure in line with population growth, greed and disproportionate distribution of wealth, pollution and destruction of natural and economical resources, obsession with sexuality, more consumerism and capitalistic ideologies, senseless suicides, on and on and on. The list of crazy acts and values that we are supposed to understand and deal with, and the limitations that we are expected to plan our lives within are growing larger but tighter. The consequence of all these pressures is a deep state of confusion and helplessness to grasp the meaning of our lives or anything around us. Many of us have already lost self-control and attempt crazy acts, such as bombing buildings and killing hundreds of innocent people. Who can really find a meaning for his/her existence in this environment when every one of us has become a part of the problems even as we try to be a better person?

Despite our children's potentialities and efforts to achieve certain goals, the impact of external limitations, i.e., social and economic systems, is extreme and capable of crippling so many able individuals. The road to success and relative happiness was much clearer in the past. Now it is full of whats and ifs and insecurities. Not long ago, we believed that education and personal initiative led to job security and a rather healthy family life. But not anymore. How have we brought this chaos upon ourselves and why do we accept living like this? Do not we have any other option? All we need to agree on at this time is that so many important factors that affect our financial and emotional welfare and state of mind are out of our controls, and in fact out of the control of those to whom we have trusted the construction and maintenance of social and economic systems.

In all, the complexity, unfairness, and irrationality of social structure are making our lives too obscure and unmanageable. Making sense about this system or coming to terms with it would continue to be the most challenging task for governments and people. Yet, for recognizing 'who we are,' we must understand and defeat the effects of these erratic forces. First, we should somehow accept and cope with the fact that understanding and justifying the existing socioeconomic conditions is beyond our ability to a large degree. The intricacies and crookedness of the social and economic environments that we have inherited, and perhaps helped create for ourselves, are unexplainable and unsustainable. Why cannot we see this and do something about it? That is amazing! Second, we must get smarter and fight the temptations of getting absorbed and/or dissolved in these systems. Third, we must find ways of flourishing as an *individual* within these substandard systems both spiritually and mentally. We must make the best of the bad situation without being pushed to despair about the whole matter of life. Handling this convoluted dilemma is quite difficult for most of us, of course. However, we must at least remember that the meaning of a person's life manifests only through his selfless and self-reliant character and not the phony social identity s/he strives to build.

Our needs and socioeconomic pressures obliterate our lives and then we blame 'life' and fate instead of social structure and our own inability to find better means of living or stopping our own role in feeding the monster ruling our world. The task of evaluating 'who we are,' both personally and as human beings, is also getting tougher with time, due to the rising personal malice and naivety, as well as socioeconomic limitations that one must face and cope with. Yet, we must strive for more self-discipline and spiritual power to overcome the forces of despair and confusion and to concentrate on grasping 'who we are.' What other choice do we have?

Natural Limitations (Physical and Mental)

Everybody deserves a peaceful life and a chance to develop him/herself to the highest levels of wisdom and piety in our supposedly civilized societies. This is a noble objective. However, our genetic and upbringing limitations always stand in our ways. In addition, both formal and social educations, at home and society, mislead people about the right values of life and their choices. Furthermore, people's delusions and unrealistic expectations turn into additional limitations that hinder their ability to learn 'who they are' and why they wish to choose a particular lifestyle. Society is causing us more confusion everyday, but we also make life difficult for ourselves by our decisions.

Our mental and physical abilities are mostly hereditary. The bone structure, height, weight, and intelligence are basic limitations, though we can influence their growth somewhat with nutrition, exercising, and learning. Despite our genetic limitations—that we must recognize and live with—, education and awareness might help a person overcome his/her personal limitations, e.g., athletic abilities or mathematical aptitude, after a long process of training and possibly revamping his/her old habits. Nonetheless, a true appreciation of one's limitations is the best way to overcome them.

On the one hand, we must envision and train our brains for their ultimate potentialities, like body builders who create massive muscles regardless of their heights and bone densities. On the other hand, overestimating our mental capacity and logic, and becoming more arrogant every day, shows our naivety. It hinders our chance for even the basic nurturing of our brains for our own benefit. Formal education per se or egotism cannot help us for real life challenges. Instead, we need to pinpoint and learn the essential means of living and relating. Learning the right stuff about life and self, including our ultimate limitations, requires patience, modesty, and special efforts, however.

Usually, parents have the motives to teach these facts to their children, if they were not so preoccupied by life themselves and could think rather objectively outside social norms and teachings. We all try to recognize our kids' talent, such as athletic abilities, memory, artistic talents, creativity, vocabulary and language, etc. Sometimes, teachers and other concerned individuals might play a positive or negative role too. Some objective parents succeed in pinpointing their kids' potentialities and limitations and possibly guiding them properly. Nowadays, however, most parents spoil their children with their raw value systems and their naïve intentions to maximize their kids' confidence and self-image. Thus, they ruin any chance for their kids to grasp their natural limitations and work out their options realistically. They do not appreciate the repercussions of over or under developed Ego and confidence that result from parental overindulgence of their kids. They only put more psychological pressures on their children and themselves by ignoring humans' natural limitations. They kill their spirits instead of helping them figure out their potentialities and limitations properly.

Gauging our mental strengths and limitations is a natural and perpetual process that starts at a very early stage of our lives, but our Ego and apathy often sabotage our chance for doing a proper assessment. The purpose of assessing our inherent limitations is to set more realistic life targets, and to enhance our self-awareness and objectivity. Ignoring our limitations, or hoping to curb their symptoms superficially, eliminates the chance of pinpointing our simpler potentialities that we can nurture naturally and often have divine and lasting purposes. In some cases, self-awareness might help a person overcome even his/her deep idiosyncrasies, e.g., jealousy or spite, after a long process of training and finally revamping his/her old habits. However, the main purpose of assessing our natural limitations is to set more realistic life targets, and to enhance our self-awareness and objectivity.

Personality Limitations

The deep effects of personality aspects, i.e., Ego, Model, and Self, on our communications and their roles for finding happiness were discussed in detail in Volume I of this trilogy. These personality issues impose severe limitations on our lives. With our false personalities, we cause ourselves many extra headaches, mainly due to losing our identity and a chance to find 'self.' Furthermore, we attract people who are incompatible with us in terms of their needs and aspirations. Thus, we go through a long process of trial and error before finally accepting that our lifestyle and relationships are only making us more depressed and desperate instead of enriching our lives. In particular, the lousiness of most relationships nowadays relates to the lack of inner power and integrity of partners, again mostly due to the shallowness of their personalities.

Self-imposed Limitations

Our erroneous judgments and decisions create a large variety of self-imposed limitations. Furthermore, we make our lives more complex and unbearable when we do not find the courage and willpower to reverse a bad decision, or at least acknowledge it. A simple example is addiction. A smoking or drinking habit may start for many reasons. A person with a good judgment would not be dragged into this position in the first place, but even if s/he were, s/he would try to rectify his/her mistake. Some people may not be mentally prepared to fight the temptations of a habit and breaking it. Not everybody can avoid or overcome the psychological effects of some earlier decisions or failures that may linger for the rest of a person's life. This is true even when s/he feels the burdens of this limitation and understands how it prevents him/her from developing self-esteem and a positive outlook on life.

Physical limitations due to the lack of exercise and activity, and psychological limitation due to negative thinking and experiences, are the main categories of self-imposed limitations. While the causes of these limitations may have been outside an individual, a determined person recognizes them as self-imposed limitations that only s/he can eliminate, and then look for workable solutions. Obviously, solutions are often hard to come by, while self-discipline, conviction, and commitment are needed too. Yet most of us compound the effects of our limitations because we remain passive or ignore the debilitating symptoms of our self-imposed limitations, instead of working on our willpower or seeking help.

We impose major limitations on our lives due to our attitudes and personalities. Sometimes, our false pride stands in the way of establishing or maintaining the kind of relationships we so dearly need. We may even destroy good relationships because of our egoism, selfishness, and stubbornness. At the end, we suffer personally the most from such self-imposed limitations that lead to substandard life conditions. We hurt ourselves unknowingly, because all these life burdens are the results of our naively conditioned mentality and personality. Of course, our judgments and values are mostly tainted by the outcome of our rearing environment and the influence of social norms, which means that our limitations are mainly of no fault of our own. Yet we are ultimately the one imposing it on ourselves with our passivity and negativity. We must understand and acknowledge that only we are responsible for alleviating these limitations the best we can. If we analyse our relationships, attitudes, expectations, and judgments more critically, we can pinpoint our weaknesses and limitations. Fortunately, many of these limitations are curable or controllable, if we really care to help ourselves.

Self-imposed limitations often result from the value system and lifestyle we adopt. For example, most people spend beyond their means and then suffer its consequences. They borrow money to acquire fancy clothing or pursue a certain lifestyle.

Thus, they make life miserable for themselves and people around them by living like mindless robots merely following the crowd. They just let their raw ambitions and greed overwhelm their ways of building and leading their lives. They torture themselves with their fantasies, neediness, inability to find love and happiness, or thirst for power and wealth. This kind of self-imposed torture and limitation prevents us from enjoying a simple life and utilizing our potentialities. Instead, we get hung up on life trivia and superficial stuff.

The Ultimate Life Limitation

Some astonishing questions and realizations shake us during childhood when we become curious about our origin and wonder what gave us life, and why. What happened that we are here in this world? Before finding a satisfactory answer to these elementary but confusing curiosities, we suddenly face a more shocking fact: Death. It remains a major and stressful discovery for a few days or weeks. Then this ultimate life reality subsides after we struggle and fail to understand its purpose, even after asking all sorts of questions from our parents. At last, every child somehow surrenders to the harsh reality of death as s/he sends it to his/her subconscious. S/he realizes this ultimate limitation of his/her being briefly, but prefers to deny it by hiding it in his/her subconscious. Thus, our understanding of death remains at the perceived reality level, which has a tendency to be rather casual about our convictions and daily affairs. Our subconscious does not emanate the force and the meaning of death truly—as the ultimate limitation of our being.

Of course, our natural ability to forget sad realities or submerge them to our subconscious helps our sanity. However, forgetting or undermining 'death' diminishes our ability, as a child or adult, to appreciate who we are and establish a profound value system. There is a potential for kick-starting our self-awareness process, but we all lose this chance. Understanding 'who we are,' our inherent vulnerability, and the reality of death—that our existence may end in a second—could have helped us stay modest and alert. We could have been much humbler if we always remembered that we have no control over our most precious asset—our lives. Instead, we insist on building a pompous character and childishly brag about our importance.

The irony is that remembering our 'nothingness' regularly empowers our character and spirit. We find a deeper meaning for the things happening around us, if we remembered perpetually that our existence is really controlled by supernatural—or at least some random—forces. At this level of high consciousness, other life limitations become more bearable, and the significance of so many of our struggles for phony success would subside drastically. At this point, we graduate to the next level: We like to learn something about (or at least create a plausible imagination of) this outside force that grants us life and death. We may then decide to re-examine and adjust the course of our lives to some extent in order to play the limited role we may have in our destiny, such as not drinking and driving or eating harmful food. We would be alert about our environment and feel part of Nature and the universe. By our constant sense of mortality, we start to appreciate our existence better, and we enjoy Nature and other creatures, as we see them fragile, beautiful, but also so vulnerable like us. We try to learn from other human beings who have offered their wisdom and experiences of life. We learn how all forms of life have developed a mechanism for defence against danger and death, but also yield at the end to the powerful forces of Nature when time comes to surrender their existence. All that defence mechanism and personal wisdom would be worth not a penny.

Thus, we should celebrate death consciously as the main clue about the meaning of life, instead of pushing it to our subconscious. Repeating the word 'death' should not cause gloom either. Actually, the more we bring this reality into fore, the more we learn about the *mysteries* and *values* of life. We appreciate the triviality of all our worries and greed. For example, when a job promotion or recognition is delayed or overlooked, we would not only handle the related pains and disappointment better, but also welcome the chance to ponder our life choices more insightfully.

Fortunately, many people nowadays try to keep death in their semiconscious occasionally by repeating the slogans, 'Life is too short, and you live only once.' This subtle awareness is supposed to help us mitigate our fear of taking on challenging adventures. It could also make us stronger and wiser if it were practised continuously as a ritual, and if people felt the true essence of these slogans. However, most people use them as an excuse for their laziness or carelessness—instead of alertness—or for justifying their pleasure-seeking mentality. Unfortunately, the slogans 'Life is too short, and you live only once' have become a scapegoat for people to get more reckless financially and emotionally. We always insist on missing the boat even when we get a worthy insight occasionally!

In all, while death brings us to the final frontier, it also gives us the best yardstick to gauge our lives and limitations with higher wisdom. Of course, some exceptions defy this general criterion. For example, when an old or terminally ill person suffers from pain and self-degradation, the situation could be a higher and more devastating limitation than death itself. In fact, death becomes a source of relief in this instance, too, as the only escape from life limitations.

Nonetheless, the main limitation of one's life is life itself, which is ultimately significant merely for the opportunity it renders us to trace and enjoy our potentialities, as well as the integrated potentialities of others and Nature, for only certain number of years. Even if we are lucky to have a full natural life, we should be wiser in allotting this most precious resource in a meaningful manner. We have a choice, and hopefully gain the wisdom too, to spend our lives on activities and thoughts that give us a sense of self-fulfilment and spiritual transcendence. And for some of us who have passed certain stages of our lives, it is now so clear that life is such a short journey and how ignorantly we, as a child and young adult, felt there was so much time to conquer life. We realize how we have wasted so much of our precious lives and mental energies on pursuing shallow dreams and pleasures.

Acknowledging our ultimate limitation—the finality and fragility of life itself—also gives us the proper mindset to distinguish life priorities and essentialities more objectively. The journey of life can become extremely joyful and beautiful once we discover that hidden inner power within us—our spirits and potentialities—and engage them consciously to show us what to look for, where, and how. Death, as life's ultimate limitation, could also make us realize that our inner strengths, which we energize through self-awareness, may possibly be the echo of an external force. We may attribute this external force to our creator, the God, the supernatural, or anything else that we did not feel existed before we learned about ourselves with a deeper sense of both our ultimate limitation and inner power. Remembering perpetually of our finality and fragility should become a major tool for raising our awareness and stirring the spiritual feelings that come from meditation.

A quote from Wolfgang Amadeus Mozart about death is interesting to include here, although it reflects only half of the picture of this ultimate reality. The other more important half, i.e., death as a device for putting our existence into proper perspective, is missing in his words. In fact, imagining any chance for afterlife imposes only a big obstacle to understand our existence. The idea of afterlife is just another way religions harm the naïve public and society. That is the worst manner of forgetting our existence.

"As death, when we come to consider it closely, is the true goal of our existence, I have formed during the last few years such close relationships with this best and truest friend of mankind that death's image is not only no longer terrifying to me, but is indeed very soothing and consoling, and I thank my God

for graciously granting me the opportunity of learning that death is the key which unlocks the door to our true happiness. I never lie down at night without reflecting that — young as I am — I may not live to see another day. Yet no one of all my acquaintances could say that in company I am morose or disgruntled." Letter to Leopold Mozart (4 April 1787), from *The Mozart-Da Ponte Operas* by Andrew Steptoe, Oxford University Press, 1988, p. 84.

Particularly, the part he says, *I thank my God for graciously granting me the opportunity of learning that death is the key which unlocks the door to our true happiness,* is really precious.

A few other life limitations are also important to discuss briefly in the next few pages despite their lesser significance compared to death.

Timing Limitation

'Timing' (for making good decisions and doing the right stuff) is an important factor for life accomplishments, because both our personally and externally imposed limitations compound with time. For example, we know that children learn multiple languages many folds better than adults, especially if exposed to them during infancy. The same is true for music, art, sports, etc. This 'timing' factor shows that our potentials fruit only within a certain window of opportunity. Even our extended efforts usually do not lead to positive results if we miss the timing for making the right decisions in life. This principle applies to all aspects of our lives throughout our existence with various emphasis and nature.

Obviously, our physical abilities and energy deteriorate with age. Our senses and brains lose their sensitivity and sharpness. Besides the limited number of productive years for achieving certain (and often essential) objectives, our decisions within those years must be timely too. Not a new discovery, but many of us simply forget this fact or are deluded by positive thinking gimmicks. We forget that we cannot do most things that should have been done long time ago. We should have made the right decisions when we had the chance to do so. Most importantly, without timely decisions, we miss life's real opportunities, suppress our potentialities, get entrapped within life's trivialities, kill our spirits, and limit our chances to succeed in many aspects of our lives later. Education and learning are obvious examples, but even simpler life decisions should be timely. On the other hand, pursuing unrealistic goals for looking proactive, or merely due to our naïve positive thinking, makes us lose great opportunities in life and look pathetic too.

Education and work constitute the primary structure of life that we automatically plan (and believe is best) for our children. However, things have not always been so structured, and even now, many children in the world do not enjoy the privileges of educational and career planning. Some are doing the opposite in fact. That is, instead of learning at the young age, they are forced to labour with no access to education. On the other hand, we may soon realize that we are keeping our children at schools and universities uselessly for no tangible benefits. It fact, we might be doing them disservice by our present policy. This principle of 'timing' must be revisited soon to ensure that both individuals and society benefit from human potentials most effectively—or at least more effectively than present. Nowadays, we are losing vast potentialities that could be better applied for personal and social benefits.

Another obvious example is the 'timing' for starting a family. Experience shows that the best time to do this is when partners have the financial resources, energy, and patience to deal with each other's needs as well as their kids', etc. Nowadays, so many auxiliary factors defer people's decision to start a family, or they raise their kids outside a family, e.g., as a single parent option. Overall, a less favourable 'timing' has become the cause of relationship conundrums in the new era, with no fault of people in this special case. Everybody is rightly apprehensive about the prospects of getting into a serious relationship nowadays. For one thing, partners' high expectations of themselves and each other, and the lack of mechanisms to find suitable partners deter us from building families. The damages caused by random dating during the years prior to marriage somewhat diminish couples' ability to relate in fact. In many cases, nowadays, we have to get into our second or third marriages, because of our failures in the earlier one(s)—mostly due to bad timing of various types of decisions. These assertions are not for condemning people's inability to get married soon enough, but rather to stress that our varied worries and life obligations complicate our decision to start a family on a timely manner. Thus, we get entrapped in a graver mental condition. Our relationships (or the lack of proper ones) damage our psyches too. Thus, not only the matter of timing for marriage is too complex and critical nowadays, but also the effect of this delay and indecision is hurting our spirits as well as our children's.

Another example about the 'timing,' is our decision about our *purposes and interests in life* in conjunction with our careers, so that we can satisfy both our financial and psychological needs. Because of bad 'timing,' many of us end up living a miserable life due to misfit jobs and careers we get stuck with. Some people switch between jobs and careers continuously to no avail. Many of us simply choose a career as it appeals to us for some irrelevant factors, out of necessity, or wrong educational background. As an obsolete requirement of socioeconomic structure, we spend many years of our precious lives on formal education and training. Then we often decide to ignore all those efforts and hardships and train or re-educate ourselves in a different field, which usually proves unwise for new reasons. Thus, our decision about the field of education must be made at a proper 'timing,' mostly the first time, after understanding our limitations, potentials, temperament, life plans and philosophy.

Living requires many major decisions, as discussed in Volume III. They reflect the importance of 'timing' in both our major and less obvious decisions. As a rule, though, our most important plans and decisions must usually be made at the young age perhaps before 30 or so. Understanding life and our purpose of living before making all these critical decisions is extremely helpful. However, as young people, we are only misled by social trends and propagandas instead of finding the right ways of learning about life and our divine potentialities. Thus, the outcome of our major life decisions often end up much less desirable than we usually anticipate. Our bad timing and decisions affect our families too, which then causes us indirect pressures on top of feeling entrapped in a meaningless and stressful life.

Regardless of our obsession for success and happiness, the bare requirement for health and peace of mind demands timely decisions for building our fundamental thoughts, beliefs, life philosophy, higher spirits, and a suitable lifestyle. We must make timely decisions about a path of life that is manageable with the least amount of stress.

Self-assessment

Engulfed by so many limiting factors like the ones discussed in this chapter, and pressured by normal living conundrums, such as work and family environments, drawing a true picture of 'who we are' and also nurturing our potentialities would be too abstract at best. Our efforts to grasp this blurry picture would also feel like a futile effort. However, with patience and determination, a personal self-assessment might provide clearer answers about our existence gradually. We must learn to pause and concentrate, with full attention, on our thoughts, actions, and feelings and the motives behind them. Then perhaps we plan to become someone worth being, if self-assessment shows the necessity for some adjustments, which is usually the case for all objective students of the truth. Exploring the depth of our 'self' requires more guidelines, of course, which perhaps some rational and professional people could put together soon. Probing rational individuals with objective viewpoints about life, can help us stay on a self-awareness path. Sometimes, a simple question by a child may raise a deep thought, which might eventually help answer some of the more complicated matters of life. Giving ourselves a chance to do the right kinds of thinking is the main step for earning our primary wisdom toward self-awareness and enlightenment.

The sign of being on the right track is the declining degree of our egotism and neediness. We start to see life less selfishly, in an objective and independent manner, instead of merely feeding our dogmatism or imitating the norms of the prevalent life structure blindly. We start to notice our nothingness instead of gloating incessantly about our importance. Only by gaining the capacity of doing an honest self-assessment, we become the best judge of our character and personality with fewer doubts about who we are. We may say something to others rather carelessly or callously at a moment of weakness, but would realize our error when we sit alone later for a sincere self-analysis. We also find the courage to go back and correct our mistake or rudeness, and perhaps get a chance to reconcile with people we have hurt. Our search for 'self' would still be incomplete, or not worthy enough, if we find in ourselves signs of prejudice, self-serving conclusions, unjustified parental influence, irrelevant social values, and greed. Only through a selfless, divine self-assessment, we may test the validity of our conclusions and judgments.

Naturally, being honest and critical of ourselves is difficult if we do not know how, or when we falsely believe in our sincerity. However, the worst case is when we stubbornly fool ourselves and believe to be honest when our hypocrisy is bugging even our own mind. Without an ability to control our prejudices, both our self-assessment and judgments of others are worthless. One way to test our sincerity is to recall past experiences and re-evaluate them according to their merits at the time. Do we still consider our response or reaction appropriate today, according to our new objective (rather selfless) value structure? Would a similar judgment today be valid using our present mindset and standards? Are we humble enough now to at least go back and apologize for our error in judgment and rudeness? If the answers to the above questions do not convince us that we have changed, then our effort to reach selfhood has not been effective yet. We should gauge the strength of our criteria and convictions used for assessing our reactions and judgments. We should convince our conscience (if we have one) about the rationality and honesty of our current judgments.

It may help to review a case from the time I was deeply sunk in these types of thoughts and testing my self-assessment efforts.

During my college years in Los Angeles, I had a friend who appeared smart by most standards. He had a B.A. in architecture and was doing his masters in urban planning. He had travelled extensively and had numerous friends and several girlfriends, while financially depended on his parents, who had strong faith in him. One day we were relaxing and chatting by a swimming pool when he mentioned his recent conversation with his father. In response to his request for more money to travel to Europe, his father had apparently told him that he could not afford or did not wish to pay for this trip. My friend was furious about his father's reluctance to provide what he thought were the essentialities of his life, i.e., travelling to Europe for a couple of months every year. Naively, I tried to explain his father's decision and added that perhaps time had come for him to develop some sense of responsibility and financial independence.

With disbelief about my stupid remark, he yelled, "They must handle my needs since they brought me into this world."

I realized the futility of continuing this conversation.

This example has a few angles for analysis beyond the obvious conclusion that this friend had been spoiled. However, most relevant here is his outlook on life and his perception of himself.

To me, his view of 'who he was,' as a 24-year-old person, appeared strange. It was also interesting for me to note how his knowledge of 'who he was,' his value system, and judgment were directly related and collectively tainted, especially since he always bragged about his sense of modesty and his energetic show of his philosophical approach toward life.

The big obstacle for self-awareness is obviously our egoism and the effects of crooked social norms cultivated in our heads, which give us wrong impressions about life. How could a reliable value system evolve from a faulty trained mind? And how could one hope to assess and analyse the question of 'who am I?' without a proper value system and self-assessment abilities? How can one even understand the concept of self-awareness and self-assessment without some basic mental preparation? The point here is not to condemn or analyse someone's viewpoint and choices. But rather to demonstrate how my friend and I were both surprised and mad at each other's comments, view of life, and 'who we were' as two young graduate students regardless of our parents affluence.

I always wished to believe that this educational incident with my friend many years back would probably have a different outcome if he could relive that moment. Had my friend's philosophy of life had changed over the years, I wondered. I imagined that his father's decision might have pushed him to adjust himself to the new realities and perhaps develop a new value system and lifestyle eventually. Thus, whenever I remembered him in the following thirty years, I imagined him as a rather changed person. Recently, I heard he was looking for a new rich wife. His first rich wife had apparently kicked him out at last.

The risk I am taking to write this story is rather calculated, as I believe this friend would not find out about my comments about him even if I gave him a copy of this book personally and begged him to read it. The only minor risk is that one of our common friends reads the story and mentions my derogatory remarks to him. Well, I do not care anyway! Yet, my openness, courage, and arrogance to include this story here show the flimsiness of my enlightenment after all these years. I admit I still have a long way to go. Why could not I resist including this story?!

Self-analysis and assessment are continuous endeavours. We become wiser by thinking more, making objective judgments, refining our value system, discussing our thoughts and beliefs with others with more care, learning more about our idiosyncrasies, and pondering all the points raised in this trilogy. Yet, some major decisions should be made at an earlier stage of our lives when we lack the wisdom we may gain only decades later after a thorough self-assessment. Depending on others for advice, such as our parents and teachers, could be risky if they cannot help youths do their own independent thinking. Thus, youths must develop and apply some quick guidelines for helping them in the early stages of their growth, as they travel through this self-disciplined learning and teaching processes.

The Final Judgment

Despite all the personal limitations briefly discussed in this chapter, we must *eventually* make a final judgment about the path of life we have chosen or like to follow. Ideally, however, we must make this judgment when we are young and have more options. While *internalizing* our ultimate limitation, death, we should always remember that life limitations compound with time and restrict what we can do and 'who we can be.' Especially our idiosyncrasies and futile aspirations should be viewed in a clearer light as we reassess their roles and significance in our thoughts and values more objectively—perhaps divinely indeed.

The main purpose of gaining a higher level of consciousness about our potentialities and limitations is to enhance our self-awareness and grasp 'who we are.' Everybody tries to deal with this dilemma intuitively according to his/her level of wisdom (cognition) throughout his/her life. However, while we passively strive to grasp our potentialities and limitations, our learning and discovery about 'self' would be evolutionary, if tangible at all. We merely wander confusedly within our infinite thought spectrum and wonder who we are. Nonetheless, this final judgment through self-awareness is important as the only vehicle for reaching a sense of contentment and maybe even happiness.

Although exploring 'self' and exploiting our potentialities are not easy for everybody, we can all learn about our limitations rather readily and benefit from our improved perspective of life immediately. Appreciating our vulnerabilities and frailties is particularly useful for earning the wisdom of viewing all other life (social) limitations with some degree of insignificance and triviality. We can then envision our life options and choose a smart way of living. Death, in particular, is a perfect tool and measure for understanding 'who we really are!'

PART IV

Struggles and Victories

CHAPTER TEN
Quest for the Truth

Our desire for a lasting sense of triumph and tranquility drives our quest for the truth. We wish to find a meaning for life as we look for salvation. Yet, all our good intentions and efforts seldom reveal anything about this mysterious truth and happiness. All along, life simply goes on, while our inner conflicts and lingering confusion get deeper. We just work harder or get lazier, depending on our personality, in order to cope and forget our sad experiences, while we doubt the value of our hopes and positive thoughts, too. Lost within a thick mental haze, our efforts and plans serve neither our natural needs nor a tangible purpose. Even our goal to stay content and 'practical' feels nothing but 'pure compliance,' although we take pride in pursuing the common goals of getting rich and famous, etc., like everybody else.

Most of us admit that our present lifestyles cause mainly disappointments and hardships, though some tentative success and gratifications give us enough hope to keep on ploughing on. All along, however, we cannot stop wrestling with a major dilemma—a philosophical doubt: Would our idiotic struggles eventually lead to a *meaningful and worthwhile* sense of victory? When? How? Intuitively, we expect some form of triumph, a logical value, or a reward for so much efforts we put into figuring out and living this perplexing life. But are we only dreaming?

On top of our crusade to grasp our reasons for living and to follow a certain lifestyle based on a thoughtful life philosophy, a cruder dilemma is whether we must accept all these 'hardships.' Not only the existence itself, but also the agony of defining and maintaining it often feels absurd. Why must we try so hard for everything, even when we seek a simple life? Are our Ego-ridden sufferings and greed-driven worries warranted in the big scheme of things—when humanity is facing its looming demise?

We hope that our hardships and experiences have some educational value at least. Yet, life's erratic events and drastic shifts in personal priorities restrict the usefulness of our experiences for future purposes or decisions. Besides, without a sound life philosophy to justify our efforts already, today, any personal experience remains merely a random event with little significance or practical application. So, does this mean we are doomed, because seldom any of us knows the reasons for his/her hardships? Hardly anybody has a sensible life philosophy for living in the chaotic perceived world. We hardly get the opportunity or motivation nowadays to even establish some real life purposes. We merely imitate others, cherish our shallow interests and desires, and strive to cope with external forces (i.e., socioeconomic facts and interpersonal issues). That seems to be the best we have learned to live.

Overall, both society and our rooted idiosyncrasies, such as insecurity and egoism, prevent us from thinking outside the box for a better means of living. We are conditioned to accept hard labour automatically as a duty for existence and perhaps gaining some pleasant experiences. 'No pain, no gain,' is a common motto. But are we really serving ourselves with our present mentality and lifestyles, especially since most of our experiences usually end up dampening our spirits? Do some sporadic joys really make up for all our pains and incessant disappointments? Do we have any other option for living? Or, should we conclude that we just have to struggle because we are born as humans and bound to live in our substandard societies with our crooked nature? Because God wants us to suffer? Or because we are stupid? These questions become more prevalent and relevant in line with the rising social chaos, life complexities, and people's inability to relate effectively.

Naturally, we like to stay positive, lift our spirits, and move forward. We have no other choice. We want to fight off negativism and lethargy, which build up gradually during our routine struggles for indefinite and intangible victory. We resort to positive thinking and motivation enhancing techniques to boost our mood and performance. We strive to accomplish certain rudimentary goals. We also hope that our deep-seated dysfunctional habits, fears, and inner conflicts eventually suffocate underneath our flimsy optimism, pleasures, and gaudy pretences—so that we suffer less.

Alas, even our optimism cannot help as long as our fixed mentality and social distractions sabotage our sacred inner quest for the truth. Many obstacles, e.g., the mirage of happiness, hinder our ability to face the reality, as explained in the coming pages. We simply cannot handle *the truth* about the sad state of our social structure even when its harsh symptoms hit us like an avalanche. Accordingly, our struggles and experiences only feed our habits and strengthen our coping aptitude. This universal mayhem cannot be remedied in near future, either, until, 1) a majority of people learn to live rather independently, and, 2) society respects individuals' freedom and integrity, instead of manipulating and brainwashing the public for economic purposes. It is hard to imagine that these two ideals would ever materialize.

Nonetheless, not knowing the purpose of our lifelong struggles remains a torturous mystery until we satisfy our personal quest for the truth. This mission is etched in our subconscious and we cannot avoid pondering it at least occasionally. We feel obliged intuitively to resolve our inner conflicts about life's realities somehow and to anticipate at least a small chance for triumph at the end!

Our Main Struggles

The main struggle we endure permanently, knowingly or unconsciously, is our inner quarrel to attain a psychological equilibrium. Mainly, we strive to distinguish between the realities of this world, as we have learned or conditioned ourselves to believe in (the perceived realities), and the truth that is waiting to emerge from inside every intelligent human (the real realities). The struggle is to understand and live with the contradictions between 'what we have become' and 'what we could be' in its purest form when God created us, free from societal influence. Generally, we try not to think about these contradictions. We rationalize who we are and what we do in order to reduce our pains. We deny our inner quest for the truth or its value. As intelligent beings, we know that wars, hunger, crime, destruction of environment, genocide, racism, drugs, and all the other manmade evils of this world are not the signs of a healthy life and mind, but every one of us is directly or indirectly involved in propagating these symbols of civilization and conformity anyway. We have become part of the social and economical systems carrying these values and diseases across the borders and brains. And we have submerged so deeply in our own egoistic pleasure-seeking attitudes and personalities that we can no longer even look up and see the storms of pain and thunders of anger passing above our heads ready to bring us, including the human history and culture, to our ends.

The struggle is to *communicate* with people about the path of inner satisfaction and self-questioning, especially with those we care so much about. Only a small group understands these abstract concepts, or are motivated enough to explore these types of thoughts. Although we can hardly communicate at these levels, the struggle for self-questioning continues within us as a natural growing process. Every time, the process may last a few seconds, hours, or days, for most of us; or may turn into a lifetime crusade for a devoted group, such as gurus, philosophers, and spiritual masters who pursue it eagerly with great devotion.

The struggle is to *believe* that the questions of, 'Who am I?' and 'What the purpose of my life is?' are truly instinctual and constitute the fundamental pillars of human identity and humanness. Life distractions and perceived realities (fighting with real realities) disturb our quest for the truth and self-questioning very quickly, before we find the chance to delve into the depth of the questions. The cry of children and families for food and shelter, personal weaknesses and desires, greed and pleasures are all obstacles to attend to our philosophical thoughts about life and our chosen lifestyles.

The struggle is to understand and *manage* our ceaseless doubts and prepare ourselves for major life decisions and demands, as discussed in Volume III.

The struggle is to *remember* how insignificant and vulnerable we are and that the value of life could not be summarized in making a living, having a family, engaging in some materialistic or emotional pleasures, fighting amongst ourselves and then leaving as ignorant as we were born. There should be some purposes for our lives beyond what we have defined for ourselves. Humans must be free from the limitations, rules, frustrations, psychological and physical hardships, drugs and tranquilizers, ignorance, deceptions, immoralities, and fears that we wrestle with a lifetime. Our existing life structure and mentality could not be a definition of a real reality and humanity, simply because we can see the evidence of Nature. How could animals, plants, fields, and farms be so beautiful and in harmony and yet the most intelligent creature on earth be so miserable, confused, and unfulfilled? How dare we ruin their harmony too? It is hard not to wonder whether we are really the smartest species on the planet or this is still another one of our egotistical dreams. Even the wildness of Nature and natural disasters are at least explainable in terms of some instinctual motives or by scientific phenomena. Yet, for humans, the pains and disasters are mostly self-inflicted and unjustifiable. Our struggle is to understand 'why?' Why are we so naive and selfish?

The struggle is to *exploit* our real potentialities and identity in order to resolve the inner conflicts about who we are and how we feel and behave. We like to be successful, but at what price! We like to feel happy, but are looking outside ourselves to receive it from others and things!—mostly by abusing and hurting them too. We like to be accepted and approved by members of family and society, but we betray one another and sell our souls in the process! We like to enjoy life, but work as slaves doing things that do not mean anything to us! We like to live in peace with others, but we do not want to let go of our egoism and sense of superiority! We like to be mentally and spiritually strong, but we fight for power to rule others! We need a simple life, but we have made it so complex to live every single day of it! We struggle to be free, but are trapped inside our shallow desires and by our dependence on others and things! The list of contrasts and contradictions never ends.

Our ongoing struggle to find happiness usually fails, too, because we look for it within a social format not suitable (or capable) for offering it. Our habits and lifestyles support sexuality, power, greed, and pleasure, but not peace of mind. We fail to recognize that gaining even some relative happiness depends on our ability to elude social values and economic realities that have crippled our natural existence. Thus, humans' struggle to find happiness would remain merely a big, futile fantasy in this environment. Yet, even a harsher struggle is to accept that happiness is a myth to begin with, which has become even more elusive when we insist on finding it in our Ego-driven professions or around our crooked friends, family, and spouses.

Most of us can directly associate with these contrasts, struggles, and dilemmas. Yet, we deliberately choose to forget about them, mostly because we feel incapable or unwilling to do anything about them. We simply accept that we are extremely helpless in the scope of the social order to change anything. (But of course we get haughtier every day anyway.) We feel our weakness to be a nonconformist and challenge all these fixed values. Yet we bask in the superficial joy of artificial pleasures, sexuality, and deceiving appearances. Fashionable clothes, luxurious automobiles, beach houses, glamorous parties, fame, casual sex, promotions and status, and all the rest of them are hard not to be attracted to. But then those who have acquired all these symbols of success and happiness tell us differently. They have come to realize that all this extravagance has really been a mirage and at the end they still feel lonely and lost, in a vast desert of anxiety and ignorance. They just repeat the same old routines and habits like robots and merely fool themselves with their own crooked thoughts and philosophies.

Nonetheless, the temptations of worldly rewards for conforming and excelling in the execution of societal rules and demands are hard to resist. This is especially true when we do not know what to replace the existing social rules with and how to acquire a new wisdom to support the required overhaul. All the discussions about 'self' realization through inner peace and wisdom feel evasive and hard to grasp for those who have not tasted it. Even for those who enjoy a small dose of this spiritual state of mind, seeing beyond the first layer of ideas and feelings is impossible and thus hard to remain faithful and advance.

Meanwhile, our ultimate struggle is to boost our spirits the best we can and run the rest of our lives in peace.

The Awareness Intersection

So, can we avoid life's traps somewhat and mitigate our sufferings? Can we overcome our inner conflicts and mental pressures somehow? If yes, how? While no fix formula exists, we each ultimately find a plausible path for inner peace if we start the *long journey into ourselves* (as Rumi puts it) toward the boundaries of the *mystical* real world. The long process evolves gradually as we feel a genuine urge to do an honest self-assessment (to look within ourselves), beyond the prevalent social criteria, to find our identity, the right reasons for living, and the purpose of our struggles. We meditate and gauge our thoughts, feelings, and experiences freely and objectively—to become more aware of our deeds and events around us. We begin to believe in ourselves and our ability to find inner peace and serenity. Soon, we reach an initial sense of contentment as a sign of approaching the awareness intersection.

On the other hand, many of us reach this intersection by accident, most likely after a big shock, a major setback, or losing our patience with common lifestyles and existence. We feel tired of depending on deceitful people and systems to maintain a superficial identity. Therefore, we sometimes arrive at this intersection by chance after having exhausted all other options and doing a lifetime of damage to ourselves and others.

Sometimes, the most common experiences of one's life, such as a family predicament, near death experience, or issues of social interest or concern, such as ecology, evoke the process of self-questioning. A sense of emptiness (of the self) drives us to look for more substance in our lives. After losing so many years of our precious lives and ignoring the sacred energy within us, we may at last arrive at the awareness intersection and notice the variety of paths that we can pursue in our quest for the truth and real reality. This may be the point where for the first time we get a notion about the person that 'we could be,' but 'have not been.'

At this saturation point, we are no longer happy despite all the pleasures and power. Our struggles to accumulate more wealth in a world of perceived realities suddenly feel so futile and infantile. Thus, we start to think harder and deeper, which may lead to a process of self-questioning and perhaps awakening. Then we see and feel things that we had never believed in or even contemplated worthy of discussion at a younger age. Thus, the process of self-questioning and awakening evolves.

Sometimes, simple questions erupt mysteriously and we get an urge to explore the depth of human mentality and humanity with very simple thoughts like, 'Why should people kill each other?', 'Who created the universe and who created the creator?', etc. These basic thoughts might raise our curiosity to also explore the truth about ourselves, including our *perceived* and *real* roles in life and society. Within this frame of mind, we gradually see the bizarre deceptions behind most perceived realities or at least get a chance for contemplation and new interpretations. We abhor the influence of the 'mainstream' on shaping our character and thus begin to reassess our association with social values and rewards of compliance.

Many other factors, including our inner conflicts, might make us convert and evolve dramatically and hastily too. It often begins with a sense of loneliness and withdrawal, which is the only venue for real thoughts and questions. A person may become physically lonely or not, which could be a contributing factor or not. Yet, what matters the most is that his mind has drifted away from the mainstream and questions the validity and value of his usual thoughts that had kept his brain constantly busy, e.g., the thoughts of workload, promotion, family needs, etc. Now, he can relax his mind and let some fundamental thoughts get a chance to emerge out of his subconscious. Sometimes, because of loneliness, emotional preoccupation, or a lack of gratifying experiences, a person suddenly arrives at the question of, 'Why am I doing these things?' and 'Whom am I doing them for?' And of course the direct derivative of these questions is, 'Who am I anyway?', and 'What is the purpose of my life?'

Many other basic questions occupy our minds during this mental explorations, too, like, 'Why must I die?', 'What have I achieved?', 'Is this really all living is supposed to be?', 'Is there anything else I could do to free myself from the anxieties I have endured in the last 40-50 years and be happier?', 'Why life feels so short and shallow, and why did not I realize or somebody tell me how quickly it goes by?', and lots of similar questions. At the end, all these questions lead to a deeper grasp of our needs and identity, after discarding our old juvenile obsessions, thoughts, and feelings that we have pampered all along to build a phony personality and life. It becomes apparent that those thoughts and feelings have been only delusions and deceiving distractions. They have not brought us closer to our souls and self. Now, we feel an urge to transcend the world of appearances into the sphere of real realities where the real *I* is waiting to be born—*a real birth due to a fuller consciousness.*

For middle-aged or older individuals suddenly the meaning and implications of death shift to a higher level of consciousness and life becomes more tangible than before. Most of us reach this point when we get older and feel anxious, lonely, and lost. Thus, we sense the reality of our mortality better and realize the vanity of our attachments. The questions of, 'Who am I and what the purpose of my life is' become more relevant and urgent. Now, we remember. We remember our existence and need for salvation if very soon we are not going to exist! Our perceived reality of 'death' turns into a real reality for existence after being buried in our subconscious as a painful fact for so many years. A conscious knowledge of death awakens the shallow individual that has been, to meet the real self that exits within him. We may even decide to write our will and testament too, at last. Many people who have had near death experience (NDE) have suddenly been awakened by a similar mysterious urge.

Nonetheless, an individual may be driven into a self-questioning state of mind for many reasons. However, it usually happens after we have tasted the futility of the values and pleasures of the perceived world.

Thus, we arrive at last. And when we arrive, we do not know what to do except the basic withdrawal and isolation from the perceived reality and people who have kept us a prisoner in their world. Our parents, teachers, friends, or anybody else never took us to this intersection when we were young and had not gone through a lifetime of misery, mistakes, disappointments, and perhaps some futile experimentation. Where we go from here is a personal choice. At this stage, we stand at the awareness intersection with several paths branching from it. We pause, study each path, and learn about not only its destination and demands, but also our personal power and objectives for following that path, the obstacles, rejections, isolations, hazards, loneliness, and inevitable disappointments—all for a possible salvation. At this point, we start to delve into certain fundamental thoughts similar to the discussions in this trilogy for many months and years before we grasp and adopt a more viable path of life. We should not choose a path hastily again before years of contemplation and self-awareness.

The opposing paths reflect various lifestyles according to the reality we can *practically* embrace, which would be a mix of values from both the perceived reality and real reality worlds. Most of us can follow only a path that stands somewhere between these two extremes after we gauge our options, strengths, courage, and stamina. The main, ultimate path is the hardest one to conquer, but if we do, we may even approach the SUMMIT. Yet, most likely, we should initially choose an easier path that we feel would lead to a practical destination for us. We can always experiment along the way to learn more about our final destination by advancing from an easier path to a new one with more demands on our time and thoughts.

Anyway, the first and most important stage is to make sure we have arrived at the intersection. It means we have decided to give ourselves a chance to step out of our phony personality and embrace our true 'self' through a long process of self-therapy. We are ready to change ourselves and challenge the values and rules that we have accepted and lived by so obediently all along. We see our weaknesses, helplessness, and lack of integrity. We feel we deserve better and believe that while happiness is an illusion, peace of mind is a rather attainable destination. We also sense a feeling of rejuvenation, control, freshness, and inner power. Then, if we are lucky enough and appreciate what has been achieved, we acquire a high level of steady consciousness that can make our enlightenment permanent and paramount. Our high spirit and spiritual strength at this stage would guide us in choosing the right path. Otherwise, we must continue to experiment until we find the right one eventually according to the level of independence we desire and can handle without the normal attachment to society and people. We do not wish to wait forever to decide which path to choose, though. It is usually better to start slowly and build momentum on the way to the higher paths of self-awareness along with a gradual detachment from the norms of the perceived world.

Some of us might have had a glimpse at the awareness intersection and perhaps paused when we were younger and touched by some thought-provoking books or discussions. Surely enough, however, we were soon distracted by the forces of the perceived world when they quickly engulfed our minds and feelings. The ideal situation would have been to arrive at this intersection by choice (not by accident), when we were young, and perhaps as part of some kind of initiation ritual. The ideal would have been that our parents had had the wisdom to know, believe, and teach us at least a notion of the 'real world,' rather then merely reinforcing the teachings and beliefs of the perceived world including religions. We wonder, 'What is elderly really good for then nowadays!?'

At the higher levels of self-awareness (and fuller consciousness), our wisdom heightens enough to capture and feel the real world somewhat more clearly. The (real) reality of our existence becomes apparent in the context of many full-conscious activities, decisions, pains, and joys that keep happening in our lives. This personal awakening affects all other aspects of a person's life when he discovers the real reality behind every concept that had all along had a different (often childish) implication and meaning at the perceived (reality) level. Many divine notions and feelings imprisoned in our subconscious and unconscious suddenly begin pushing up toward our conscious mind. For example, as we grasp the beauty of Nature with deep awareness, we acquire a novel impression about the overall majesty of creation with all its intricacies, which we still cannot fully comprehend, but appreciate at a magical level. The real reality of Nature reveals itself to us if we learn how to seek it. From a high level of consciousness, this beauty and the feeling surrounding it manifest a new sense of being and sacred attachment. The limited perception of beauty by one's eyes turns into a limitless understanding of 'magnificence' with mind, thoughts, and feelings—a state which could never be explained by superficial interpretations in the perceived world. At such unique states of consciousness, we are awakened by an experience or thought and introduced to a new way of seeing things and living. These types of experiences confirm our progress on the new path, if we grasp and nurture them properly as deepening symptoms of awakening and wisdom.

Unfortunately, many of us do not get an opportunity to reach the awareness intersection, or we arrive too late. This is particularly sad because it takes a long time to travel from here to a decent destination while we suffer a lot in life for absolutely no reason. We need the inner power when external forces have the highest impact on our lives. We need our confidence and self-reliance more than ever when we are being dominated and exploited—when we are young with naïve aspirations and imaginations. But we do not have the right tools and minds, because we are trained merely for living in the perceived reality world—a world made merely of fantasies and illusions. Nevertheless, if we happen to arrive at the awareness intersection, it is better than not arriving at all.

Human Logic's Reliability

Following a divine path of life for attaining wisdom and enlightenment does not sound logical to us. As practical and rational people, we remain sceptical about these intangible concepts, as they cannot be explained by scientific proofs or at least plausible theories. Yet, many philosophers and spiritualists argue that not all concepts, e.g., inner self, can (or should) be explained by science in the way it is developed today. The intricacies of the universe are too complex to be explained by any human logic and science. For example, the concept of infinity and the idea that universe has been, and will continue, to expand indefinitely is beyond our brains' ability to visualize and comprehend. For one thing, we cannot grasp the idea that some event or thing has no ending. Second, we simply imagine that if something is expanding beyond its limits, it is doing so into another space that must have already existed. However, this seemingly logical perception does not apply to the universe and so we remain confused. There was this theory, of course, until recently, that the universe will eventually stop expanding and start a reverse process of contraction. This theory is even more difficult to absorb or relate to, because the whole thing returns to 'nothingness,' as it had been prior to the Big Bang. All the space would be gone too! Then the newer science claims that in fact the universe will expand forever. What does 'forever' mean? Nonetheless, human logic is willing to adopt these findings as a possibility worth contemplating—as a scientific foundation—at least as plausible hypotheses for further speculation and analysis. Therefore, the question is how much trust we should have in our logic and science, even when they fail to make sense, e.g., about the universe expanding forever. At the personal level, in particular, it seems that we are trusting our logic and common sense too much naively. We become arrogant and stubborn about our ideas, because we imagine we have reached definite conclusions based on our presumed superb logic. It is a major irony indeed to rely even in small measures on human logic to unravel the truth about our existence and the universe. What an Ego!

On the other hand, despite its severe limitations, humans' collective logic and science have been following a systematic and proven track. A continuous development of ideas has turned into workable theories, tools, and machinery that have accomplished specific purposes. The progress of science has been cumulative, disciplined, and according to a systematic approach (all limited to certain laws and rules we have created in our perceived world, of course). Furthermore, these scientific principles have been tested within the natural settings of the universe and have proven to comply rather nicely with some of the specific laws of nature. Travel in the space and landing a spaceship on other planets or on the moon, breaking the nucleus of atom and extracting huge amounts of energy, discoveries at the bottom of the oceans where no light has ever reached, the amazing technology of computers and cybernetics, and horrendous amount of medical and other scientific knowledge that we have accumulated, especially in the last 50-60 years, seem consistent with the basic laws of nature. It is easy to show that the logic we are using to explain events and phenomena, to visualize new possibilities and theories, and to set newer scientific objectives, are working nicely in line with the general laws of the universe, all subject to our brains' limited capacity, of course. Since we use less than 5% of our brains, we can hope that eventually humans can explain more facts about the universe and life. Our brains, logic, and scientific knowledge are still at a primitive stage, yet it appears that we have followed some form of logical process and a scientific foundation; we are not dreaming logic, although our personal logic often becomes dreamlike.

At the same time, we must remain alert about a possible bottleneck. That is, human brain and logic seem viable and reliable only to the extent they fit nicely with the natural laws of the universe, e.g., building an airplane to defy gravity, finding a cure for a disease, etc. Human logic is not driven by some mysterious, inherent power within us, but it is only a tool for making an inference based on past experiences and specific methods to verify what is out there. And even at this level—for making plausible inferences—our logic has not yet helped answer the majority of questions and phenomena that the universe challenges us with. Our intuition and intelligence are inherent, but our logic is man-made according to our intuition and intelligence. In all, outside its application to natural laws for scientific purposes, we have no other criteria for measuring the meaning and power of human logic for deciphering other complex features of our existence and thoughts. Even for applying human logic to scientific research, we must usually go through a long process of trial and error, and experimentation of random ideas (e.g., for finding a cure for cancer), until finally someone stumbles upon a solution. Thus, at best, we are fitting our logic to the requirements of science to prove natural laws. Again, this means that our logic is not an inherent and reliable tool, but merely a dynamic means of focusing our thoughts and processes. We do not even accept human *intuition* as a logical process or tool. Everybody seems to have his/her own logic and thus we are often incapable of agreeing even on simple principles.

Accordingly, scientific discoveries have been based on a rather random generation of ideas driven merely by human logic and also tested within the scope of human logic in compliance with the natural laws of the universe. Therefore, both science and human logic find their limited validity only based on their capacities to explain or control a natural phenomenon or work in harmony within certain previously tested parameters. Beyond this limited scope, neither science nor human logic has an independent capacity to guide or enlighten us, especially considering their inherent high interdependency.

Our logic is incapable of speculating, let alone solving, the question of, 'Who created the creator,' because we cannot develop even a basic hypothesis for this dilemma, never mind inventing a method to test it in a natural setting. Of course, the fundamental question that stirs and stands firmly behind the question of, 'Who created the creator' is still the simpler dilemma of, 'Who or what created the universe?' Our logic has been able to explain the process of creation at a much smaller scale, nevertheless, such as the creation of an embryo or a cell. If our logic has been helpful to explain this relatively smaller phenomenon, can it possibly work eventually for explaining the larger picture, such as the universe, and reveal more about the real world?

Nonetheless, our logic and science remain limited by the level of human intelligence, which is presently functional mostly within our perceived world, and only for speculating about some of the simpler natural laws. They may also offer some plausible notions about the existence of a real world. For now, however, they are inadvertently and inconsistently applied mostly in the perceived world to answer merely our basic questions. Yet, we are hoping to cross over from our perceived world to the real world with the use of our logic. We often believe that both levels of creations—the creation of the whole universe and the creation of a cell or embryo—are parallel fundamentals of the real world. Thus, we conclude that our logic and science are viable tools for explaining the rest of the questions in time, if and when our brains develop enough capacity to ask the right questions, which are testable in a natural setting.

We should take one step back and confess that even our impression or definition of the reality (including the universe and Creator) could be highly flawed. Are we merely inventing a fictitious real world that we assume exits, because our brains suggest that such a world (the universe and possibly even God) should *logically* exist? Are not we assuming that a real world must exist, simply because our perceived world is merely a figment of our illusions and limited by our imaginations?

Many of the scientific laws and human logic may be erroneous because we do not understand much about the real world, and definitely our raw perceptions obstruct our learning process. Yet, we believe that the universe is a major phenomenon that constitutes the real world. If we deny this principle, everything becomes only a figment of human perceptions, including the concept of creation and the creator, all the science, and anything that any philosopher or a prophet may say about spiritual souls and divinity. However, for now, even from within our perceived world, we can imagine the existence of a real world, based on a unique mix of personal experiences, logic, and inferences. We can attribute these testable physical phenomena, and the logic that explains them properly, to a world of real realities.

In all, we like to believe that the universe stands beyond our perceptions and thus belongs to the world of real realities. We cannot deny its *real* existence outside of humans' thoughts, logic, and perceived connection to a real reality. This is the world (a kind of reality) that would have existed according to the same laws and phenomena regardless of our knowledge or perception of it, or even our existence. We can make this assertion because we can safely assume that we are merely *perceiving* the whole concept of existence and the universe. This is a major assumption; but our logic insists that it is a reasonable one. We believe it is reasonable even though the theories of quantum physics suggest that we, as observers of events, influence their outcomes.

Now let us go one step further and declare (with near absolute certainty) that everything other than human perceptions belongs to the real world. This includes all the things, animals and plants, and even our occasional pure thoughts outside our perceptions. The only thing that keeps us humans away from the real world is our (diverted) perceptions of this world. How strange! What a discovery! However, in spite of its cynical simplicity, it is interesting to see how the complex issues of duality of the worlds that we belong to can be a notion understandable even by our naïve common sense. Our perceptions have become so strong and so much part of our realities that a whole new world has been created—the world of perceived realities that includes weird notions about the real world too. Therefore, the good news is that we can walk right into the world of real realities as soon as we doubt the validity of our perceptions in the world of perceived realities. No pain, meditation, and special efforts are required, at least not at the entry level, if only we can get rid of our idiotic perceptions. This is how the naive notion of one dimensionality of wisdom paths, as suggested earlier, might actually make sense too. Although it is not easy to rid ourselves from the imprinted notions of the perceived world, we can see the entrance to the real world once we stand at the awareness intersection. MAYBE!

By definition, the perceived world is only a manifestation of our minds. Therefore, we may begin to distinguish the authenticity of values and concepts only through awareness and by retraining our minds. In that sense, the strength and clarity of our minds determine how effectively we can separate a perceived reality from a real one. Nevertheless, the power to distinguish the two levels of realities must come from, and flourish within, our minds and logic eventually, despite all the initial (existing) misperceptions registered in our brains and logic.

In a few centuries, humans might learn to not only distinguish the signals they receive from inner and outer sources as perceived or real, but also apply some of the real ones in their everyday life in hopes of fortifying their connection with the universe and the world of real realities. Future humans might grasp the universe and the real world through their REAL thoughts, which would grow only when people become free of perceived values, habits, and attachments. At this point, we can only speculate that everything out there belongs to the real world. Only how we humans connect to them puts them in the perceived or real realms for their limited grasp and purposes. Only what we do with objects and thoughts make them perceived or real. Embracing this simple notion is a prerequisite for entering one of the wisdom paths toward the boundaries of the real world.

An even simpler idea can be generated from this discussion. We can suggest that humans' mind grasps outside information and values at two levels, perception and comprehension. At the perception level, we accept the information superficially at its face value, or according to an existing criterion applied by an stimuli, logic, and previous conditioning—e.g., values reflected in prevalent social norms. A simple example is when one is asked to listen to a piece of music. The music is heard and perceived to satiate one's taste or not. A classical, country, or exotic music of foreign lands may feel weird to people who have not been exposed to these kinds of rhythms. The response would be, 'Yes, I like it,' or 'No I do not like it.' The music is evaluated against some prejudged and perceived notions. It is merely another act of *perception* without any special attempt to comprehend it. At a comprehension level, however, we can feel, and mentally connect, to each individual note of the music and understand the message it is communicating without making a reference in our mind (if we can) to any other music we have heard before. Few people can achieve this level of consciousness, though.

For reaching the 'comprehension' level regarding our acts and judgments, and for delving into our thoughts about a special issue, we must mainly get detached, perhaps through some form of meditation, from our existing mental prejudices. Attaining this rather divine state of mind sounds illogical and impossible for most people, though. Yet only at this level of consciousness, we can envisage and follow the path toward the real world. At this high degree of self-awareness and mental synthesis, we learn to run all aspects of our lives rather harmoniously. We can bring our minds to this 'comprehension' level in order to understand the meaning of many concepts and communications satiating our lives.

The validity of our logic and science outside of our perceptions is debateable from many different angles, though that is not the purpose of this book. The goal here is only to reflect our random inclinations to believe in, or doubt, the validity of our logic and science. This very similar type of whimsical mindset is equally at play when we wish to establish our beliefs and convictions. We cannot be easily persuaded to engage (and believe) in a philosophical debate or abstract sensation that appears illogical or contrary to the existing scientific knowledge or personal beliefs.

Overall, we must haggle with our dilemmas about human logic and science and find reasonable solutions for our personal purposes and for directing our lives. On the one hand, we cannot, and should not, discard our urge to explore exotic ideas that have been called supernatural, spiritual, or myths despite our scepticism. We must assume that, with an open mind, we always have a chance of finding other life paths that could never become obvious to a rigid mind, even if all kinds of evidences were in front of the person. Thus, it seems that we can (should) never trust our logic fully. Our narrow logic cannot make too much sense, e.g., for grasping God and supernatural, when in fact our intuition or imagination goads us to believe in myths or some other reality beyond the perceived world.

On the other hand, we cannot second-guess the validity of everything, (not even the perceived facts) that we have been able to prove by using our logic and science, on the ground that they may be only our perceptions and not real. Human logic and knowledge have evolved rather purposefully and systematically over millenniums, although they remain extremely limited due to the frailty of human brain (including our perceptions). We cannot refute the validity of events and things that happen to us in the perceived world on the ground (or suggestion) that everything we do and see in this world is only a dream or an illusion. It sounds illogical to believe that we may be awakened from this dream to enter the real world—e.g., to go to heaven. The basic logic tells us that any attempt to create an illusion of an unknown phenomenon, by using the analogy of an existing event, is most likely a fallacy and leads to other forms of illusions. That is, using the analogy of night dreaming to imply that we could be awakened from our present state of ignorance would not be of much help for explaining our relationship to the real world and who we are.

Overall, the state of human logic and knowledge about our world can be summarized as follows:

1. Many unexplained questions remain about the universe, and about our role in the journey we call life.
2. Humans' present logic and science cannot provide the right answers, at least not for near future.
3. Our logic and science cannot either prove or refute the existence of supernatural and spiritual phenomena.
4. Some evidences, or at least claims, suggest the existence of supernatural and spiritual phenomena.
5. We have all felt some kind of special energy within ourselves and experienced unexplainable connections that we call luck, coincidence, telepathy, etc.
6. Most of us are giving a benefit of a doubt, even if it is in our deepest subconscious, to the existence of a real world beyond the perceived world that we love so much because it seems easier to relate to and sense.
7. We have come to assume that human being is a super being with special connections to his creator, merely on the ground that we have used our brains more effectively and created more things. The fact that we think, have logic, and master some form of science, is assumed to make us different from other animals. Humans' unique abilities and spiritual urges are undeniable, yet there is no evidence that humans should be given any preference over other species in terms of divinity and their connection to the supernatural. Well, we have had prophets and spiritual leaders who have made us feel special. However, why we should be considered special in the kingdom of the creator of the universe is not clear. Other animals have instincts, some ability to use logic and think, too, though their mental development is perhaps in its primitive stage. And perhaps they have or will have a spirituality dimension, too, which we do not know about. Just wait a few million years! Even plants are being proven to have some type of intelligence and possibly consciousness.

8. Humans' existence is most likely only a minuscule, purposeless, by-product of the creation and not a divine scheme, even though we have divine potentialities and spirituality drives. Nobody can prove otherwise. Therefore, accepting some unfounded prophecies about humans' immortality and priority in the universe is only a clear indication of humans' poor logic and gullibility.
9. Our varied curiosities, questions, and doubts have a direct impact on our way of thinking and making important decisions. They affect our lives, and cause us agony and anxiety, yet we remain unable to ignore or do anything about these inner urges.
10. Our deep inner needs and conflicts persistently boggle our minds and make us feel obliged to create logic and science to resolve personal and life's uncertainties to reach some degree of mental equilibrium and peace.
11. We realize that answers to socioeconomic problems of the 21st century cannot come easily, because human logic and common sense are extremely deficient, especially outside the scientific applications.
12. Solution to human misery cannot be found within the context of our existing socioeconomic structures, but rather require a new source of energy, stronger logic, and deeper thinking. For example, we would never agree amongst ourselves on the mechanisms of governing our countries or even the simple issue of controlling our national debts and budget deficits, which are so desperately needed. And of course, we have a long list of socioeconomic problems. The bottom line is that our personal logic and common sense are in no way accurate and reliable, but they seem to be all we have and can depend on.

In the final analysis, it seems more plausible (and logical too, perhaps) to assume that human logic and science would never be able to explain so many phenomena and questions about the universe, Creation, humanity, our relationships, etc. Yet, we do not wish to acknowledge our ignorance and use this awareness to at least stop judging everything and everyone so adamantly. We do not wish to admit our mistakes, not even in those cases where our crooked actions and selfish beliefs are unexplainable even by human logic, science, or plausible theories.

CHAPTER ELEVEN
Beliefs and Convictions

It is time to agree that humans' logic and common sense have failed to create social harmony and peace. Instead, they have goaded us to fight one another relentlessly or seek superficial pleasures in hopes of hiding our pains. They cannot even help us cope with the chaotic symptoms of the socioeconomic structure—which is itself the creation of our poor logic and common sense. This is what our logic and common sense have told us to do! At personal level, our logic and common sense are even less reliable and useful compared with the methodical logic used in social and scientific settings. Our unique emotions, insecurities, and genes make our logic and common sense too varied and shaky. Thus, we feel more helpless every day when logic cannot help us communicate among ourselves or address even our mundane life issues and relationships, let alone drive our fundamental thoughts and life philosophy.

The impotency of our logic, science, and religions to bring us together for a more meaningful life kills our spirits too. We feel unfulfilled, without a sense of identity beyond all our seemingly logical perceptions and needs. We feel soulless, without a basic touch with the real world, which appears mythical and illusive according to our logic. We feel anxious, without a reliable grasp of the perceived reality world engulfing our existence. We feel lost and lonely, without knowing the purposes of our deeds.

Without a reliable logic to help us, we feel even more frustrated and vulnerable, while we plough on through life aimlessly and sense its vanity. We feel perplexed when we cannot satisfy our inherent urge and curiosity about spirituality and reach a relative stability in our lives.

Under this common, stressful condition, some intelligent and lucky people may eventually succeed in building their beliefs and convictions to compensate for the shortfalls of human logic. They build some type of beliefs and wisdom to guide their lives, instead of depending on logic and common sense per se, or letting themselves get absorbed in social norms or religions blindly. The option of doing nothing about our rowdy logic and living without at least certain beliefs and convictions is torturous for many people. At the same time, becoming arrogant and dogmatic with some primary beliefs, religions, and raw convictions would only make our lives even sadder and more stressful.

Our personal experiences, contemplation, and meditation gradually develop our basic convictions, which then provide the platform for building the foundation of our thoughts and life philosophy. Conversely, a solid foundation of thoughts and a smart life philosophy help us stay focused and objective about our beliefs. Our beliefs and convictions must make sense collectively toward a specific, and usually divine, goal. Obviously, our genetics, intelligence, and even luck play major roles in the way our beliefs, personality, and outlook on life develop. Our personal experiences and their impacts on us are always unique, so our conclusions and convictions can hardly be generalized for common purposes. For example, if a person 'sees it when he believes it,' it does not mean that others can also apply this crude logic or depend on this forced method of self-conditioning to build their convictions. This imaginary condition—blind faith or perhaps hallucination—would never work for everybody and it should at best be considered only another method of mental conditioning (self-hypnosis) with no benefit. As another example, this author's experiences and the way they have affected his convictions cannot be replicated or simply adopted as proofs of the supernatural. They are mentioned in the following pages not for depicting any evidence of the real world or even a basis for his beliefs. They are just examples of things that happen to people and merely help them ponder the possibility of another reality and thus perhaps to redefine their purposes of living and being. The fact that these types of real or abstract experiences happen to us only raise our curiosity about the existence of a real world beyond our perceptions—but nothing more. They are merely additional clues about humans' vulnerability, which we must take into account for building the foundation of our thoughts and beliefs to augment our logic—but nothing more. These examples merely show the sanctity of our spirits in pursuit of life way beyond the power of our logic. The following personal experiences have helped this author in gauging his beliefs and positive doubts and possibly goading his search for self-awareness—and nothing more.

Abstract Experiences

'Abstract experiences' noted here merely signify those events and feelings that do not happen regularly in one's life. The use of the term 'abstract,' also reflects the infrequency, fragility, and the difficulty of explaining these types of experiences by our logic. Otherwise, the author still remembers those odd experiences as quite vivid, sensational, and shocking. Other individuals have reported similar experiences too.

In a beautiful spring afternoon, at age 13, I left a relative's house to go home by myself. I walked alone in a shady, long alley that led to the main street. The only sound came from the water dashing down a narrow creek, which ran in the middle of the alley with the rows of huge plane trees on both sides of the stream at around ten feet from one another. Suddenly a bizarre sensation overwhelmed me and I felt that 'I' was separated from my body.

I could no longer feel my steps or any other movement of my body. It kept walking by itself and 'I' just watched it from the other side of the stream. Both shocked and delighted, 'I' was looking amazingly at the body, as if watching a shadow walk by itself. *Who is the person sauntering so determinedly on the other side of the stream?* 'I' wondered, although I realized it was my body and the question felt odd all by itself. It walked effortlessly and unconsciously, and 'I' followed it for about 45 seconds without worry or even wishing to change anything, although I was quite aware of the lost control. The body was a fully independent 'entity' outside 'I'. And 'I' was, more than anything else, perplexed by this mysterious development. The whole experience and the fact that 'I' remained in charge of thinking and wondering at that instant felt magical. 'I' did not wish for it to end. Then as 'I' felt content, my sense of consciousness began melting again and 'I' noticed that the special sensation was fading fast. The more I tried to maintain myself in that state of separateness, the faster 'I' was pushed back inside the body and in three seconds no trace of the body was on the other side of the stream. Gradually, my steps got heavy as usual. I felt myself walking again, as I dragged my body in the last few feet out of the alley. It felt as if my super consciousness lost its power and freedom as soon as it merged with the body again. 'I' felt the heavy load of my body all over again.

My subsequent efforts to repeat that out-of-body experience, the same day and later, proved futile. I could not recreate this odd experience of separateness of my body and 'I'. It happened unexpectedly once again, though, two years later, but it lasted only 20-25 seconds. I did not smoke cigarettes, drink liquor, or eat anything out of ordinary that could have caused this sensation (or hallucination) of separateness in those two occasions. Despite my efforts years later to reach that state of separateness and perhaps divinity, it has not reappeared to me—not even through meditation. By aging, some obstacle—perhaps the conditioning strength of the perceived world—has prevented it from recurring. The experience could have not been caused by a sickness either because my awareness had in fact increased during those particular short spans of time, and then the sensation had halted abruptly and my normal level of consciousness restored.

Now, I realize that those questions and feelings, during the state of separateness, most likely came from my thoughts and conscious mind that possibly resided in 'I', but definitely not in my body. Or perhaps, the questions were posed by 'I', a separate entity or soul, which controlled my conscious mind and thoughts while the body seemed fully isolated and walking on its own power. These logical musings are quite puzzling, as I recall my conscious and thoughts staying close to 'I'. Either my thoughts and conscious mind were hanging in midair—as a third entity by itself—when the questions were being asked (by 'I'?), or 'I' was in control of my conscious mind and raising the questions. The main question circling in my head was, 'What or who that body is then?!'

I realize that mind can play tricks on people, but the naturalness of the sacred sensation and profound questions overwhelming me in those limited seconds, make it hard to believe it was merely a trick. Even it was, its nature and purpose remain mysterious and divine. A similar experience by Dr. Jacob Needleman is explained in his book, *The Heart of Philosophy*, Alfred A. Knopf, 1992, page 64.

"There was one experience of a certain kind that only much later in my life did I understand. I remember it down to the smallest detail. I had just turned fourteen. It was a bright October afternoon and I was walking home from school. I remember the trees and the colourful leaves underfoot. My thoughts were wandering when suddenly my name, "Jerry," said itself in my mind. I stopped in my tracks. I whispered to myself: "I am." It was astonishing. "I exit." I began to walk again, but very slowly. And my existence was walking with me, inside me. I am fourteen years old and I am.

And that is all. I did not speak about this experience to anyone, and for no other reason than that I gradually forgot about it."

I did not mention my out-of-body experience to anybody either. I simply could not understand it or even attribute any significance to it, as though it had been a rather normal event at the time, perhaps as part of a ritual for reaching adolescence; or, too weird to share with others. Besides, I could not explain it easily, not even as much as I have tried to explain it in these pages. I cherished this experience privately with awe for many years until more recently when I shared it with a person or a group on a few occasions during our conversations about the supernatural. This story probably sounds odd and unbelievable to people who have not had a similar experience. But it has always remained as a thought-provoking moment of my life (and perhaps a clue about the possible peculiarities of the real world), even though it lasted only around 45 seconds. Out-of-body condition is reported in million instances during near death experiences—NDE—by the way.

Nonetheless, if somebody asks me about the meaning or significance of this experience, I would have difficulty answering. What is the sensation of separateness and what does it prove or show? The basic reaction to, and significance of, an experience of this nature is merely in the possibility of body and mind separation becoming a reality for the person who experiences it, even if it is for a short interval. I know what happened and I know that it was no dream and no influence of any outside agent and it happened in both occasions without prior meditation, thinking, expectation, or any other kind of mind provocation. It happened unexpectedly in full force instantaneously, twice. It could not be self-hypnosis and it could not have been mental or physical illness. So, what was it? Perhaps one explanation is that, at those ages, a child is starting to move away from the state of childhood and getting ready to enter adolescence. While our minds are reaching the maturity to ponder the realities of the world, the very first inner quest for knowing our self, and the purpose of life that we now have learned something about, emerges naturally, perhaps as an instinct. Maybe as a scared instinct to get to know who we really are(!), which perhaps surges more freely from within us at younger ages. (It probably has difficulty manifesting thoroughly even during childhood, and thus these odd sensations, because it is so flimsy and tentative when it occurs.) However, as our minds are formed by the rules and values of our perceived world, we lose our capacity totally for experiencing this natural instinct. As our minds get clotted with rigid perceptions and we get more absorbed in the perceived world, we lose our instinctual abilities to see and feel the connection we may have with our bodies and the real world. Our divine potentialities get buried deeper. Thus, perhaps we grow up completely ignorant about another dimension of life—which should have become apparent to us and revealed our essence otherwise—all thanks to the vast influence of the perceived world. Is it then possible to say that humans of the Stone Age were better aware of, and connected to, the real world, maybe like dogs or some other animals which sometimes seem to have supernatural powers?

This experience suggests the possibility of mind and body separation, although we may not know exactly how and why. This is, of course, not in contradiction with the idea of body-mind connection. In fact, they reinforce each other. The unique feeling of body-mind separation and the absurdity of the separation experience, as noted above, reiterates their connectivity at all other times while we are physically alive. A more relevant question is whether this separation can occur only while body is alive, or whether 'I' would survive even after the body is no longer providing the blood, nutrients and oxygen that brain requires to stay alive. Is 'I' in my brain or only *using* it? If the former is true, then our human logic dictates that a separate 'I' would not continue to exist after death. With the brain rotting after the body dies, there would be no more brain cells to think or constitute the 'I' that some may believe to be my brain, my thoughts, and my conscious—although 'I' and my brain appeared to be separate during those abstract experiences. The other possibility is that 'I' is separate from all physical aspects of my body, and my mind is only a communication device (an intermediary) to connect the body to 'I'—perhaps as my soul, as part of the overall universe consciousness. With this theory, death would destroy the communication mechanism, i.e., brain cells, but 'I' continues to exist in whatever medium and meaning (perhaps not a form) that would apply to it, as it existed both before I was born and after I die. This latter idea of a separate 'I' outside both my mind and body, and that 'I' existed before I was born, poses a new dilemma, though. We can ask, "If 'I' existed before my body and mind were created, why I do not remember it, and if I do not remember (know) it, then 'I' is something that has no meaning in the context of the life I am living now." It seems appropriate at this point to leave this whole question of who 'I' is aside for now, except for making one more odd speculation:

One very remote possibility that we may entertain based on this last theory or idea is that, the reason we cannot remember (or know) that elusive 'I', which exits outside our bodies and minds, is because our communication channels, our minds and thoughts, are not tuned in properly. If our thoughts and minds were purified and aimed diligently toward the real world, there would be a good chance that we would remember (and know) the 'I', or the 'self', that we really are. Is the ultimate 'self'-awareness for this end?

The possibility of separateness of 'I' and body is merely supported by some abstract, but *real,* experiences. Yet, I am inclined to believe (but never certain) in the existence of 'I', as an entity outside my body and brain that could be contacted through my thoughts if I know or learn how. My big reservation is that why was 'I' initially separate from my body and brain? Or, putting it in a more direct phrase, 'Why was 'I' given a particular body and mind and sent to this world to have a short life in terms of the body and the mind? Why connect 'I' to a body and mind in the first place? Why manifest 'I' within a body and mind? And why did not 'I' remain as the 'I' that always existed independently? Why was I born into a physical life we soon learn to love so much in our perceived world despite so much suffering we must endure?' One plausible answer is that perhaps every one of us, as individual 'I's is transformed into a body and mind form, for a short term, for a specific purpose and mission. And now we have to know what that mission is! So far, we all seem to have failed to figure this out. Can we ever solve this mystery? Is the main mission forgotten because of the overwhelming interference of the perceived world? Accordingly, this answer remains plausible only if 'I', and everybody else's spirit too, can find the purpose of being here and living in a chartered body. Otherwise, death is the end of 'I' too.

Another abstract clue about the possibility of a deeper dimension of humans comes through night dreams for some people. The type and depth of these dreams vary for individuals. Some people, like me, dream every night almost the whole night. These dreams are often quite complex and have many interesting features that I have been studying for years as part of personal curiosity. Some of the main points boggling my mind are noted here. For one thing, we recognize ourselves distinctively in the midst of the stories in our dreams. In fact, the 'I' in the dream has a high degree of consciousness about its existence in those places and events and the manner it behaves, thinks, and feels. The settings and landscapes in these dreams are often quite strange, splendid, and colourful by themselves, which raise the question about the possibility of (and the reason for) brain creating such unworldly images only during the dream and not when the person is awake. Another amazing feature of these dreams is the accuracy and delicacy of logic, emotions, planning, evaluation, negotiations, high awareness, questioning and reasoning, arguments, sequence of events that 'I' gets involved in. It seems rather imprudent to imagine that only brain's activities could generate such refined accuracy and complexity only randomly without any specific objective behind such long sequence of events during a dream. All these perplexities of dreams make the author spend time to study them occasionally. Yet the sophistication of these dreams is not only amazing, but also a cause for speculating about the separation of 'I' from daily life during our sleep. Is 'I' in our dreams a clue about our spirit by any chance?

Anyway, take all the above speculations as philosophical gibberish that has no value other than giving us a chance to exercise our minds, test our idiotic logic, and possibly build our personal beliefs and spirit.

Real Experiences

Some of us believe that our destiny is set at birth. Our genes play a major role in this matter, anyway, even if we do not believe in God's role or luck, etc. Some people even accept that every event has a purpose as an integral part of their destinies. They place their faith in their fates as part of their fundamental life philosophy. This mentality helps them deal with unpleasant events, thoughts, and feelings—as pain and torture would always engulf humans' lives. We may not understand the purpose of an event right away, yet it sometimes manifests as a blessing later. Many little events might turn up to be small miracles for definite purposes. In all, by adopting some faith and adapting to simpler notions of the real world, we may learn to set our expectations and attitude more modestly, make life tolerable or even joyful, and perhaps fulfil some genuine purposes too.

Real experiences mentioned here are only some examples of small miracles in the author's life. Similar miraculous revelations (divine interventions perhaps) happen to everybody occasionally. But, what goads a person to suddenly believe in some realities contrary to the perceived world's norms and values?

I grew up in a family void of religious or spiritual beliefs. I became a pragmatist with little patience for speculation and naivety. Seldom did I believe in miracles, the supernatural, or spiritual claims. I always depended only on facts, reasons, and hard proofs. As I faced critical decisions and doubts in my life, however, I realized that some matters could not be analysed by facts and hard evidence. I became full of doubts as I had difficulty making decisions and, at the same time, felt helpless and exhausted. I felt desperate and frustrated when decisions were not made or delayed for days and months, and sometimes years, due to the lack of adequate information or my severe doubts about all my options. On the side, things happened regardless of my (in)decisions and I started to realize that most of my thoughts and decisions, even after substantial analysis, turned out not to be necessarily useful in the hindsight. On the other hand, many events that were out of my control turned up to my advantage in unforeseeable ways.

Many events, which I now consider little miracles have not only affected my life directly, but also changed my way of thinking and attitude. They have goaded me to adopt certain beliefs, including those related to the inevitability of life's destiny. By writing about a few of these experiences, I am merely offering some examples of how even a pragmatist learns to break the barriers and move away from a lifetime of conditioning habits and values to explore new principles.

The first example relates to my presumably smart decision to return to Iran in 1976 after nine years of education and work in California. Living in Los Angeles had been a learning experience by itself, with lots of opportunities and disappointments, not to mention the traffic and smog. At the end, I decided to return to Iran and work at positions and salaries unattainable even in the United States. The amount of money I was making and the luxurious furniture and automobile that I bought in Rome provided a dreamlike lifestyle for me in Tehran. While enjoying a liberal and shallow life, it soon appeared that my routines were flimsy and habitual with no ultimate purpose. I was wasting my life away in what could be called a dreary mix of pleasure and vanity. Yet, I had no thoughts or plans beyond my daily adventures. I was really living in the NOW! After three years, the Islamic Revolution happened, I got married, my daughter was born, my father who lived in Los Angeles fell seriously ill, and the war with Iraq started.

Life's absurdity became more apparent when every night we had to run down to the basement to protect ourselves and our families from the bombs and missiles that Saddam Hussein, with the aid and guidance of the United States, was dropping on our heads. The idea of so many young men and boys dying every day in the proclaimed holy war against Iraq, made life seem too vain and chaotic. The pictures of so-called martyrs who were given a key to heaven and lured into this despicable war of Egos and human folly were infuriating. At the same time, my brothers in Los Angeles indicated that my father's health was deteriorating very fast in the incentive care unit of a hospital where he remained in comma. The borders and airports were closed and leaving the country became illegal. No freedom and no life. The situation was completely hopeless and I felt helpless.

My wife and I considered emigration, but the task of abandoning our familiar life and starting all over again seemed insurmountable. We had doubts about so many issues, especially our risky future in a foreign country even if we could get permanent residency and decent jobs. Many potential risks and uncertainties hindered decision-making. Our small savings could not be transferred out of the country legally, and illegally it was not worth much. At this time, the government of Iran allowed people with serious health problems leave for getting medical attention in other countries, accompanied by a related person. I decided to use this loophole to go see my father in his last days. The authorities insisted that my mother, who was in Iran at the time, could go help him, but not me. Of course, they did not know that my brothers were in Los Angeles already. This information would have closed the door on me completely. After two months of haggling and insisting on the fact that my parents were separated and my frail mother could not speak English, the officials reluctantly issued a permit for me to leave Iran, without my family of course. Thus, I started to plan for my departure.

The bank I worked for was nationalized and I had become a government executive, but under scrutiny and suspicion. Thus, I did not talk about my plans to leave the country to anybody in fears of obstacles that some bank official could cause spitefully or whatever. Just a few months earlier, I had hired a new employee educated in the U.S. One day, he came to see me unexpectedly and turned in his resignation for going to Canada as a landed immigrant. In a few minutes, he told me a lot about Vancouver, where he was planning to live. I did not know much about Canada or even considered living there. Yet, before going home that night, I had already decided (more like a sudden inspiration) to try to move my family to Canada. This was contrary to my initial plan to return to Iran after visiting my father. That night I told my wife that I would not return to Tehran, so she and our daughter should somehow manage to join me as soon as I got our permanent residency from either Canada or the U.S. I realized that my job in the next few months or years would be tough and risky. However, I did not care as if driven by a divine force.

Another major obstacle was getting a visa. The U.S. government had prohibited entry visas to Iranians regardless of their background due to the hostage situation. (Some 50-60 Americans were labelled spies and kept hostage by the Khomeini's regime.) I called my good friend, a French businessman who knew some people in the economic attaché of the U.S. Consulate in France. He said he might be able to help me with the U.S. visa if I could go to Bordeaux and meet him. So I left my wife and six-month-old daughter for an unknown adventure, with my wife's blessing of course. It was extremely difficult for me to leave them behind in the midst of all that chaos, but it seemed that now I was on a holy crusade.

I learned the day before my departure that my boss, a top executive in the bank, was flying to Germany on the same Lufthansa flight. There was no time and too much risk to switch my flight. Thus, I disguised myself partially to avoid an encounter at the airport or during the boarding. From my seat in the economy section, I could see him in the first class. I hid in my chair until we were outside the Iranian air zone. Despite the sense of freedom after so long, I was too sad and worried about my family's welfare amidst the mayhem in Iran. But personally, I was a free man again. At least, I did not have to play a fake personality to cope with the Islamic rules anymore and fear everything and everyone.

Once the plane was over Turkey, I went to my boss. He was shocked. I told him that I was hoping to go to Los Angeles to visit my dying father. "You're not coming back, are you?" he asked with stress and resignation. He complained for my clear disregard for the protocol and not informing him formally. Now I was even more certain that my return to Iran was risky. At least I had lost my lucrative job and a chance for any worthy career in Iran.

I went to France, my friend helped me with the U.S. visa—an impossible task in those times—and I flew to Los Angeles. There, I applied for immigration to the U.S. and Canada. It turned out that my lawyer for pursuing the U.S. immigration process was a crook and, after all the money I paid him, the process was taking much longer than he had promised, despite my years of work experience in the U.S. Meanwhile, the economic recession in Canada had created complications and, after ten months of waiting, I received a letter from the Canada Consulate General in Los Angeles stating that, in accordance with a recent government communiqué, all applications based on educational merits were turned down. First, I took the rejection gracefully and accepted my bad luck. Then, a mysterious voice whispered in my head that it was not necessary to take this rejection letter final and return to Iran. Perhaps I should do something. During all this time, my wife kept calling me and crying on the phone for their hardship in Iran. She was also losing hope to be ever allowed to leave the country and join me. At that point, I had spent the worst ten months of my life.

I wrote a letter to the Canadian Consulate in Los Angeles. The words reflected the basic truth in a logical manner, but somehow with a passionate tone that I did not know I had in me. The words came to me from a divine source I have learned to depend on when I *really* have a legitimate need. My brothers insisted that my efforts were useless considering governments' bureaucracy, especially when the order had come from the Minister of Immigration or the Prime Minister himself. In about two weeks, I received a phone call from the Canadian Consulate and was invited for an interview in ten days.

After the interview, the Consular General told me that giving me an immigrant visa was against the new rules, but somehow she was inspired to help me. Then she introduced me to her husband, who also worked in the Consulate. Finally, a decision was made to proceed favourably with my application. However, first, the whole family had to undergo a complete medical check-up. I forwarded my family's package to Iran to complete according to the requirements of the Consulate General of Canada in Tehran.

Despite the good news, I was concerned about my wife and daughter while the war escalated and so many obstacles remained for my family's exit. My wife informed me on the phone that she had found some individuals who smuggled people out of the country for an exuberant fee. For my wife and daughter it meant paying our leftover savings after one year of no income and large expenses, including the bribes in Iran, lawyers' fees in L.A., etc. Still, the main issue was the risk of my family's illegal border crossing, considering the severe punishment of many who were captured. However, my wife was adamant to flee, ignoring my pleas to wait at least until I had some documents for her to use for travelling to the U.S. or Canada. She thought that the opportunity to flee was too precious to bypass despite its dangers and risks. Thus, she fled Iran with our daughter after completing their medical checkups and sending them to the Canadian Consulate in Los Angeles.

For my medical check-up, I went to a reputable medical clinic and visited a few physicians for various tests, X-rays, etc. I knew about my old hernia that needed an operation someday. However, I had postponed the surgery since my job did not require heavy lifting and I did not have any pain. One of the doctors noticed it and insisted that I had to undergo an operation or I would have difficulty emigrating. He was arranging fast for the operation and calculating the horrendous costs for a person without insurance. I told him that I had to think and let him know the next day. I was worried about my family in the deserts of southern Iran in their attempt to flee and then arriving in Pakistan, which was even a worse prospect. And now, the doctor was insisting that I would not be allowed to go to Canada with a hernia. I did not want to jeopardize the immigration process or my family's situation, if hernia was indeed a problem. Without a visa to travel to Canada, my family had to live as refugees in a country for sometime. On the other hand, undergoing an operation would have been time-consuming, expensive, and risky. This was still another major decision to make under duress.

After considering my options, I took the risk and told the good doctor to report the hernia, but I would not undergo an operation in the middle of all the commotion around me. Later on, when no problem came out of my hernia, I realized how much deceit or exaggeration a supposedly professional doctor is willing to assume just to make some money from someone's desperate situation. The hernia story shows another quick, risky decision I had to make when I was not in my best state of mind.

The journey to Pakistan border through the deserts of southern Iran is quite difficult and unhealthy, especially during the summer time. My wife had told me that she would not be able to contact me for around ten days until they had arrived safely in Pakistan. Arriving in Pakistan would have its own risks, I knew.

Preying on Iranian refugees' desperation, some Pakistani police and officials could extort as much money from them as they could, and still surrender them to the Iranian police for showing their cooperation with the Iranian government.

The details of the hardships my wife and one-year-old daughter endured to complete their frightening and torturous journey is a long story that I skip here. It would be a horrific and lengthy tale all by itself. When she called me from Islamabad in Pakistan, I had just received instructions from the Canadian Consulate to go for the final paperwork and getting the immigration documents. She told me that after giving big bribes and constant humiliation and intimidation by the Pakistani police, they had finally gotten an exit visa. She had also learned that Spain was the only destination in Europe that did not require a visa. Therefore, she had purchased a ticket to go to Madrid.

I went to the Canadian Consulate the next day and explained my wife's situation. With the Consular's monumental help, all the documents were completed the same day. My wife's and daughter's papers were mailed to the Canadian Consulate in Madrid to be delivered to my wife. I gave the instructions to my wife on the phone about their visas and the plane tickets to go to Vancouver in onc wcck from that date. She had gone to the Canadian Consulate in Madrid every day, but papers had not arrived until the last day when she was booked to fly to Vancouver. She could make the flight and we met after one year in the Vancouver Airport, on September 18, 1982. My wife was extremely thin and tired and my daughter did not recognize me. My bank colleague who had first told me about this great city came along with me to the airport to participate in this re-union. He certainly deserved to be a part of it, as destiny's instrument to give me the insight I needed in one gloomy day in my office back in Tehran. It was my fate, but more importantly, it was the destiny of my kids to live in Canada, where they would definitely have much more opportunities.

Many coincidences and small miracles had intervened to move to Canada. Even my father recovered fully and lived a healthy and active life for another twenty-five years—the same person whom the doctors in one of the best U.S. hospitals had pronounced terminal. To me, it was the destiny making its way through all the obstacles to bring us to Vancouver; a city that is full of natural beauty—my ultimate compassion—and freedom. Miracles are perhaps mere coincidences, but they sure feel supernatural to me. Therefore, I have built my beliefs around these personal experiences and tiny miracles.

All my life, so many things have happened to me that had initially appeared negative or positive, but in the hindsight, have found a different meaning and interpretation. All the lost job opportunities and promotions, which were given to less qualified people due to discrimination, have turned out to be a blessing for me. I believe so now, as all those disappointments made me find my new ways of thinking and living. Some of the negative events that saddened me at the time have actually stopped me from getting into a life of continuous struggles for more status and money. I realized it many years later, though, when I got a chance to think and meditate. In fact, those setbacks gave me the opportunity to do the real things that matter to me now the most. This type of transformation or transcendence can happen to everybody once we see and appreciate the clues from the real world. When I bought a house full of weeds and no landscaping, it felt like a complete disaster to me and I did not have the financial priority to have them professionally done. Thus, I took on the job of cleaning and doing things with my own hands, which was laborious and dirty. However, that job gave me a chance to learn to work with my hands and on my knees, something that I had never considered necessary after so much education and false Ego. Not only my gardens turned beautiful and a source of enjoyment, but also I learned more about the beauty of flowers and plants and how they grow, blossom, and multiply. This experience brings a deep sense of appreciation for some intrinsic values that only a labouring gardener can enjoy. I feel a special connection to every plant inside and outside my house. I would not have enjoyed my garden as much as I have, if I were not the person creating it, even if it were ten times bigger and more beautiful than it turned out.

Therefore, I have come to believe that it is not always the initial perception of, and reaction to, events that determines their final value and impact on our lives, but rather the subsequent surprises that come later when we see the outcome of our efforts and patience. The beauty and purposefulness of the real world reveal themselves from beneath our initial perceptions and expectations once we pass the test of fortitude and conviction.

Another experience started as a negative incident and then turned into a positive aspect of my daily life. It happened after a car accident that resulted in softening of my back and neck tissues and constant pain. I tried many different treatments, including physiotherapy, chiropractor, and painkillers. These treatment methods induced some temporary relief, but the pain always returned. One year later, I visited a specialist who prescribed an exercise routine to do at home. Those simple exercises, along with some light weightlifting later on, improved my condition after a couple of months. Now these exercises have become part of my daily routine. I do not have any more pains and my overall health would not deteriorate even if I stopped my routine exercises. However, after becoming more conscious about my body (subsequent to a debilitating car accident), I have learned more about both my physical and mental requirements and the importance of keeping them in good shape. My spirit has risen drastically since the accident due to the dramatic change I had to make in my lifestyle. Now, I even appreciate my healthy-looking stature after getting rid of the extra fat, fatigue, and short breath. The sudden awakening made me quit my heavy smoking, too, after thirty years of addiction. I have, in the process, learned to believe that for a healthy mind I should have a healthy body. Therefore, I look back at the car accident as a wakeup call that changed my outlook about physical requirement and health. I learned to take care of the body that must help me for a long time to come. Prior to this event, I did some minor exercises only when I had time and motivation. Now, I have made a habit of it.

Many other Real Experiences with similar outcomes have changed my life outlook in a systematic manner. They have amazed me in terms of likely miracles that often seem to happen behind the scene. They are great examples of destiny and decisions working in a mysterious combination and leading to such wonderful conclusions. Of course, not all of my plans and decisions have been successful. On the contrary, I have faced tremendous failures and disappointments due to both my bad decisions and what we may call bad luck. Yet, these negative experiences have only made the power of positive ones even more crucial for sustaining my sanity and keeping my beliefs in that mysterious energy that intervenes when necessary. Of course, I also believe that while our destiny pushes us forward in a certain direction incessantly, our decisions or indecisions play a prominent role in the outcome, and we must be prepared to face the consequences of our right or wrong choices.

A Sense of Victory

After going through major stages of life and making millions of decisions of various natures, along with my indecisions due to my doubts, I feel ready to tally the final score. It appears that a combination of fate and my decisions (or indecisions) has been responsible for around 70% of my present life standing and overall success, mainly in terms of finding a simple lifestyle and tranquility. The other 30% of my life outcome has been negative. Those experiences have caused me deep agony and stirred my doubts about the validity of my fundamental trust in destiny. The irony is that the 30% setbacks have been related to the major decisions of my life, including my doomed marriage and other companionships, career, and developing my true potentialities. I made horrible mistakes in all those main areas with my hasty or naive decisions. Only the mere positive outcome of those 70% routine decisions, related to less significant life issues, and the support of that mysterious fate-maker have saved my sense of relative optimism and determination. Of course, I have never been able to completely eliminate my doubts about the existence of a divine entity behind the scene. I would never know the mystery behind the seemingly life-changing miracles or the validity of my interpretations of them. Yet, overall, I prefer to keep my convictions intact, especially when I ponder all the seemingly miraculous revelations throughout my life.

Overall, my educated belief in the inevitability of destiny has emerged gradually from experiences that were positive or negative at the beginning, but found different interpretations when the real meanings of those experiences revealed themselves many months or years later. This belief has moderated my sense of mere pragmatism that in the past directed my actions and decisions. And this relative reliance on fate reduces the agony of dependence on the information that we receive from all the crooked sources in the perceived world.

Yet, I have discovered something important about fate aside from all the above conclusions. I have learned that fate is highly correlated to the type of person I am. I should not expect good outcomes and health simply because I believe in fate. No way! Rather, my experiences have taught me that good things happen only when I am truly compassionate, selfless, and realize the need for bettering myself every single day. That is the most important lesson that our beliefs and convictions can teach us.

Our personal contacts with an external force or energy—when we touch some blessed moments—are scattered throughout our lives, from childhood, which is a state of curiosity and apprehension, until we reach a stage where our experiences feel more tangible and expressible. We feel that we have travelled on many paths, but, often, they had been only trials and errors, experiments that caused change of heart, change of thought, and change of direction, wonderment and maturation. We usually encounter two types of experiences. The first kind may be classified as *abstract experiences*, which are direct signs of the existence of a real world. The other kinds of experiences are simple life situations that suddenly feel like magic or a blessing. They are signs of the real reality, too, while the messages are often received in an indirect way. We may refer to these events as *real experience* only to distinguish them from the abstract ones.

The abstract and real experiences quoted above are some of the clues that have influenced my outlook (positive doubts) regarding the existence of a real world. My understanding about, and contact with, the real world is surely limited and remain very much at a philosophical level. Yet, it has made a significant influence on my way of thinking, feeling, and doing things, hopefully in a better and more humanistic way. And that is all that matters. I may never walk on the same path that a diligent guru walks, but I am convinced that whatever little knowledge and beliefs I have accumulated from my life experiences would guide me in dealing with the uncertainties and doubts that would continue besieging me on some days. Accordingly, this would be the message I advocate in this book. That is, a middle ground between full spiritualism and atheism is a sensible path that most of us would feel comfortable to adopt. All we need to do is to make an effort to know who we are and why. And then, we may review who we think we are in the context of things we must do, decisions we must make, doubts that we must cherish or overcome, and relationships that we love to have with other individuals and our environment as a whole.

Earlier in this book, a question was raised about a person's choices when he arrives at the intersection of wisdom paths. Now is perhaps a good time to answer that question.

The path that we choose when we arrive at the awareness intersection would be personal according to the degree of our beliefs and doubts regarding the existence and relevance of a real world compared with our seemingly practical way of thinking and living. At that moment, we are realistically aware of the struggles needed to maintain a balance between our inner quest for the truth and the social request for conformity. We realize and accept this challenge, which would continue to consume our energy for the foreseeable future and yet keep us in conflict with others and within ourselves. We attempt to define a workable middle ground that would, on the one hand, keep us in touch with our need for the realization of 'self' and our inner actualization, and, on the other hand, help us adapt and perform the role that we are expected to play in society, without getting absorbed in it or by it. A middle ground path would be the path of self-awareness and wisdom that we would use as a point of reference in dealing with our decisions and doubts most effectively, perhaps in the form of fairer and wiser consciousness.

The middle ground path may prove to be a trial effort for transcending into higher wisdom paths in a natural manner through gradual growth. We definitely cannot jump or fly to the Summit, but rather we should walk gradually and attentively by testing our wisdom every step of the way. Like a mountain climber, we should kccp onc cyc on the Summit and one eye on the next step, which is often just our contact with the world of perceived realities. We must first make sure we are standing on a firm ground before taking the next step. This is where a solid foundation of thoughts and a workable life philosophy can help. A middle-ground-path life philosophy, as defined and suggested throughout this trilogy, would be a guiding light for things we do and decisions we make. This wisdom could alleviate our suffering during the course of life. And it would be the wisdom that would guide us in helping other human beings in any way we can, with the hope that it would bring us closer together and in touch with Nature and our spirit.

The most important thing to remember, however, is to sense and honour our arrival at the intersection (of truth), which has an extremely high significance of its own. We have finally passed beyond the foggy layers of the perceived world and noticed that we are not the person that runs around in this world constantly causing all sorts of anxiety and stress for our 'self's and other human beings. Now, we can see the absurdity of all the unnecessary struggles that we considered a requirement of social living, the wealth, the status, the sexuality, the power, and the rest of them. We are now willing to re-evaluate social requests from within our inner quests for the truth. And this arriving at the intersection with all the revolution in our thoughts and attitude towards life is what we may consider the ultimate VICTORY.

PART V
Common Sense and Self-awareness

CHAPTER TWELVE
The Conflicting Roles of Our Doubts

While we emphasize on our decision-making capability and assertiveness as appealing personal attributes, we suspect the value of our 'doubts' and the state of 'doubtfulness.' In fact, we often consider our doubts self-imposed limitations that cause procrastination and hinder the opportunity of chasing our ambitions. Yet, many of our doubts are blessings, if we understand their nature and use the right balance of doubts and decisions in life. Of course, we also benefit from a balance in the number of conscious decisions to 'do not make a decision,' compared to occasions when decisions are needed urgently.

We face an enormous amount of doubts and decisions just for running our daily affairs. Moreover, we ponder many doubtful ideas about life, while feeling obliged to justify our existence every day too. Our most daunting doubt is about the possibility of a non-physical existence. We try to satisfy our spirituality need (mostly through religion) along with a vision of afterlife, which sounds like killing two birds with one stone. The usefulness and relevance of these dilemmas and doubts are not too important. Rather, the fact that our minds are too preoccupied and waste so much energy on these doubts and questions demands a review. Why God has made us dwell on so many doubts, duel with so many decisions, and still lose most of our life's opportunities, is a big mystery.

The level and depth of our doubts have increased in the recent decades due to the deterioration of many social and personal factors, which are discussed throughout this trilogy. For one thing, we have lost touch with our natural instincts to think and decide independently or gauge the purposes of our doubts. Our instincts are largely subdued, as we like to rely more on society to give us the clues and values for living. Our leftover instincts are not trustworthy nowadays, either, e.g., when our sexual drive pushes us to marry a jerk or submit to our partner's whims at the cost of losing our identity even around our close family members. We cannot trust even our intuition, often rightfully. While our philosophical and routine decisions sometimes benefit from our intuition partially, we seldom depend on it for serious decision-making, except in emotional situations, which leads to another bunch of hasty decisions and disasters.

The rising social complexity and uncertainties have raised our stress and doubtfulness about all facets of life, including our own and other people's integrity and intentions. As we get moulded deeper every day into our shallow identities and routines, our ability to make natural observations and decisions has declined and we have lost more of our 'self.' The quality and reliability of information, which we are supposed to use for our decisions, have diminished rapidly in society too. In fact, all kinds of misinformation and false information are deliberately introduced in societies to influence and direct the mass in a desired direction. Capitalism and consumerism depend on market performance, which is driven by normally false advertising and propagandas to sustain our fat, incompetent social structure at our expense. Accordingly, we have no reliable life vision or a chance of redemption within a fast declining social environment. We are in a kind of black hole where there is no hope for escape. We just follow this common life path hypnotically and our insecurities keep mounting.

So we have become cynical and more doubtful about the whole purpose of living and struggling for such intangible results. We often doubt even our identity as we try too hard to prove our individualism, and we doubt our sanity in the midst of this chaos. The average intelligence of the public has increased in line with the evolution of science and social interactions, yet the degree of social gullibility has skyrocketed. Thus, the quality of our decisions has declined and we face shoddier destinies and deeper disappointments. To get some relative relief, we have become obsessed with the idea of finding love and happiness *at least*, which has turned out into another painful fantasy. And also the cause of more doubtfulness.

In all, without our instincts, reliable information, or personal convictions, our decisions have become too mechanical or emotional. As we feel more dependent on social values to set our life objectives and path, the rising uncertainties and doubtfulness have contained and contaminated our minds. We often feel trapped within an ambiguous mental state and forced to tackle too many dilemmas about all aspects of our lives, including social structure, the creation, spirituality, and human nature. We ponder these quandaries and the related notions publicized merely in terms of philosophical ideas and scientific concepts if we find time, patience, and intelligence. Yet, we usually do not dare to consider, or express our view of, the world differently from the common perception of it. Or we simply put our trust in religions, while we often doubt their validity deep down anyway.

We have extreme doubts about both our inner (self) and outer (social) relationships. Our doubts also increase as our artificial and authentic needs clash, while superficial social trends and structure also cause more inner conflicts. Within this state of doubtfulness, we remain helpless to reconcile the necessities of either our inner or our outer world. We have doubts about our potentials, daily routines, and destination. We have doubts about the purpose of life in general and our efforts within this obscure social structure. We also have major doubts about all the religious and philosophical ideas. Especially, we are too keen to grasp our personal and humans' role within the universe, as if proving our connection to it would resolve so much of our problems. We have doubts about the possibility of soul. In smaller scales, we have doubts about the purpose of our dreary existence and we have doubts about trusting anybody to help us with our dilemmas and decisions. We have doubts about our feelings and thoughts. We have doubts about our looks, so we check the mirror all the time in hopes of getting some kind of a clue. We do the same thing subconsciously with our conscience—the inner mirror—to deal with our doubts about our characters. Yet, only 'gullibles' (gullible persons) and 'egoists' may ever overcome their wide range of lingering doubts.

The Nature and Level of Our Doubts

Several layers of doubts boggle any intelligent person's mind. At the bottom of our fundamental questions lies our doubts regarding our identity and destiny—level one doubts. We like to know who we are and what we can logically expect to get from life in general. At the next level, we have questions and doubts about the means of satisfying our basic needs and coping with the demands of social living, economy, family, health, and day-to-day living. Regardless of the ultimate purpose and divinity of life, there is still the reality of hunger, disease, desires, and 'time' as dominant dimensions of physical life. We are forced to make decisions and have deep doubts about the conditions that rule our physical and mental growth, social order, and value systems. And then at the third level, we question and doubt the means of happiness and spirituality. We want to grasp and possibly reach a state of inner peace and happiness, aside from our urge to know our identity and decipher the secrets of creation, and regardless (or in spite) of our unending struggles to satisfy our basic needs. These three levels of doubts are shown in Diagram 12.1. They affect our lives differently and deeply.

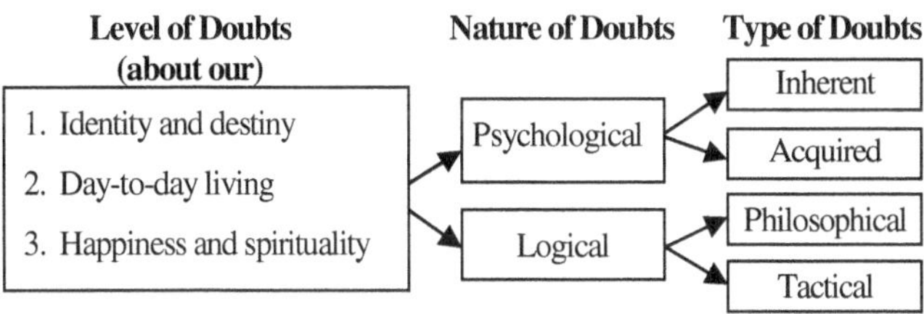

Diagram 12.1: Level, Nature, and Type of Doubts

The Scope and Effects of Our Doubts

A vast number of dilemmas boggle our minds according to the three levels of human doubts noted in Diagram 12.1. These doubts are either psychological or logical in terms of their nature. Examples of *psychological* (and instinctual) doubts include thoughts like, 'Am I handsome?', 'Am I talented?', 'Is my spouse cheating on me?', etc. Parallel to the same questions, *logical* (intellectual) doubts consist of, 'How important being handsome is?', 'How to make a living if not talented enough?', 'How to react to my spouse's infidelity?', etc.

Psychological doubts are either *inherent* due to our genes and human nature or they are *acquired* through personal experiences and building our idiosyncrasies over years. Logical doubts are two types too: Philosophical and tactical. *Philosophical* doubts relate to our options and choices in terms of *what* to do and *why*. *Tactical* doubts relate to *how,* in terms of implementing our choices and options and coping with socioeconomic environment (despite our philosophical disposition and apprehension).

Regardless of the nature, type, or level of doubts, they all affect us psychologically somehow. They might even indicate or cause our deep inner conflicts. As we strive to make good decisions, while facing major doubts, we are constantly in conflict with our convictions, integrity, and conscience, and thus cause our own stress. Especially in terms of our logical doubts (e.g., regarding our sex appeal or wisdom), seldom can we find easy answers to depend on and move on. Even when we choose a life philosophy to relieve ourselves from constant pressure of choices and doubts, we often doubt our philosophy of life itself. Always, various temptations and external forces try to shake the foundation of our thoughts and philosophical inclinations.

Our rising inner conflicts create even vaster psychological doubts, as we must deal with more uncertainties nowadays due to the deterioration of socioeconomic conditions and decision-making variables. In this chaotic environment, self-doubt also increases fast, while we struggle to build an authentic identity, understand our roles, and make timely decisions.

Some of our simple doubts eventually turn into fundamental life dilemmas and philosophical paradoxes, which then cause even more doubts of different natures—to the point we eventually doubt even our sanity. For example, a main human dilemma is that, while we desire to live long, most of these living years bring us only suffering and disappointments. Thus, we doubt the purpose and value of living long, or at all. Even the fortunate group who has their basic needs satisfied have vast doubts about many issues, as they keep searching for that elusive happiness and tranquility their entire lives in vain.

Unfortunately, life is becoming too strenuous to allow a stable state of mind. It mostly consists of struggles for understanding and satisfying our basic needs, confronting people, and trying to survive. The majority of us must rely on economic conditions and job market to make a living. Meanwhile, the level of work related stress has become the main cause of heart attack and other illnesses. So, the purpose of our efforts becomes, at least philosophically, quite doubtful. Personal aspiration and artificial needs keep increasing, too, and putting more pressure on people's psyche. The lack of job security, deficiency of market economy to offer decent and dignified job opportunities to people, minimal freedom in doing things that one really enjoys doing, family problems, relationship conundrums, and the stressful demands of social living at the early stage of the 21st century make the desire for a long life absurd. Sometimes we think that living longer is simply an unfair sentence to lengthier torture.

On the one hand, our rising cynicism about our incessant misfortunes and the vanity of our struggles makes us doubt the chance of human life having any purpose, especially in terms of finding happiness. On the other hand, we have an intrinsic urge to satisfy our minds about, and fill our lives with, happiness, which we think we *deserve* and somehow feel intuitively to be a natural expectation for human life. Our naïve innate belief about happiness emanating sooner or later goads our search, struggles, and doubts. We remain stubbornly hopeful that life has a meaning, although nobody appears to have a definition of it after so many centuries of speculation and search. Nevertheless, these rotating waves of pessimism and optimism about happiness and existence create serious doubts about the possibility of finding tranquility and justifying the purpose of a long life in such a hectic environment.

These kinds of thoughts and doubts about life are not merely the symptoms of an individual's depressed mind. Every one of us can relate to these experiences quite readily, though the degree and frequency of these negative experiences vary among individuals according to their level of tolerance and naivety. The theme of this book would appear too negative compared with the more appealing ideas suggested in positive thinking books. Unfortunately, it is depressing to talk about the true reality of life, which mainly consists of our doubts, the enormity of major life decisions in the new era, our obsession to find happiness at all cost, sufferings, ongoing struggles, and stressful daily routines that we cannot avoid.

The whole topic of 'philosophy' has evolved in response to our humanistic experiences, doubts, and expectations, and in line with our struggles to find a reasonable (if not absolute) inner happiness and tranquillity. The basic premise, which we can easily relate to, is that 'peace of mind' is the only tangible definition of happiness and tranquillity. And yet, the characteristics of our lives, causing such extreme level of doubts and struggles, give our minds very little, if any, chance to achieve a steady peaceful state. Not only our life routines, but sometimes even the prescriptions of positive-thinking advocates make the burden of our struggles heavier and further from the truth. They only expand the type and nature of our doubts in all directions.

Therefore, it is necessary to discuss depressing topics in this trilogy, including our personal limitations and capacities, the rude and negative aspects of life and humanity, the doubtful value of positive-thinking practices, the role of our doubts and beliefs, etc. These philosophical explorations are not meant to dampen our search for possible relief and hopefully peace of mind. Rather, they are for increasing our alertness and tolerance, to find the right path to peace and tranquility. Some tone of pessimism in this book should not be taken as a complete rejection of life and the precious values that are inherent in it. On the contrary, the point is to find those virtues in life that can bring us the ultimate peace of mind just by aborting our fantasies, fruitless thoughts, negative doubts, and corny lifestyles.

There is a beautiful world out there behind the illusions and superficialities of the perceived world. It is accessible to all of us while we are 'alive' and can learn to enjoy it with a peaceful mind. This world reveals itself only to those who consciously and forcefully search for it intelligently by denying some of the given rules of our social living, if we can give our brains a break. Yet it seems that only through constant thinking and planning we are able to barely sustain ourselves in this super-active and demanding world. Even when we take a couple of weeks of vacation to give our minds a rest, we have a hard time not thinking about work. We doubt the possibility of a world outside the objectives of organizations and we doubt our identity without those objectives, especially for more prosperity and power. It is perhaps not easy to grasp the idea of a beautiful world beyond the mayhem we live in, and perhaps it is even more difficult to forego the habits that we believe are essential for our survival and social living. It is sad how we humans neglect our ability to do amazing deeds, create splendid thoughts, and make everybody feel peace and tranquility just by realizing our divine potentialities instead of nurturing the demons within us.

Our Doubts about Human Nature

Our doubts and cynicism about the purity of human nature is particularly troublesome. Our experiences and interactions with people give us all the reasons to seriously doubt their honesty and integrity. Our perceptions of people with whom we exchange services, friendship, compassion, and love build our perception of human nature. Our own impurities, such as jealousy and spite, taint our perceptions of humans and their nature even more. Our reactions reflect how others have dealt with us, how damaged we are ourselves, how we judge the purity of human nature, and the kind of attitude we find suitable for ourselves to live in society without getting hurt all the time. Overall, people's low degree of purity and integrity, especially our parents, spouses, teachers, and colleagues infect our outlook on life and raise our doubts at all the three levels noted in Diagram 12.1. Mistrust and cynicism have become an epidemic and our societies would suffer from these personal deteriorations tremendously. Corruption has spread fast, and the lack of personal integrity and basic morality has blemished human nature and humanity beyond repair.

Humans' great appetite and aptitude for wickedness is just amazing. However, even more astonishing is some individuals' exemplary goodness, compassion, and ability to cooperate to achieve what we consider a 'humanitarian' cause. It feels incredible when humans' divine potentialities erupt from their deep existence and their spirits enrich everybody, including the person himself. Sadly, however, these individuals and occasions are so rare we cannot spend too much time to discuss and fuss about them when the overall human canvass is painted in dark colours and people are getting more corrupt in general every day. In fact, humans' divine potentialities appear so beautiful and heavenly because these experiences are rare beyond our normal expectations.

We sometimes wonder about the extent of human impurity, but we are mostly amazed and impressed with the simplest sign of purity in some humans as if we were watching some aliens on our planet. Ironically, these occasional human goodness causes more confusion and doubts for us, as we wonder for the millionth time that perhaps humans' real nature is supposed to be pure!! Alas, it seems we are only dreaming about this possibility. A good metaphor about human nature is the universe itself. While many brilliant, enlightened individuals always shine like stars and give us some level of hope about the possibility of a better life, the deep, dark nature of the world and all its frightening features threaten our existence like black holes and asteroids.

Our doubts about the purity of human nature have affected our relationships extensively, too. We have a hard time choosing a spouse and have a harder time maintaining a marital relationship. We have little trust or faith in our bosses and organizations we work for. We are suspicious of the intentions of our friends and colleagues and are paranoid about our politicians and public officials. It is not hard to see how we have reached this level of doubtfulness about our nature as our societies and relationships have become more complex and stressful. Yet the question is whether we can ever overcome our doubts about the purity of humans and humanity. And if not, how can we live together when our trust toward one another, and social structure as a whole, is collapsing so fast.

As another symptom of our rising doubtfulness, we strive (quite rationally) to become more analytical than instinctual. We search for solutions as an ongoing, routine activity of our lives and we pretend to be analytical. But even if we have analytical aptitude, and could behave like an objective person by restraining our emotions, we still have to depend increasingly on external information. We are still at the mercy of others—their actions, moods, and behaviours—in order to make effective decisions, e.g., for getting along with our spouse in a mutually agreeable setting. In all, our experiences with all the words and promises, information, and individuals' integrity have made us too doubtful to relax and put our guards down in order to build even some relative sense of harmony in our lives. Without confidence in our judgment and instincts, the seeds of cynicism have spread vastly in our minds, and then flow subconsciously into our actions and relationships.

Naturally, the rise of socioeconomic complexities and uncertainties would also continue to create more doubtfulness about everything. A major problem would be our increasing suspicion about the intentions of others even when they could be sincere, at least once in a while. We are already badly distrustful of the integrity and effectiveness of the social systems that we depend on, even the judicial system, police, bureaucrats occupying sensitive government posts, clergics, etc. With all these suspicions and doubts, it is too hard to imagine the kind of life we may have in a few decades, if at all. All we see in ourselves and others is stress and suspicions and thus can predict only more stress, anxiety, and doubts.

In particular, we hate to witness the depth of the wickedness of people who are close to us and we love so much. But then, our reactions to them, others, situations, events, or dialogues reflect the effects of our latest view of human nature, plus a sense of cynicism about the purity of our own personality and judgments. Our self-evaluation of our purity and integrity—if we ever get brave enough to internalize our thoughts and know ourselves—makes us feel sad and helpless. We resent both our vulnerability and aggressiveness, and for being forced to adjust our behaviour according to situations, individuals, and events, outside our standards and ethical convictions.

As a result, most of us carry severe doubts about the purity of human nature and our own. Sometimes we feel more optimistic and sometimes less, and of course, some of us like to have more faith in the purity of human nature than others. Yet, we all doubt the future of humanity seriously, as we witness the materialistic interests of individuals always supersede their moralistic values and integrity, and their Egos overwhelm their relationships with others to the point of becoming ruthless, and so vastly self-centred.

More than half a century ago, Carl C. Jung portrayed a picture of the Western man in his book:

"... a complete picture of Western man - assiduous, fearful, devout, self-abasing, enterprising, greedy, and violent in his pursuit of the goods of this world: possessions, health, knowledge, technical mastery, public welfare, political power, conquest, and so on. What are the great popular movements of our time? Attempts to grab the money or property of others and to protect our own." Psychology and the East, First published in 1978 by Art Paperback, page 110.

We have come a long way since Carl Jung made his succinct observation! Not only all these noted traits of Western man have been intensified many folds, but also we have successfully spread these degrading features of humanity to all corners of the globe under the name of democracy and human rights. Now, the whole world is infected with Western values and personalities in proportions unimaginable to Carl Jung. Ironically, we feel so proud of these values too!

Our most recent pictures of the Western man confirm that things will continue to get even worse and our faith in the future of mankind will grow shakier. We can blame population growth and people's higher expectations and greed, while at the same time the resources are declining and economic systems are becoming less efficient and effective. Rich is getting explosively richer, poor is getting pitifully poorer and the middle class is sinking faster into debts and depression. All these features of our crooked mentality affect humans' perspective of life and increase their doubts about humanity and themselves. Their unfulfilled needs raise their hostility, frustration, and loss of purity.

Obviously, human purity has declined in reverse proportion to the expansion of urbanization, automation and computers, and submissive devotion to capitalistic way of life. Even when some experts, who are responsible for the economic welfare of their first ranking countries, finally admit that capitalism is not going to work, still some arrogant authorities insist on their naïve, self-serving propagandas about generating more wealth for the rich and reducing their taxes.

Modern societies and the socioeconomic motifs of capitalism reinforce only more of the same things: corruption, deeper impurity of human nature, higher dependence on external information with lower confidence in its reliability and integrity, and naturally more anxiety, cynicism, and doubtfulness of all sorts.

As noted above, some individuals learn to explore the hidden divine potentialities within them and thus attain selflessness and inner peace that enrich other people's lives too. These angelic manifestations of goodness by some people is always refreshing and often shocking to us. Yet, even more amazing and bizarre is humans' general eagerness to neglect their ability to do amazing deeds and create splendid thoughts simply by activating their divine potentialities instead of following superficial social norms and only nurturing the demons within them.

Managing Our Doubts and Decisions

We can escape neither our doubts nor major life decisions. Planning our lives is an intuitive urge for intelligent people, yet our success depends on how well we analyse our options, doubts, and decision factors in a timely manner. Planning is a complex task, especially since we suspect the reliability of information, social structure, and human nature. On the one hand, being proactive is becoming more important every day, considering our dynamic—and often confusing—socioeconomic environment and the rising contamination of information base. On the other hand, we must understand the nature and importance of our doubts for managing our decisions objectively and patiently, while also making sure our doubts do not cause more mental stagnation.

Naturally, the practical purpose of our doubts is for keeping our guard in society to avoid making hasty decisions and getting hurt. However, as a more important and personal purpose, maintaining some degree of doubts helps us keep our sanity and humanness, because certitude only makes us too dogmatic, arrogant, and stubborn. Without our 'doubts,' we do not get the opportunity for self-awareness. Without our 'doubts' we forget how insignificant we humans are in the large scheme of Creation and the universe. Without our 'doubts,' we would be even less instinctual and natural. And without some doubts about the existing social structure and values, we would never look for an alternative lifestyle, in which our thoughts and behaviours are not manipulated, our Egos and sense of superiority are not boosted senselessly, and our lives are not so shallow and aimless. Carl Jung states:

"Where there is faith, there is doubt; where there is doubt, there is credulity; where there is morality, there is temptation." Ibid., page 123.

At the same time, we can also say that, "Where there is no doubt, there is no genuine faith; where there is no doubt, there is both arrogance and credulity; where there is no doubt, there is no real test of judgment; only where there is no temptation, there is no need for doubt."

Even our most rigid scientific and mathematical knowledge have only relative—and thus doubtful—definitions and consequences. Our theories and personal experiences are normally based on a list of assumptions and inductions surrounding the time and space dimensions, stringent conditions, and presumed properties of some phenomena or event. The theories of relativity have shown how our perception of time and space have been misleading. Theories of quantum mechanics have shown that we cannot predict the location and speed of particles with certainty at any particular time. And these *erratic* particles are the basic constructs of the universe, the molecules, the energy and matter.

Everything we see and talk about has only a relative meaning and interpretation according to situations and conditions that prevail at that instant. Of course, there are things that we judge with a higher degree of certainty and we need not mislead ourselves about them, even though an ultimate interpretation may raise some doubts about their real (and ultimate) certainty. For example, a married person has no reason to doubt the fact that s/he is bound in a relationship with certain characteristics. It is a given fact, even though someone may challenge the whole concept of marriage and argue that a piece of paper cannot be an inherent determinant of a marriagc; what is marriage? What is it supposed to be? We know about the birth and existence of our children with close to absolute certainty. There is no practical advantage in having doubts about these facts, at least relative to the present social circumstances.

Our doubts stem from our ability (or inability) to see and acknowledge the 'reality' of something. Gary Zukov states how we define our reality in his book, *The Dancing Wu Li Masters*, Morrow, 1979:

"'Reality' is what we take to be true. What we take to be true is what we believe. What we believe is based upon our perceptions. What we perceive depends upon what we look for. What we look for depends upon what we think. What we think depends upon what we perceive. What we perceive determines what we

believe. What we believe determines what we take to be true. What we take to be true is our reality." Ibid., page 312.

The jest of this statement is that perceptions determine our 'reality.' However, how closely this *perceived reality* could ever approach the 'real reality' beyond people's personal urges and perceptions? How far off the chart our perceived reality is? We can safely assume that the 'real reality' is the entity not dependent upon or subject to our limited vision, logic, knowledge, and desires. It is the reality that continues to exist beyond any existence that we can ever envision.

While we erroneously accept many of the perceived features of our world as certainties (facts), we ignore that many life concepts can benefit from some degree of doubt, starting with some doubt about the validity of what we are conditioned to perceive. Hence, our differences begin with our personal approaches in defining the real reality compared with our raw perceptions. For example, our personal beliefs about God's existence is handled differently by various groups:

- Some believe in God's existence with complete certainty; **'Yes'** group.
- Some believe in God's inexistence with complete certainty; **'No'** group.
- Some doubt God's existence; **'May be'** group.
- Some challenge, or question, the meaning of God to begin with; **'What?'** group.

Each group applies its own logic and approach according to its state of mind and personality. The first group consists of those who draw their faith from cultural, parental, or social influences. They have been conditioned to feel absolute certainty about God's existence. Although a small group of people might have had special personal experiences that have convinced them of God's existence, no evidence exists for the rest of us to agree with them or understand the depth of their experiences. Unless a person is logically (what is logic?) convinced about God's existence, s/he would be a fool to believe in such a strong claim only by the influence of others or cultures. S/he is only emotionally stirred to put total faith in hearsay and take it as certainty. How can such people consider themselves even slightly intelligent? This is a question that other groups often ask.

The second group consists of rigid individuals who deny God's existence because they have not personally seen any evidence or experienced it directly. Or even worse, they insist on their personal (humanistic) logic to prove the impossibility of God's existence. However, one may argue that the lack of proof and knowledge is not an evidence for the rejection of an idea. In particular, in the light of human's very limited knowledge and logic, and considering the vast domain of debatable science and unanswered questions and phenomena, it is silly to use the argument of 'no evidence' for rejection. How can a bunch of atheists consider themselves even slightly intelligent? This is a question that other groups often ask.

The third group maintains a level of doubt with respect to God's existence. For this group, there is not enough evidence to accept God's existence. However, their modesty and logic let them keep some doubt about the possibility of such existence. They simply cannot convince themselves to reject this possibility, however obscure the possibility in terms of our social and scientific claims in favour or against it may be.

Finally, the fourth group consists of those who attempt deviously or objectively to question (or sometimes confuse) the issues. For example, God as a creator may not make sense to them, or they may challenge several aspects of God's definition to such extremes that the whole issue becomes merely philosophical. For making their arguments and building their beliefs, this group is seeking some kind of evidence that would be less susceptible to humans' tainted logic.

Deep down in our psyches, most of us live somewhere within a domain that contains all these four possibilities. This domain depicts the boundaries of our intelligence, doubts, and thoughts. After all, our beliefs are built around our dynamic personalities and Egos, which are themselves a reflection of humans' evolving intelligence, doubts, and thoughts. We all belong to a point on this domain. Obviously, the most desirable points are those along the broken line that extends between the 'doubtful' and the 'philosopher.' The 'yes' and 'no' groups are the extreme imbalance positions where gullible and egocentric individuals fight one another relentlessly. Therefore, if we can envision a kind of balance for the level, nature, and subject of doubts, the 'Maybe' and 'What' groups are perhaps the ones that most likely have reached that balance, although they are the most doubtful groups. It is important to know where we belong on this domain, as our personalities and Egos affect the quality of our lives as well as the lives of the people we deal with.

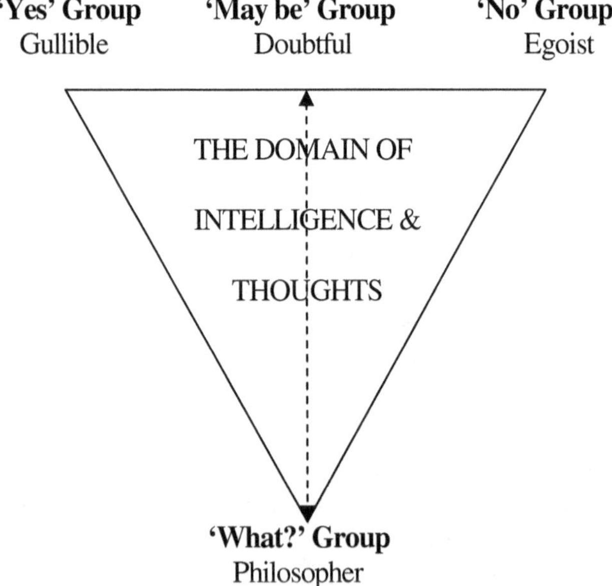

Diagram 12.2: The Domain of Intelligence and Thoughts

The debate over the existence of God is a useful example to show that majority of us can be safely classified into these four classes in terms of our naivety, personality, and Ego. Perhaps a small, undecided group cannot be easily classified in these terms, but the rest of us have personalities with a tendency to fit within one of these four classes, though perhaps not at these extremes.

As a proof of our thinking ability and decisiveness, we all have a tendency to convert our doubts into certitude prematurely in hopes of reducing our stress. Our goal is to convince ourselves about having our doubts dealt with. Everybody does this intuitive exercise to rid him/herself of the anxiety of stagnation in the state of doubtfulness that absorbs so much of his/her mental energy.

'Doubtfuls' seldom overcome their fundamental doubts about life, lifestyles, and social values. On the other hand, 'gullibles' and 'egoists' find their answers very quickly by sticking to their rigid viewpoints and personalities. The philosophers are active doubtfuls who keep testing and explaining their observations of various phenomena and options. They never give up and some of them might sincerely feel that they may (or must) find the secrets of the universe and life with some degree of plausibility.

Philosophers are different from egoists in the sense that when they are less doubtful (or even certain) about something, they can provide some credible description of their thoughts. This is something that an egoist cannot provide. Besides, philosophers usually remain flexible to view other evidences, even if they seem contradictory to their views.

Only 'egoist' and 'gullible' groups claim that they are certain about things in absolute terms. Therefore, they make their decisions much faster than others too. On the other hand, if a person is not gullible or egoistical to insist on a certain conclusion, s/he surely needs a refined personal wisdom to help her/him for decision-making and developing a value system.

A main step to gain personal wisdom (self-awareness) is to have a balanced level of doubts about things, to avoid dogmatism and quick judgments, and to have a process of evaluating options and consequences. The primary rule of self-awareness is decision-making under a balanced doubtfulness condition, with perhaps some philosophical inclinations. This implies that decision-making and doubtfulness are not opposing conditions, but rather complementary and useful. Wisdom contains some degree of scepticism and doubtfulness. Wisdom is the ability to manage one's scepticism and doubtfulness in order to make the rationale for a decision somewhat more reliable. Managing our doubtfulness is the art of grasping and acknowledging the purpose of such scepticism; it is the process of internalizing and meditating on the question or issue at hand.

In our daily routines, we may belong to one group or one point in Diagram 12.2, but pretend to be at a different point for many reasons. Even an egoist often presents himself as a liberal and perhaps even a philosopher just to play along and get social acceptance with his phony communications and pretences. A 'Yes' person who agrees with everybody and everything, does not accept for a moment what a sheepish, inferior personality he has developed for himself. Instead, he may speak of courage and even be rude to others in order to hide his gullibility. A philosopher is, by trademark, a bewildered person looking beyond the realities of our (perceived) world in search of the truth and his real self. But, even him, the philosopher, has to come back to the world of perceived realities frequently and pretend to cope with the general rules of social living and conditioning. A keen philosopher or even a credible scientist might develop strong religious beliefs, too, in some unusual circumstances.

The idea of being doubtless is absurd and contrary to the notion of personal wisdom. Returning to our original example, doubtlessness about God's existence is the prescription of religions, some spiritualists, and even some positive thinking schools. These authorities promise that firm beliefs would give us the power to see the unseeable, to experience the unthinkable, and attain mystical wisdom. But in reality hardly anyone can be free from 'doubts' permanently. Our doubts are the remaining inner instincts that we can depend on. Our doubts provide a chance to reassess our perceptions and hopefully see some clues from the real world. Our doubts, when applied in right measures, protect us from gullibility, and may even incite our creative thoughts. When we attempt to lose our doubts, we take on unnecessary risks or make commitments that we may have to carry and regret a lifetime. For example, it is good to have deep doubts while choosing a spouse; this would stop us from depending solely on our emotional state of mind when mistakes and risks could have grave repercussions.

While wisdom requires doubtfulness, it also demands decision-making in a timely and responsible manner. Thus, self-awareness dictates both alert decision-making and intelligent doubtfulness. The intensity and type of doubts, of course, vary from situation to situation and according to the type of decision. Under normal conditions, personal wisdom manages these doubts if it is developed over time through honest meditation and reflection. Conversely, decisions driven by egoism or influenced by personal emotions reflect our ignorance about the value of wisdom that comes only from measured doubtfulness.

The Benefit of a Doubt

Dilemmas, doubts, and decisions goad our thoughts during most, if not all, of our waking hours. We cannot avoid them because they help the inherent structure of human conscious and because they determine our life direction and destiny. We have even introduced these concepts in our procedural and administrative principles and practices. For example, when a jury deliberates on a verdict, it is instructed to vote guilty only if it has 'no *reasonable* doubt.' Therefore, we have defined a criterion (reasonableness) for the most important decision in our judicial system based on the level of doubt, according to the strength of the evidence presented during the trial. In this sense, the convict is given 'the benefit of a doubt.' His guilt is not established unless it is proven beyond a reasonable doubt. Furthermore, the level of doubt allowed varies depending on the nature of a charge. A higher degree of doubt is allowed for a criminal charge compared with a civil charge even when related to the same case. These seemingly just criteria in some societies are, of course, not followed in many countries, as they are not compatible with their ways of life and thinking. The idea of 'reasonableness' remains vague and subjective in the mind of every juror too.

Our decisions are intuitively driven by our doubts, except that the decision criteria vary for different types of decisions and according to the circumstances, person's mood, personality, etc. Often the difficulty of personal decisions is not due to the lingering doubts, but rather the lack of a reliable criterion to measure the doubts against. The rule of thumb usually is that the higher the criticality of the decision, the softer should be the reasonableness of doubt (i.e., need for more scrutiny and doubts). Also, for personal decisions, the decision-maker alone and at that special instance has to establish who or what should be given the 'benefit of a doubt.' In some instances, we may have to be more forgiving and sometimes less, and sometimes we may even feel hostile and unforgiving. These internal emotions, which may be of short or long term nature, are the added dimensions influencing our mind about the idea of the benefit of a doubt and our judgment about the reasonableness of a doubt. We often have difficulty to remain objective. We may even submit totally to our emotions and ignore the importance of being rational and making objective decisions. We may fool ourselves or hurt somebody else when we forget how important our decisions are, as well as the role of the decision (or doubt) criteria, i.e., the principles of the 'benefit of a doubt' and the 'reasonableness of a doubt.'

Acknowledging the inherent role and force of dilemmas, doubts, and decisions in our lives, we also face the ultimate challenge to control, balance, and master them in an efficient way. Life's mundane duties and decisions should not absorb us.

Rather, we should doubt our present mentality and lifestyles and instead spend time to gauge the essence of life. Away from the mass of superfluous thoughts wasted on self-preservation decisions, doubts, and dilemmas, we should strive to contact our true self for self-recognition. The ways we are conditioned to see, and think about, life in terms of dilemmas, doubts, and decisions are astounding. And the amount of mental energy wasted to maintain the balance among them, just to keep our sanity, is enormous. We are not here on this planet only to solve problems and find solutions, or are we? We are not here to fight and destroy one another for satisfying our false pride, fat Egos, and endless greed, or are we? We should cultivate a great deal of doubts about everything we have been doing to humanity so far, or should not we? Our thoughts must be refurbished to give us a new vision of humanity and meaning of life. We need to relax our minds and free our thoughts to see the beauty of Nature, the intricacy and greatness of our inner selves, and to establish our real sense of life. Or do not we? We need to tame our desires to attend to some of our spiritual contents.

"Those fettered by desires cannot perceive the Clear Light. Desires crave for external fulfilment. They forge the chain that fetters man to the world of consciousness. In that condition he naturally cannot become aware of his unconscious contents. And indeed there is healing power in withdrawing from the conscious world - up to a point. Beyond that point, which varies with individuals, withdrawal amounts to neglect and repression." Carl Jung, *Psychology and the East,* First published in 1978 by Art Paperback, p 125.

All these great ideas about revamping our mentality are, of course, easier said than done. How can one break away from the conventional and self-sustaining ideas and forms of life that have passed through many generations and become an intrinsic reality of our being? No easy answer exists. Yet we may start with discipline and perseverance for gradual self-awareness. We can assess the rationale for our decisions and doubts and then try to validate them with our convictions, instead of accepting them as facts or acting upon them casually. We can question our dogmatism, naivety, value systems and their purposes. Self-awareness is a process, not a sudden awakening. The latter only seldom happens, but gradual self-awareness, through meditation, reflection, and simple mental practices, which we all are capable of, can lead to enlightenment. Our doubts help this process immensely.

CHAPTER THIRTEEN
'Cultured' Common Sense

Our reasonable doubts and common sense are the only tools we have to make our judgments. Yet, we cannot stop doubting the value of our common sense. Can we trust it at least for measuring the reasonableness of our doubts? Can we rely on our common sense for making decisions and managing our doubts? These circular arguments raise only more doubts about humans' capacity for making good judgments. We already refuted the validity of human logic and common sense in Chapter Eleven. All the evidences in society indicate that our common sense is flawed. In fact, we can witness how sadly our world is run mostly through 'common nonsense and senselessness.' Is not our common sense driven mainly by our misperceptions and egoistic judgments? The answers to these questions are important, because common sense seems like all we have to handle our doubts and decisions. Outside information and the advice of experts and friends may help to gauge our options, too, but ultimately we must depend on our common sense to tackle our doubts and decisions. Usually, the outside information and people's advice have limited value or are tainted by malice or emotional factors, anyway, or they do not quite apply to our circumstances or personality. Especially when it comes to major life decisions, such as career, marriage, or divorce, the value of outside information and advice becomes quite questionable. We could rely on our experience, sometimes. But, major life decisions are usually made only once in our lives, mostly when we have no experience with those matters.

Therefore, it seems that we have no choice but to rely, largely, on our common sense to play two roles. First, *as an analyst*, accumulate, sort out, and assess the information, advice, logic, emotions, and any personal experience that may be available, and measure them collectively for resolving the question or decision at hand. Second, *as a judge*, choose an option that seems viable beyond any reasonable doubt. A good judge would not make a hasty decision while he has some doubts about the validity of some of the facts before him or about the risks of choosing a wrong option. At the same time, a good judge knows the risks of delaying a decision forever without a justifiable cause. The combined responsibilities of *the analyst* and *the judge* constitute a definition of 'common sense.' Naturally, our analytical and judging abilities are driven by our foundation of thoughts, intelligence, personal life philosophy, predominance of personality aspects, etc.

Thus, on the one hand, we must admit the weaknesses of common sense, as it is contaminated by our erroneous perceptions, incomplete information, biased advice, inexperience, and misleading emotions. On the other hand, our common sense can be elevated through awareness, as we build our foundation of thoughts, life philosophy, general intelligence, analytical abilities, and objectivity. In all, while a definite answer with respect to the reliability of our common sense seems impossible, we must become the judge of its strength personally through self-awareness. We must assess the quality of our common sense personally and determine whether it can be trusted at least on some occasions.

The notion of 'common sense' suggests that a decision made on this basis should appear prudent to a majority of people who are common (average) in terms of intelligence and judgment. This is not quite the connotation used here though. Common sense, in the context suggested here, is meant to merely reflect a person's analytical and judging abilities, which realistically differ amongst individuals. In fact, common sense nowadays must supersede an average person's analytical and judging abilities, because people are highly influenced by tainted social values, emotions, egotism, and greed. A useful *personal* common sense should exceed the normal sensibility and logic of commoners. Therefore, our decisions made according to 'common sense' are not supposed to be necessarily acceptable to others, nor should they be in line with prevalent social values in order to be valid and valuable. We are responsible for our decisions and doubts in reference to our personal 'common sense.' The only condition is to ensure that our approach and process are not biased and rigid.

Common sense for our purpose requires independence in analytical evaluations and objective judging of our unique *personal* dilemmas and decisions. However, the phrase 'common sense,' as applied here, is also for discussing *common issues* in a *commoners' language* for a *common understanding* of a majority of us. For example, this author considers himself to have an average intelligence, experience, and knowledge. Thus, the materials selected for discussion in this trilogy are intended to reflect the thoughts and experiences of a common person compared to a pure scientist's or psychologist's way of thinking. Accordingly, the validity of the discussions is expected to be evident in the way the general public may understand and associate with a good majority of these thoughts and discussions easily, and find those conclusions sensible for *practical* purposes. At the same time, people's viewpoints are challenged on some occasions or their curiosity is raised. Some may agree with the discussions, conclusions, and the approach the author has taken to present them, and some may disagree with certain points. Yet the overall intentions and suggestions of the author must be at least clear to them. Most of us, including social scientists and psychologists, agree that social and psychological principles hardly submit to solid generality or conclusions for a global application. In the absence of scientific proofs and principles for many of our behavioural and relationship dysfunctions, we have no choice but to rely on our common sense to judge ourselves, others, and the complex relationships that prevail amongst us. We can try to learn from one another's experiences and thoughts to enhance our understanding and feelings of ourselves and others, while bringing some sense into our socioeconomic systems and relationships too. Nevertheless, it seems reasonable to depend more and more on our common sense, as well as the sensible wisdom of others, to sort out our personal and social problems and eradicate their causes, and then find practical means of living together in some harmony and peace. One major objective of 'self-awareness' is to polish and enhance our common sense. And books like this must rely on common sense to explore and draw tentative conclusions about our needs and behaviours.

Developing Our Common Sense

About fifteen years ago, I set out to write this book with the intention of exploring the contentious issues and ideas for living in the new era. I began this journey by using straight 'common sense,' analysis, and discussions. Soon I got more involved in the project and thus dissolved in much deeper exploration than I had initially intended. In the process, I found out more about myself and the depth of humans' interactions with one another and life. So much of my unconscious beliefs and dogmas surfaced vividly and bridged the mental gaps that usually distort our thoughts and raise our doubts. In a sense, the amount of concentration needed for developing various concepts put me in a much deeper state of self-awareness than I had ever envisioned possible for me. In fact, this whole experience turned out to be a precious practice in self-evaluation and self-therapy. By itself, this self-therapy proved of great value to me. This personal gain happened as I lived through each stage of the book for months and followed my thoughts evolving both in general and specific terms. The experience had a definite value for me in exploring my unconscious needs, defects, motives, and internalizing some of my fundamental thoughts and beliefs. Although I realized my inability to change myself drastically, I learned to adjust my mentality, attitude, and life path to make things easier for myself and others. All these general observations plus my personal convictions also made me realize that understanding and feeling life is a unique challenge that each of us must adopt by creating and following a similar soul-searching process privately. I am not suggesting that we all write a book, which by the way may not be a bad idea for learning about ourselves at least. Rather, I think we should spend enough time and concentrate, in some form of deep meditation, on various issues and ideas raised here, plus everything else that one may find relevant for living nowadays. Everybody can test the assertions and conclusions in each chapter by applying them to similar or unique aspects of his/her life. This exercise would not only provide deeper insight and firsthand experience, but also give the person a chance to explore each concept and internalize it. This is the best way to turn our raw judgments into a 'cultured, personal common sense' and make better decisions.

We may associate with some statements and conclusions in a book or study, but personal convictions solidify only through personal feelings and experiences. Nevertheless, when we associate with some suggestions and conclusions, it confirms our thoughts about those issues, and it helps us overcome some of our doubts about the validity of our approach or decisions. Some ideas or issues may be easier to apply directly to one's personal life than others. And, sometimes there are no concrete conclusions, but only some general thoughts—provoking notions. In all these cases, we should take the matter in our hands for analysis according to our situation and our 'cultured common sense.' For example, the answer to the question at the beginning of the chapter about 'evaluating and judging our doubts and decisions through common sense' remains mostly a personal matter, depending upon one's degree of self-awareness, rather than a universal guideline or conclusion. Accordingly, the validity of a 'general common use' for everybody's use would be rather unwise.

Any valid conclusion comes from an objective review of our questions and doubts, even though no ultimate proof or certainty may be available. Unfortunately, even if we could provide a scientific finding for any question or phenomenon, there is no guarantee that the principle or law supporting this finding stays valid forever and applies to all individuals equally, not even in pure science like medicine. For example, despite the overwhelming evidence linking cigarette smoking to lung cancer, many non-smokers get lung cancer, while many heavy smokers live happily without inflicting lung cancer. Furthermore, no amount of knowledge seems enough to convince everybody to quit smoking. This attitude is quite ironical as well as a proof of social science's difficulty to draw firm conclusions about people behaviour.

Our doubts stem from a much deeper and stronger unconscious impulse, and thus often cannot be affected by straight logic and emotions—though sometimes even our flimsy logic or emotions overwhelm all the facts and our reasonable doubts. The point is that even our seemingly most obvious 'common sense' is not fully capable of helping us with our doubts. Yet, the stronger the foundation of our thoughts and common sense, the better chance we would have in recognizing the source and validity of our doubts. Even most intelligent individuals have some doubts about their 'doubts,' maybe even more than common people do. They cannot decide whether their 'doubts' are due to their weakness in decision making or due to their justified scepticism about the problems and unresolved issues standing in the way of a decision. That is, we have doubts about not only many life issues and dilemmas, but also the rationality of our doubting habit. The intention is not to make the discussions complex. Rather, to point out that we suffer more of our doubts about the rationality of being a doubtful person than from our doubts per se. In essence, our chronic cynicism is a type of personal defect that may be resolved only by experience, awareness, and enhancement of our common sense.

A major doubt that we all share relates to our uncertainty about our mission in life. Many points and ideas about life, and the possibility of being a happier and freer person, have been discussed in this trilogy for nurturing our common sense. Whether this goal has been achieved, and whether those discussions would really help us learn something about ourselves and our relationships remain a personal judgment and ability. A relevant quotation from Krishnamurti reflects how these discussions and thoughts may be perceived and interpreted. He says:

> *"When we are young we say, 'well at least I'll be happy'—sex and all the rest of it. As we grow older we say, 'my God, it is such an empty life', and you fill that emptiness with literature, with knowledge, with beliefs, dogmas, rituals, opinions, judgments, and you think that has tremendous significance. You have filled it with words, nothing else but words. Now when you strip yourselves of words you say, 'I am empty, void." Truth & Actuality,* J. Krishnamurti, Gollancz 1977, page 70.

The Value of Our Thoughts

We cannot help wondering if our thoughts and words are merely a way of filling our voids. Or whether our incessant contemplations are only for subduing our lingering doubts and sufferings while we seek our mission in life—at least for grasping a simple means of living. We cannot help noticing our regular attempts to hide or suppress our fears by resorting to philosophy and words. Sometimes we even fool ourselves or others by fantasizing about a more tangible reality beyond our mortal existence, including the possibility of our souls eventually joining eternity. We know no evidences exist about immortality, except for the messages of some alleged holy books, yet a good majority of us develop our own senses of spirituality and personal philosophies regarding how our souls would resurrect after death. Are some of us knowingly exaggerating with our fanciful predictions, certitude, and foolish philosophies, while an opposing group remains quite cynical about the possibility of a real reality behind our raw perceptions, thoughts, and imaginations? Are all these philosophizing and fantasizing for filling our voids then? This may in fact be true if our feelings about life remain shallow at the level of words and scattered thoughts—despite our sincere efforts to find the truth. Thus, the answers to the above two questions are 'yes' and 'no' respectively in this author's opinion.

Normally, we do not (and cannot) engage in *conscious* learning and thinking only to keep ourselves amused or to subdue our feelings of emptiness. At least some of us have a deep conviction and serious intention to transcend beyond the limited wisdom that we have learned to be possible and normal. And for approaching this level of enlightenment, we believe that whatever we learn must be felt internally and practised externally so that we realize the real significance of a thought or experience. Those thoughts and experiences are significant enough in themselves without any need for us to go overboard and fantasize about eternity and immortality, or even worse, become too dogmatic and certain with our wild visions or philosophies.

Not believing in the value of our thoughts, words, and personal experiences for signifying our lives would futilely add still another dimension to the domain of our doubts. That is, we can doubt the value of our thoughts, feelings, and actions to the point of living like a bum. But then we would doubt the value of living like a bum too! It would perhaps be easier on our minds and souls if we could stop questioning life and living, and instead viewed existence as an obscure phenomenon that should be pursued passively without getting philosophical and curious about it. It is possible indeed. But how we get to this realization is another significant process and a major decision all by itself. We cannot simply wake up one morning and decide that we want to not care about all these thoughts and doubts that are not going anywhere and are not helping us anyway. If we have grown up as a normal person with average intelligence and curiosity, we have developed urges to think and demand explanations for many questions that life throws at us continuously.

Being inquisitive and progressive are inherent urges of humans, and giving it up is not a straightforward possibility. Accordingly, even 'not caring' about the meaning and philosophy of life must be a conscious decision in order to become a reality and find its significance. Choosing any life path or philosophy must be an alert decision in itself. Otherwise, we get even more confused not only for lacking a particular vision or plan for life, but mostly due to the inconsistency of our activities and decisions. If we have not made a conscious decision to relieve ourselves from certain, or all, thinking and decision-making, we must have been forced into this numbness unconsciously, perhaps by some external forces or stimuli, which we have not been able to elude. We are simply a victim of some psychological strains or social coercions killing our senses completely. In this case, we have no ground or criteria for recognizing the meaning and purpose of our actions and thoughts. Which means, we must stop assuming and pretending that our minds are clear and functional. Instead, we must admit that our minds are indeed infected by this social epidemic, i.e., the weakness to think and decide independently, *for whatever reasons*. Then perhaps we could do something about the matter.

The point is that our thoughts about life, our mission, and all kinds of doubts that emerge in the process are instinctual and have special significance for our mind and being. They are fundamental and natural requirements of our existence that reflect the vitality of our soul and our allegiance with life dimensions beyond our normal perceptions. The reality of our soul becomes evident in our doubts about the purposes of earthly life. Our search for the truth is indeed an intuitive struggle to access our enigmatic soul. Our positive doubts about the meaning of life and all the rest of it are actually due to our estrangement to our soul. Having doubts is the right clue that we have souls and a rationale for searching it. Accordingly, our doubts also indicate that we have not found the essence of our existence—our souls. As such, our doubts provide a great incentive to continue our search. Only when we find our souls, our doubts dissolve and the inner peace evolves.

Especially when we are young, other than being lured by the temptation of a happy life—the sex and the rest of it, as Krishnamurti puts it—, we are also driven by our untamed Ego that refutes our vulnerabilities and naiveties. We do not have time or patience to think and go beyond the obvious physical aspects of our surroundings. As a young person, we are merely attracted to superficial lifestyles and physical enjoyments that maximize our pleasures. This mentality is obviously too shallow, especially in these demanding ages when major life decisions require a solid foundation of thoughts behind them. On the one hand, we need high capabilities in judgment, independent thinking, and decision making to break away from the superfluous family values and social conditioning. On the other hand, we lack a reliable platform upon which these independent thinking and decision-making can flourish. Our strong doubts about social values are quite reasonable and rational, but we lack solid values and philosophy to replace them with. The youths, especially, must have major doubts about their radical (but naïve) values, which they like to introduce as their new vision of life—supposedly with more emphasis on independence and freedom. They must question the validity of their new values and know how they would possibly enrich their thoughts and lives, and how these values should help them with their real needs, especially the contradictory ones like independence and cohabitation. Merely resisting our obsolete, unfair social system cannot solve our problems, make things easier, or change the values or structure of society.

Resisting, denying, or escaping the problems of living without initiating viable long-term alternatives is only a reflection of our naivety and egoistic belief in our invulnerability. The challenge for the youths, in particular, is to find real solutions for our sick societies without making it even sicker—which unfortunately is the way it is going nowadays. Yet, they seem extremely naïve and vulnerable these days, which makes the prospect of a more harmonious social structure too tenuous.

Life's Dilemmas and Decisions

Some particular dilemmas boggle our minds intuitively all our lives, mostly as part of our genetic programming and biological drives. They direct us in a subtle but persuasive manner to make some kind of *philosophical* decisions, so naturally in fact that most of us do not even realize our constant strive to handle them. These dilemmas and our keen curiosity challenge our psyche as a characteristic of living—mostly unconsciously or subconsciously. Their main purpose is to *regulate* our thoughts and convictions, as well as the general direction of our lives. The fundamental thoughts discussed in Chapter One of Volume I are of this nature. They are meant to help us make some *philosophical* decisions about:

- the purpose of our lives and means of finding peace of mind,
- setting our general life philosophy and convictions,
- staying objective in our judgements instead of letting over-optimism (positive thinking) or cynicism (negative thinking) mislead or cripple us.
- choosing social and personal value systems and ethics,
- discovering our divine potentialities,
- understanding our *real* needs, and
- realizing the scope and importance of major life decisions.

Naturally, our consciousness about these types of dilemmas and decisions increases with personal level of intelligence and self-awareness. Thus, it is plausible that the above fundamental thoughts and dilemmas would feel more explicit and urgent as human wisdom increases in the next millennium or so. Nevertheless, we all ponder these *philosophical* decisions in some manner, at least subconsciously, but seldom deal with them directly and effectively. We hardly scrutinize on them, or merely come up with some perfunctory answers and ideas and move on. In our busy and complex society, most of us never find the opportunity to appreciate the impacts, importance, or even the existence of these *philosophical* dilemmas and decisions throughout our lives.

Another group of *routine* decisions help us directly for performing our daily life functions, in line with life structure. They consist of decisions about:

- our long-term life objectives and a plan to work toward them, e.g., education, lifestyle, financial needs, wealth, social adaptation, means of finding happiness, etc.,
- the type of personality we wish to develop or present to others for coping with social demands, pursue our aspirations, and maintain our identity and integrity too,
- our risk oriented opportunities and their timing, including investments, savings, budgeting, etc.,
- understanding and applying our genetic potentialities,
- managing our careers, professional interests, and social responsibilities,
- the means and criteria to choose a spouse, and
- our duty toward our children, how to nurture them, and the role we must play.

Social demands and personal needs force us to make these *routine* decisions regularly and consciously. Still, even for these expected decisions, our mental preparation is quite inadequate.

Thus, we usually end up making hasty or forced decisions mostly when we are in love or running out of time, patience, or options.

Unfortunately, even for those of us who somehow contemplate both philosophical and routine decisions, and then question our motives in some depth too, still the answers are never absolute, and the outcomes of our seemingly rational decisions are never predictable or satisfactory. Furthermore, we constantly find new priorities and preferences that make us view things differently in various stages of our lives. Thus, the value of our fundamental thoughts and philosophical decisions might appear questionable and in need of regular scrutiny and occasional refinements.

All these facts reiterate the difficulty (and importance) of making decisions due to the dynamic nature of our perceptions and environments. Yet, having a decision platform during every stage of our lives helps us function consistently and rationally. Fundamental thoughts and philosophical decisions are the only means of supporting our routine decisions to some extent according to sensible criteria.

As intelligent creatures, we pursue life and our long-term plans by continuous processing of information and acting upon the orders (decisions) disseminated by brain cells. Our brain activity and quality to process information and make decisions is a separate discussion. This book concentrates merely on the mechanisms of *decision process*, including decision-making elements, conditions, and criteria, which are discussed in more detail in Chapter Sixteen.

PART VI

Doubts and Decisions

CHAPTER FOURTEEN
Positive Doubts

We study our doubts to learn more about their sources and to assess their effects on our wellbeing. For one thing, we should ascertain whether our doubts are a symptom of our weakness in decision-making or a sign of unresolved issues and problems begging for attention. Nevertheless, based on previous discussions, our doubts can be divided into two main categories in the way they affect us either positively or negatively. Positive doubts are justifiable barriers for making decisions due to information deficiency or the ambiguity of a question. Negative doubts reflect a mental state where facts are reasonably known, the question is clear, options are obvious, and still we are incapable of bringing ourselves to make a decision. We usually present all kinds of lousy evidences and excuses to defend our logic and justification for delaying a decision. We may believe our doubts and hesitation are justified by the lack of information. However, it usually relates to our fears of risk, failure, and humiliation, if not mere laziness to act.

The significance of distinguishing positive and negative doubts lies in their opposing effects on our perceptions of life and personal image. Positive doubts reflect wisdom and patience and it helps self-awareness and growth, whereas negative doubts cause tension and a poor outlook on life. Of course, even positive doubts may inflict anxiety, suffering, and emotional pressures on us as we continue to struggle with the dilemmas that all doubts create. However, with a proper view of positive doubts (and their distinction from negative ones), we usually reduce the overall inner tensions as we redirect our efforts more effectively, from eliminating our doubts to understanding them.

Accordingly, positive doubt justifies our indecision due to obvious incompleteness of information or evidence. More importantly, however, positive doubts prevent us from becoming dogmatic and arrogant, while we give ourselves a chance to ponder some notions or clues about certain values or realities beyond the plausible facts of the perceived world, e.g., the irrationality of immortality. Positive doubts keep our minds open about the possibility of human soul and other mythical concepts like happiness, God, love, truth, trust, etc.

Overall, as its basic function, a doubt is positive (or significant) for two reasons: First, it reflects the alertness of our natural instincts to question (and stay doubtful about) the validity of any conclusion that is not supported by adequate information and evidence. Second, it prevents gullibility and undesirable consequences of hasty or emotional decisions. Other important effects of positive doubts are as follows:

- They provoke thinking and insight.
- They prevent undue risks, which are not measurable due to the incompleteness of information and evidence.
- They make us look inside ourselves for clues and answers.
- They are usually a sign of humility and control of Ego.
- They are usually a sign of patience, experience, and wisdom.
- They often reveal clues about myths and the obscure realities of life, which require our understanding and coping, compared with the inevitable facts of life (e.g., social chaos or the impurity of human nature) that we keep fighting with or blame others or ourselves for.

The level, nature, and types of doubts were shown in Diagram 12.1 and discussed in Chapter Twelve. Grasping the *nature* of our doubts is an important task of self-awareness, as it pinpoints our outlook on life, explains the sources of our tensions, and perhaps eventually helps us put many facets and facts of life in their proper perspectives. To use a metaphor here, positive doubts are like 'good cholesterols' that we had never heard of or knew their importance for our health. Rather, we had always focused on bad cholesterol (negative doubts) that we knew are harmful to our health and wished to get rid of. The nature of positive doubts (both psychological and logical) can be grouped into the following categories:

1. Social (doubts about our lifestyles).
2. Personal (doubts about who we are).
3. Interpersonal (doubts about who they are).
4. Supernatural (doubts about the essence of life).
5. Spiritual (doubts about our connection to non-physical spheres).

Social Doubts

Socioeconomic doubts reflect our apprehensions about the way we live in a social setting that has been imposed upon us and an economic system that is incapable of satisfying our basic needs in a consistent and fair manner. We feel like slaves, dependent upon prevalent rules that everybody seems to believe in, despite all the pressures for making a living and supporting our families. Hence, we cannot stop doubting the legitimacy of these systems that so overwhelmingly dominate our minds and all facets of modern societies. We cannot stop doubting our sanity for submitting to the ways and values of socioeconomic systems. We cannot stop doubting that we are being exploited in some form and degree, and that we have no effective way of defending ourselves, because we want to belong to social living and not rejected altogether. But then, these are our lives that are being wasted in pursuit of futile social and economical values. If we cannot save ourselves, nobody else would care or question our sanity for living the way we do. At the same time, we feel helpless to challenge or change the values and structures that have so solidly rooted themselves in the hearts and minds of people. Most of us are now addicted to the superficial rewards of compliance to the existing rules and values. We are also doubtful, rightly so, about our resistance and opposition making any impact. We have already discussed how limited the expected level of our influence on changing the existing systems can be, though doing whatever we can is still valuable at least in terms of personal satisfaction.

Anyway, socioeconomic doubts make us feel trapped. We doubt the usefulness of our thoughts and the value of our struggles in general, especially if we have not explored our other positive doubts to understand our spirituality and values as a person. We may suffer consciously or subconsciously not only for our inability to improve the situation, but also for being personally an active part of the prevailing chaos. These negative doubts about the role we play in the maintenance and promotion of socioeconomic systems and our substandard way of life can be quite devastating for a conscientious person. While we must accept these irreversible facts of life to a large degree, we can do certain things to alleviate the effects of such feelings at least a little. This can be achieved mostly by turning these negative feelings into positive doubts and thoughts. *How?* you may ask.

For one thing, we can re-examine our doubts about our involvement with socioeconomic systems. We may feel more positive by trying to find solutions that minimize our dependence on these systems. Finding new ways of living results in joyful experiences and higher stamina to cope with the shortfalls of social living. Finding practical solutions to live more independently would bring us gratification. At the same time, we understand the complexities of alternative lifestyles, our limitations, and all the sacrifices we must make to find our 'self' and true identity. We would definitely benefit from our new way of living and our new outlook on socioeconomic systems. While we accept our inability to make drastic changes, we learn to cope with the pressures of these social systems somehow just for survival.

Our doubts about our role in this chaotic environment become more positive when we accept our responsibilities and monitor the degree of our involvement. We would think more positively once we relieve ourselves from the feeling of guilt as a culprit in supporting such greed-based and inhumane systems. We can justify our position and optimism, by accepting the fact that the alternative to our passivity and low involvement would lead only to more isolation and irresponsibility, which would cause even more social havoc than helping the situation. As long as we do not directly promote the values that are exploitive, discriminatory, and corruptive in general, we can have only positive effects on this system and positive doubts about our associations and involvements. Our positive doubts would concentrate on few positive changes that we can bring about in spite of all the obstacles, controversies, and disappointments. We may still have doubts about the effect of our efforts, but they are positive doubts in the sense that we do not give in to despair completely. Most important of all, our positive doubts at this level are valuable for enhancing our outlook despite our limited social life. We continue to doubt the value of life within the prevalent social structure, gauge our means of adapting, and try to keep ourselves in tune with our own values and convictions. We continue to doubt the value of our sacrifices and efforts for a peaceful life. It would be a positive doubt, though, if we use self-fulfilling, ethical criteria to follow a sensible path of life. We may deviate occasionally from our criteria, but we can return to our fundamental beliefs and bring ourselves right back on track.

For building our perspective of socioeconomic structure, we should view and accept its shortfalls as an extension of human defects caused by all of us. We have collectively built, and are maintaining, a superstructure that best reflects and fits our nature, abilities, and flaws. We may believe that these systems are developed democratically or by sheer autocratic forces that some groups have imposed on majority. In the final analysis, however, our submissiveness to these defective ideologies and authoritative figures is a real human deficiency that we cannot deny or change. We admit that people accept the prevailing socioeconomic rules because of their naivety or greed for social rewards. Despite our vast imagination to think of ourselves as a capable and superior species, we can refer to socioeconomic chaos around the world to reconsider and refine our conclusions about our abilities—human nature and intelligence. When we see socioeconomic systems as a symbol of our ignorance and incongruity in vision and goals, we can then better cope with the realities of human imperfection. We can never eliminate the negative effects of socioeconomic problems, but can minimize our negative doubts by recognizing their real sources and causes. We can stop thinking of these systems as some independent phenomenon that can (or should) provide fairer and freer life for all and bring order and control to all values and ways of thinking. We have continuously tried to make our legal systems stronger and fairer. Yet we are witnessing more violence, corruptions, and frustration with the way justice seems to work. Does not this suggest that we humans are quite eager and capable to circumvent our laws and rules of coexistence when it is not to our advantage to abide by them? And does not it suggest that in spite of our seemingly good intentions to bring order to our lives, we prefer chaos and we are responsible for the world's demise as well? Is not our greed and arrogance killing us? Has not the effect of present social structure made us so sick and cruel to kill one another as a means of releasing our frustration with society and life altogether? Grasping the reality and nature of socioeconomic systems makes our doubts positive, because we stop envisioning them as some independent structure that has its own will and capabilities. We realize that it is merely our thoughtless creation. The only puzzle is that how much longer we can afford to be so selfish and silly.

Personal Doubts

Personal doubts consist of questions we have about our own abilities and (the strength of our) personalities. These are the most difficult kinds of doubts for us to understand, accept, and turn into positive attributes, simply because we cannot see our faults and flaws. In fact, for most of us, the problem arises from 'not having personal doubts,' which shows how our Egos prevent us from having a real appreciation of 'who we are.' Having 'no personal doubts' shows our naive presumptions about our perfection and knowing 'who we are.' We have already discussed the difficulty of knowing who we really are. Thus, having 'no personal doubts' is only a reflection of our Ego being in command. Individuals with lesser Ego are usually more honest and humble and carry some degree of personal doubts. This does not mean that they do not have any personal confidence or are doubtful about all aspects of their personality and abilities. Rather, out of their pure confidence and modesty, they have also gained enough wisdom to doubt the validity and truthfulness of many aspects of their perceptions, actions, thoughts, and traits.

Personal doubts prepare us mentally for accepting criticism from ourselves and even from others without becoming overly agitated or threatened psychologically. It reveals our grasp of, or willingness to explore, possible personal defects that hinder our relationships, communication, and growth. Of course, in an extreme case, personal doubts may portray our low self-image and confidence. At this extreme, our self-doubts are 'negative doubts' that taint our outlook on life and attitudes as will be discussed later. Indeed, self-doubts may have to be treated clinically if negative impacts of social withdrawal, paranoia, and insecurity are prominent in one's life. However, contrary to self-doubts, balanced personal doubts are constructive in the manner they help us explore the causes of our problems and find means of improving ourselves.

Almost everybody has personal doubts in some form and degree. The difference is in the level of consciousness and willingness to allow these doubts circle in our minds and how we use them to stir our thoughts about 'self.' Some of us may stubbornly insist on the appropriateness of our actions and behaviour, and believe wholeheartedly in our rigid interpretation of events and situations that we create or participate in. By hindering self-evaluation, which is a goal of personal doubts, we deprive ourselves of the opportunity of knowing who we are and why our lives contain all sorts of sufferings and imbalance. We just continue to perceive the world and our mission in life according to some predisposed values that we have inherited from our parents or learned in society. Without personal doubts, we hinder our personal growth, in addition to all other repercussions of imposing our imperfections upon others and causing our relationship failures.

'Not having personal doubts *ever*' is a rare case and merely a sign of a person's psychological disorder or even insanity. In most cases, we are only hesitant in acknowledging our personal doubts while trying hard to repress our natural instincts to deal with our doubts and defects. We fear listening to the inner voices that send subtle messages about who we are, our defects, and mistakes. We elude our conscience that often tries to interfere in our affairs. Usually our Ego plays an active role in defusing these voices and suppressing our urges to doubt what we do and who we believe to be. But, despite all these efforts and struggles to get rid of our personal doubts completely, we still hear the nagging voices inside us and feel the anxiety that results from our actions or behaviours, or from other people's reactions. Our options are to either continue to resist our personal doubts and the feedbacks we receive from our inner voices, or open up our minds to the possibility of some benefits in attending to our personal doubts. We can explore these doubts in some depth, and recall them proactively for more direct messages. We can look for sources and causes of our doubts and the personal defects they usually pinpoint.

Often, we subtly question the value or validity of something we do, or we condemn the manner we deal with an issue or situation. Some clues reveal our personal flaws and ignorance. Nurturing these questions and thoughts raises our self-awareness and lead to positive doubts for exploring our lives more realistically. We try to use this information to detect our defects and their sources, and to keep them in mind for future decisions and actions. However, how successfully we can apply our wisdom to future events depends highly on the extent of our idiosyncrasies at any particular point now or in the future. Remembering a bad experience would not necessarily prevent us from repeating our heinous acts or behaviour when the source of that experience, e.g., our greed or jealousy, is still dominating our behaviour and beliefs. Most of us make the same mistakes repeatedly even when we have personal doubts about our judgment, and even when we know the repercussions of our actions. Unless we can effectively control our defects, we cannot stop our compulsive behaviour and problem-causing mentality. The only remedy is to raise our level of understanding and self-awareness about our defects, and use this knowledge and energy to control their effects on our lives and relationships.

Personal doubts, however, are not important and positive solely for pinpointing and overcoming our defects. They are also positive in the manner they help us internalize our thoughts and experiences. In a state of doubtfulness, we are more receptive to input and information that erupt around us and in our heads. We find our contemplation a positive experience to think through various aspects of our lives and become more aware of the values and issues that spur our foundation of thoughts and guide the structure of our lives. This is a process of self-awareness instigated by doubts. However, personal doubts' positivity, including its learning and tranquillity effects, depends upon our mentality and attitude. With little personal doubts, we do not challenge ourselves enough and at the same time do not benefit from the divine feelings and tranquillity that comes from every challenge and learning. With too much doubts, however, we suffer from the anxieties of self-doubt and our inability to make decisions or deal with life matters effectively. We must come to terms with our doubts somehow eventually.

Unfortunately, our value systems and cultures have created a misperception in our minds about the meaning and context of personal doubts. We are conditioned to attribute personal doubts to high self-doubt, a lack of determination, and low self-image. In fact, we try very hard in our dealings with others to hide our personal doubts by portraying (or pretending) an image of toughness, self-confidence, and assertiveness. We like to appear decisive and confident. We lean toward the extreme of showing or believing in a personality of a 'doubtless' person by becoming intimidating and rude in our work and family relationships. We ignore that personal doubts are not only normal and acceptable, but also necessary and healthy. The only trick is to differentiate personal doubts from self-doubts. The latter is an extreme case of a suppressed personality with very low self-respect and self-image due to negative past experiences. Having personal doubts, on the other hand, is a positive virtue that stems from our natural instinct to understand 'self.' Self-doubt causes anxiety, paralyses a person, and leads to indecisiveness, whereas balanced personal doubts cause patience and calm, which help us alleviate our defects, empower our relationships, and raise the quality of our decisions.

The Case of Self-doubt

But 'How can we differentiate our negative self-doubts from positive personal doubts?' 'How do we know whether our personal doubts are emotionally and psychologically balanced and positive?' Especially, when we are in a doubtful moment or situation, 'How do we distinguish the *nature* of our doubts?' Doubting the nature of our doubts is a big dilemma indeed all by itself.

For one thing, it is important to remember that self-doubt is merely an extreme case of personal doubts. At this extreme, our questions and doubts are not focused and controllable and thus result in confusion and sufferings. Balanced personal doubts, on the other hand, only instigate our urges for meditation, learning, and relaxation. Therefore, our mood is an indicator of the kind of doubts we are facing. Self-doubts (like any main personal defect) feel like a cage that holds us within its tight boundaries. As much as we try to free ourselves by thinking about freedom—what we want to be or can be—still we cannot escape the cage and thus get anxious. We may even look at the world outside the cage, which reflects the open horizons of potentialities (purity and ethics- in contrast to our general defects), but we cannot get out there in spite of our desires and efforts. We are imprisoned within our self-doubts (defects). Conversely, having personal doubts is a state in which we are free to go outside the cage already. The cage door is open, and we are only trying to establish what path to follow toward which horizon.

Self-doubt usually erupts during a crisis, when we must make a specific decision. We face a challenge, but are paralysed by our self-doubt and a lack of conviction. However, balanced personal doubts are not related to any specific and immediate need for decision or action. We are simply evaluating our values, purposes, reasons for living, or our past reactions to certain situations and relationships.

Personal doubts are also a means of strengthening our life philosophy, whereas self-doubts come from a lack of life philosophy and personal convictions. When we spend adequate time and effort on personal doubts on a regular basis, we attain an understanding of who we are and what we want to do. This life philosophy eliminates, or at least minimizes, self-doubt, because we have profound value systems and criteria to depend on when we face a decision or action; we do not have to go through a frustrating process of evaluating our values when our mind is already occupied by the nature of a particular dilemma we are facing.

We can often detect the nature and type of our personal doubts. If we continuously face, and suffer from, self-doubts, then the remedy is to go one level deeper to the roots of our problems, review the nature of our personal doubts in general, and build a valid foundation of thoughts to support our actions and decisions. We may have to initially set aside our immediate decisions and postpone an action; or we choose the most conservative options quickly to focus on building our life philosophy and convictions by assessing our personal doubts.

Self-doubts are especially destructive when instant decisions and actions are required. A simple example of a soccer player is relevant to mention here. He had just been put in a breakaway situation and was carrying the ball forward very fast elegantly. The only obstacle was the goalkeeper, who started to run toward him with a loud roar. Everybody noticed the forward's brief loss of confidence and losing his momentum for only a fraction of a second. His very marginal self-doubt made him lose his momentum. His tiny self-doubt (partly stirred by the goalkeeper's rush and roar) simply deprived him of a beautiful and sure goal. He shot the ball impotently into the goalkeeper's hands instead of all the open space in the net. In life, we face these situations all the time when others intimidate us easily due to our momentary surges of self-doubts.

In most cases, our self-doubts result from our interactions and communication with others and the authority they impose upon us. We feel more vulnerable in their presence, and cannot think as clearly and objectively as when we are alone. We may also have a weakness to resist others, because we love them or need them. But this love and need is most likely a sign of our self-doubt and dependence on others. A remedy that usually works is to pre-establish our position before confronting the individual we love or has authority upon us. In order to minimize the influence and effect of others on our wishes and decisions, we should first come to term with our doubts. Otherwise, we would always be swayed away from our position when we confront people who like to exploit or manipulate us or those whom we love. We then regret, and feel frustrated with, our weakness later.

The irony is that while our self-respect and self-image suffer from our perception of other individuals' authority over us, we doubt the ability of individuals whom we do not find a sign of authority in. We detect their self-doubt as a debilitating feature of one's personality. Our tendency is to do not respect others as much when they do not exercise or reflect some authority or power. However, honouring people's authority does not necessarily mean we like them. On the contrary, we mostly like people who are vulnerable, because we have a better chance of manipulating them or at least associating with their self-doubt and suffering. These are all symptoms of our defects and social conditioning, which affect our perceptions of others and ourselves in relation to them—the following topic.

Interpersonal Doubts

Interpersonal doubts consist of our questions about, and lack of confidence in, the purity of human nature and our relationships. Viewing our relationships with suspicion and pessimism is unproductive, although warranted largely. It causes suffering when we attempt to, or think that we can, change people or expect them to be different—a little more perfect. The other side of the coin can, however, show a more positive point of view when we learn to accept other individuals' defects and shortfalls as an undeniable and unchangeable reality. That is, our 'interpersonal doubts' can incite a positive perspective of our relationships once we appreciate the limitations of human beings and their inherent defects. When we learn about the sources of human defects and their natural weaknesses in grasping and complying with the rules of ethics and piety, we become more tolerant of other people's impurities. Naturally, we can limit our exposure to defective relationships, but at the same time, we must stop seeking perfection and understanding. The importance of interpersonal doubts stems from our eventual admission to the inherent impurity of human race and learning to live with this fact in a constructive manner.

It is hard for us to admit our inability to force or influence others to think like us. Even when we accept this fact, most of us still believe that, by logic and discussion, our partner might eventually see the merits of our ways and change on his/her own. We hope that people convert based on their own convictions eventually even when we cannot play a role in convincing them. Maybe they think deeper about what we tell them and eventually change their minds on their own. However, for our sanity's sake, we must stop hoping. We should just adjust our expectations rather than waiting for others to change. Learning to do this is the task of interpersonal doubts. Through this process, we attempt to adjust our expectations, rather than being irritated and annoyed by deficiencies we witness around us. We have a natural ability to make this adjustment if we can overcome our sense of hostility, false pride, and competition. It is like watching an old black and white movie that could be an annoying experience considering all its technical deficiencies. However, while the flaws keep rushing before our eyes throughout the movie, we can still enjoy it if we lower our expectations quickly according to an objective new criterion. Accepting new criteria for judging others and situations, life becomes tolerable or even joyful. We humans have personal defects that are often irreparable. But we also have a great talent in adjusting to new thoughts and situations if only we stop being stubborn and resist being dogmatic and vengeful.

Of course, creating new criteria to lower our expectations just for the sake of tolerating some annoying people or situations is not easy. For example, how can we explain or develop criteria for our doubts about a relationship that suffers from mistrust between partners. They have doubts about the validity of their relationship, but also they doubt the viability of other personal options after separation. In some cases, partners may even enjoy their physical contacts, but lack mental connection. Thus, they cannot erase their doubts about the intentions of the other partner, while trying to tolerate each other's guts too. Many difficult situations like this develop in our lives at home, work, and society and we continue to suffer from our doubts about our options and our duty to cope. Too often, indeed, we doubt people's intentions and the kind of games they are playing. In addition, we doubt the level of patience and tolerance we must exercise without losing our sanity and self-respect. Finding proper criteria to subdue our egoism and reduce our expectations, nevertheless, remains the best remedy for dealing with interpersonal doubts, unless we can invent a seemingly more constructive solution. We may think of many seemingly rational options, but they are most likely only rash conclusions from our hurt sentiments and vengeful urges, which would prove to be quite destructive for us in the future. Once we have satisfied our urges of spite and revenge, we would feel void and empty, now with even less options to build our lives around.

Supernatural Doubts

While we struggle with social, personal, and interpersonal doubts (as discussed above), we are also burdened with many inner conflicts and questions about our identity within the context of this humongous universe. These supernatural doubts include our curiosity about the origin of life, its possible divine nature, and the possibility and kind of our connection to it—in hopes of some relief from all the hassles of mortal life. We feel obliged to explore the role and significance of these doubts and curiosities for our existence. We imagine that finding something about our relationship with the universe can help us make the right decisions about living and set our life priorities wisely.

At the same time, we often try to undermine mythical phenomena and supernatural thoughts, because they boggle our minds vainly and we get tired of wasting our energy on mystical matters. We do not seem to get anywhere with our most natural doubt, i.e., Creation, or the possibility of any purpose for existence. We try to ignore the shoddy clues or evidences of a real world beyond our vision of the prevalent social structure. Sometimes we wonder why our crude curiosities should agitate our minds so regularly. After all, we wish to remain practical about our interpretation of daily life and appear logical in our encounters and thoughts. Yet lingering doubts about our perceptions of reality bombard us forever, while eluding them seem rather difficult and unnatural too.

Nonetheless, wondering about existence is an innate urge that directs our thoughts and choices. Trying to suppress these instincts would not only cause stress and sufferings, but also deprive us from a minimal touch with our spirit and a bigger reality that stands beyond our physical world. Obviously, at the end, we still cannot answer most of the questions or remove our doubts about the real essence of life, but we achieve two things. **First,** humouring our curiosity about the universe provides a better (simpler) grasp of life and a positive outlook despite our lingering doubts. We might even realize our nothingness, curb our Egos, and thus live more peacefully. We also get a chance to explore the wisdom that others can offer and the one that resides deep in our unconscious. **Second,** viewing life in a finer perspective helps us transform our confusing, negative doubts (which we try to ignore or deliberately misinterpret) into positive doubts and energy. Thus, we build our spirits to manage our daily challenges and struggles. We develop a wiser lifestyle and grasp the nature of our social, personal, and interpersonal doubts a bit more deeply. We learn to draw energy from Nature.

The five categories of positive doubts (i.e., social, personal, interpersonal, supernatural, and spiritual.) are related and complementary in building and explaining the foundation of our thoughts. Collectively, they indicate how we perceive life and how we live it. Unfortunately, we are often so deeply absorbed and distracted by our artificial habits and pleasures, we do not find time and incentive to look beyond our limited vision of life. Some just adopt a religion to satiate all their inner voices and curiosities, simply because they are too lazy or naive to grasp the meaning of their positive doubts and explore their urge for spirituality independently. For a great majority of people on this supposedly prolific and compassionate planet the situation is even worse. They are facing so much misery and daily challenges of work, war, famine, and family problems that their minds cannot wander and wonder beyond their urgent struggles for survival. Of course, in their busy heads, still the question about the essence and purpose of living circles, perhaps in a stronger sense, because their sufferings are too deep and permanent. Yet, despite the continual encounter with life's fundamental questions, they have time to concentrate only on their immediate needs and challenges of survival. They are too lost and engaged in daily routines to entertain even the possibility of turning their essential and existential questions into positive doubts for a chance to nurture their outlook on life. However, for the rest of us, who enjoy a higher degree of personal freedom and economic possibilities, remaining constrained by socioeconomic structure per se is a definite failure. Pampering the prevalent lifeless structure with our greed and neediness is even more pathetic and a crime.

Of course, modern societies impose their own obstacles for nurturing our supernatural curiosities. In fact, most people get so deeply absorbed in a mechanical and physical life that cannot feel or care about the nagging voices regarding the metaphysical world or even the benefits of finding answers. They somehow convince their brains that these questions and thoughts are fruitless, irrelevant, and a waste of time. At the other extreme, many of us keep struggling with our doubts because we cannot get the basic questions about the essence of life out of our minds. All our lives, we feel incomplete and agitated for our inability to relax while so many absurd questions about life burden our exhausted subconscious mind too frequently. Especially, nowadays, many of us like to know the meaning of life.

The evidence of our efforts to cope with our unrelenting curiosities about our connection to supernatural is all around us in the form of religions, superstitions, spirituality notions, myths, etc. During humans' rather short history, we have invented and adopted so many shoddy ideologies in search of a better meaning for life to soothe our sufferings. However, we have so far only caused ourselves more confusion and inner conflicts by making odd interpretations about the essence of life or adopting crude ideologies, such as 'living in the now,' according to our erratic moods and insecurities. Most of us believe nowadays that the purpose of human life is to find happiness! So we seek refuge in extravagance and other exaggerated means of living in search of happiness and out of desperation, simply because no other answer satisfies our curiosity about existence. Our conditioning habits and attachments stop us from finding any other meaning for life. We speculate, theorize, or philosophize many possibilities, sometimes according to scientific evidences and human logic, yet they all remain mythical and contradictory at the end. A great body of scientific knowledge is also accumulated, especially in the last century, about the workings of the universe. However, we are still unable to answer many fundamental questions about life, while our curiosity keeps increasing in line with the rising social vanity. Therefore, we mostly suppress these nagging questions somehow and dismiss our supernatural doubts, or even turn them into negative thoughts and cynicism, e.g., atheism. Some use drugs, alcohol, and other artificial stimuli to escape their basic instincts seeking answers about life. In the worst-case scenario, of course, we just adopt a religion to mitigate our sense of helplessness.

The consequence of our varied approaches to define life and deal with our supernatural doubts is that we have difficulty nowadays to understand one another and relate effectively. Our inability to resolve all these dilemmas is causing the social mayhem we face and suffer from daily. In fact, the extremely wide range of people's interpretations and doubts about the nature of the universe and our connection to it—the big picture of existence—is amazing. Naturally, people perceive life differently according to their intelligence, lifestyle, and realism. Yet it is quite depressing to witness this deep mental incongruity—mostly due to religions—causing so much conflict and quarrels among humans.

As part of supernatural doubts, we also talk a lot about destiny, which we believe is some form of fate, luck, or karma. It seems that we are in a kind of joint venture with God, in the sense that we make decisions, and pursue many challenges, while ponder and rely on the mercy of some supernatural power to support our decisions and challenges. Our religious teachings definitely have a lot to do with this type of (tenuous) mentality and approach. No religion dares to say which attitude is more realistic, i.e., a rigid planning for our lives or depending merely on God's mercy. So we are told to do both! Our faith in fate also reflects our personal experiences of certain events happening around us so miraculously, and all kinds of coincidences that we cannot attribute to anything other than fate and the interference of a supernatural power watching over us.

We can never understand destiny, but may get a sense from those subtle clues that emerge from our experiences and the way our spirits occasionally make us *feel* connected to some obscure power. Naturally, the closer we come to our souls through self-awareness, the more we witness and accept the role of destiny in our lives. We can never overcome our doubts about the nature and role of destiny, but we can feel and use the positive energy that results from putting some faith in it. We might even stop doubting (and accept) our triviality within the universe and the fact that all parts and particles of life are somehow interrelated. Although we are such an infinitesimal piece of this grand phenomenon, we are still influenced and driven by the same forces of Nature and rules of existence. Even though we cannot see these inherent connections, there should logically be meanings and explanations infinite folds more fundamental than our Egos normally envision, even beyond our seemingly unlimited boundaries of science, imagination, logic, and thoughts. Therefore, destiny could simply be the effect of all these necessary correlations between human conscious and the universe.

Overall, our thoughts and doubts about supernatural phenomena can affect us in two opposite manners. We could let them play a negative role on our psyches when we judge their peculiarities lightly and naïvely instead of taking them as clues about other possible dimensions of existence. Alternatively, our doubts start to become positive and productive if we nurture our curiosities and let life's odd clues arouse our imagination and doubts, to explore and envision other dimensions of being. We can try to achieve this enlightenment through philosophy and spirituality, on our own, without recourse to religions, mainly for bringing a relative sense of purpose and tranquility into our lives.

Spiritual Doubts

While supernatural doubts are general regardless of our spiritual beliefs, spiritual doubts are for defining the nature and purpose of our connection to the universe or God.

In our minds, we have a mishmash of concepts about immortality, God, religions, and spirituality. We have grown up with religious models that proclaim God as the creator of life, who gives us both a physical form and a non-physical identity we call our soul. We are exposed to these ideas even when not born into a religious family. Some individuals claim contact with spirits and some present evidences of spiritual existence. But, at best, all these claims remain doubtful for almost everybody with some common sense. They are speculations and models we have built with our limited intelligence and gawky perceptions. Yet, we cannot deny that some possible truths or significance might exist for some of these thoughts and imaginations. We cannot refute the possibility of some kind of reality, including human immortality, existing beyond our perceptions.

As a pure *instinctual* urge, our sense of spirituality raises our *logical* 'spiritual doubts' to explore our essence as a human for daily living. However, spirituality feelings and doubts also raise our curiosity about the possibility of immortality and a fuller dimension of being. We wonder about our connection to another form of life or the world of realities that engulf all our physical beings and perceptions. Has a super being created us and watches over us? Are we only what we are in this world, merely a biological form per se? Or our physical existence in this world is only a shadow of what we really are? We are both optimistic about our immortality and fearful of death. Only fools may guarantee eternity, and thus we remain doubtful about our destiny after death. Even dogmatic individuals face the surges of doubts despite their hypocritical persistence about certain convictions. Religious fanatics also reveal their fundamental, hidden doubts by committing outrageous sins regularly while insisting on God's punishment of sinners. Everybody loses his/her blind faith in God (and begins to doubt all the nonsense about eternity). It happens after we suffer enough in life or when our sinful urges override our beliefs. Of course, doubtlessness is often only a *show* for justifying a radical life philosophy that supports our wicked desires and inherent weaknesses. Thus, spirituality doubts are about both our daily deeds and our possible immortality.

In our pressing lives, most of us deal with our spiritual doubts in two ways: 1) We perceive or accept spirituality as a soothing (defence) mechanism merely of human creation. We may value it somewhat according to our upbringing and intelligence without appreciating the purpose of our nagging doubts about spirituality. We ignore our curiosity about this rooted high personal need in all humans and for satisfying it properly; and thus feel unfulfilled. 2) We stick to our religions (or dogmatic beliefs) in the fear of mortality. In both cases, we lose the opportunity of exploring spirituality personally. We do not experience it truly as a tool for freeing our spirit and knowing our 'self.'

Alternatively, we can be creators of our thoughts, actions, and feelings, if we grasp spirituality personally instead of either rejecting it as an irrelevant factor or accepting it blindly in the form of a religion or a cult. We can sense divine feelings when we do things for others who need our attention or care; when we go for a stroll in Nature and connect to simple forms of life that surround us; and when we enjoy the masterpieces of other humans. These experiences reveal our radiant spirits. We distinctly feel them ascend from our physical form to some higher spheres of sensation and awareness. Some of us can be in touch with our spirits much better and more frequently than others can. This capacity evolves through the power of positive doubts that trigger profound thoughts, continuous experiments, and the eagerness to delve deeper in these states of divinity. These sacred sensations are valid signs about the existence of our spirits and the possibility of human spirituality. We cannot find spirituality in churches and mosques just because people gather in those places for some rituals. Rather, we can find spirituality in our own backyards, in our hearts, and in the footsteps of geniuses like Beethoven, in devoted people like Mother Theresa, in vast colourful fields, in deep woods, in the flight of a seagull, in magnificent mountains, and in the music and arts of many masters who have enriched our souls and stirred our thoughts.

Spirituality is not something to depend on others to explain to us, and it is not restricted to afterlife topics either. Spirituality also is not far-fetched dogmatic beliefs that religions and cults try to teach us. Spirituality is a basic sincere personal experience beyond global description. It starts with a sense of selflessness.

We can exit our physical form occasionally to experience a non-physical existence even if we are not still dead. Our positive doubts and thoughts can lead to these creative visions of existence and our connectivity to it. Within this sphere of spirituality, we grasp a sense of selflessness and responsibility to all other facets of life and their rights for existence in their own ways. These experiences not only enrich our physical lives, but also support our positive doubts about the possibility of our eventual rise to higher spiritual spheres we have already visited in certain occasions. We must personally create these divine experiences, beliefs, and the ultimate form of transcendence by exploring our positive doubts about spirituality.

CHAPTER FIFTEEN
Negative Doubts

The five categories of 'positive doubts' discussed in the previous chapter goad us to see ourselves, others, and the universe in a proper perspective and come to terms with life. In essence, only our positive doubts can mitigate the effects of our negative doubts and our sense of helplessness.

Conversely, any doubt that cripples us from making decisions unduly or hinders our thinking and acting abilities is negative. Negative doubts are distinguishable merely by their natures and effect on our outlook and attitude. They cause depression and persistent indecision, unlike positive doubts that raise our curiosity and awareness. They reflect chronic suspicion and cynicism, or merely relate to a lack of confidence and analytical ability. Over the years, negative doubts (including self-doubt) grow and become an integral part of our psyche due to a combination of:

- Personal defects (genetic or acquired)
- Bad personal experiences
- Negative outlook on life
- Mental weaknesses
- External factors and forces (seeming facts of life)

As a normal state for humans, our 'personal doubts' should goad us discover our inner self and choose a simple lifestyle and philosophy. Otherwise, they turn negative and cause mostly self-doubts and cynicism. Understanding and defeating our negative doubts (including self-doubt) require a rather magical stimulus or motivation to suddenly change our attitude and outlook on life. Still, it would be a hard undertaking, because only through a long process of self-awareness we can revamp our old mentality and reset our life values. The process often begins when we question our way of life and existence thoughtfully outside our normal cynical manner. Suddenly a 'positive doubt' about our present attitude triggers our mind toward a higher drive for self-awareness. In a sense, a 'positive doubt or thought' starts the self-awareness process. This sounds like the chicken and egg cliché! How can we focus on any type of positive thoughts or doubts when our defects and self-doubt are crippling us? How can we raise our spirit when suffering from deep depression? We feel helpless, vulnerable, and pressured by volatile and sneaky external forces. Our genetic defects incite, direct, and control our perceptions and judgments, too, and we feel overwhelmed by negative thoughts and doubts. All along, people's actions and misrepresentation of facts hinder our grasp of the meaning, the sources, and possible remedies of our negative doubts.

Nevertheless, defeating our negative doubts requires high spirit and inherent strengths, including willpower, intelligence, determination, experience, wisdom, analytical ability, logic, morality, and objectivity. We might have lost touch with these basic instincts and become, for example, a ruthless person incapable of using his/her basic sense of justice, fairness, etc. Nonetheless, these instincts are within us if we really will to use them to overcome our negative doubts and the excruciating dilemmas of life. It only requires building a more authentic value system and a simpler lifestyle. We need a solid platform and personal interest for gauging our perceptions of life in a more fundamental and honest manner.

The problem is that we often ignore our lingering positive doubts, because they only seem to add to our stress. Yet, this passivity hinders our self-awareness and learning from our inner voices. We lose even these occasional chances to rescue our souls. We do not give our doubts and thoughts enough chance to flourish, to internalize our occasional comprehension of reality. We suffocate any flares of awakening that sometimes shake our sad existence in hopes of raising our spirits. Sometimes, the truth wants to reveal itself and we ignorantly bypass the opportunity. For example, we may go to the funeral of a dear friend who has suddenly died of a sloppy diagnostic mistake by his physician. During the ceremony, we sit quietly and think about our precious memories together and then realize how vulnerable we are and how unpredictable life is. We continue to gauge our life values and philosophy, but doubt their meanings and significance. We might even think that major changes in our lifestyle and thinking are required. We seem to have learned a lesson from this depressing experience.

The sadness from our friend's death opens up a window to new life horizons if we can internalize these positive doubts. The moment of 'truth revealing itself' comes from these kinds of experiences leading to positive doubts about who we are and what we are doing. We often decide to adjust our attitude and bring our Ego under control. However, unfortunately, we do not stay with these streams of thoughts and feelings long enough to absorb them totally. In a few days, if not hours, we allow external distractions disrupt our refreshing dynamic thoughts or allow them fade away gradually in the midst of our daily hustle and bustle. Our priorities change again and old habits and thoughts take charge of our lives. We return to our common problems and pleasures, negative doubts, and forget all about the message of the truth that our friend's death was trying to convey to us. We are often blessed by the flickers of positive doubts, but are dragged down quickly and subdued by our attachments to the symbols and conditions of our demented lifestyles. On the other hand, negative thoughts have well-established roots that are so tough to overcome. We love them too.

Sometimes, we misread and mistreat, intentionally or inadvertently, the message in our positive doubts. For example, the experience of a sudden death of a friend or a family member makes us doubt the value of our struggles and worries. Yet, we emphasize on a narrow aspect of the message, and believe the answer lies in choosing a life of carelessness and recklessness. We mistreat the concept of *not worrying* by undermining our responsibilities. We misuse the messages that come from our positive doubts to justify our negative doubts (cynicism) and weaknesses. We get deeper into addictions and more pleasure, become lazier and more carefree, and forget that we still need to have a meaningful life purpose. Obviously, the way we interpret our doubts and thoughts reflects how positive or negative they are for guiding us toward a diviner path of life. Misinterpretations only confuse our state of mind and obscure clear thinking; they reflect our fears, naivety, and shallow personality.

Many of our positive doubts turn into negativity and negative doubts when we do not understand the right messages in them. When we face some dilemmas and doubts, we often feel helpless and become passive and idle, instead of delving into a proper mode of contemplation and self-analysis. Therefore, instead of expanding our life horizon through some positive doubts, we cause self-imposed depression with our negative doubts and cynicism. We get crippled and indecisive. We bypass the opportunity to turn these debilitating conditions into deep reflections that incite further activity and creativity. With positive doubts, we can instigate our search for alternative ways of living and thinking—and for revamping our negative doubts and thoughts. This mental transformation requires some efforts and ingenuity, of course. To become at least relatively free from the rules and domination of socioeconomic order, we must work harder every day with a positive attitude and expect less. For example, many of us crave the opportunity of self-employment to relieve ourselves from the tyranny of organization work and all the negative doubts it exudes. Finding the right self-employment opportunity and earning a decent living, however, requires more insight, sacrifice, and willingness to be satisfied with less.

Taking a passive decision (by ignoring our inner voices and positive doubts) and hoping that the issue or question has no merit for consideration is often a sign of laziness or irresponsibility. We hope to be relieved from our doubt and its psychological effects. We hope to erase an irritating inner conflict by ignoring it, at least for now. We try to live in the now! However, in reality, we continue to carry our doubts, both positive and negative ones, in our subconscious. And they would continue to irritate us now and forever no matter how much we pretend to be living in the now. Any doubt, positive or negative, is still overwhelming and a cause of anxiety and depression if ignored. Even our positive doubts cause inner conflict and unrest, although both our doubtfulness and indecision may indeed be justified. We cannot simply put some thoughts or questions out of our minds permanently with the excuse of not having the proper information or evidence required for a reasonable judgment and decision. Laziness gives our negative doubts all the nutrition they need to spread their roots in our psyche and cripple us.

The pressures of our psychological doubts (i.e., stress and anxiety) depend on our mindset at any particular time. Even positive doubts, which usually open our minds and improve our outlook on life, may cause stress until they are used effectively for self-awareness and adjusting our mentality. Meanwhile, we still feel the frustrations of life uncertainties and the agony of handling our defects.

In all, we must detect the sources of our negative doubts, review our life (mis)perceptions, make mental adjustments, and revamp our personal and social sources of negativities, including our cynicism, suspicions, self-doubts, and paranoia. We must build a solid foundation of thoughts and life philosophy through self-awareness and personal commitment to turn our negative doubts into positive ones.

The End of Doubts...

We all wish to abolish our doubts quickly and behave like an assertive person, but resolving our doubts is not straightforward or easy. Actually, we should not push the process prematurely until we know the true nature and roots of our doubts the same way we must know the cause of our depression first before finding a cure for it. Especially, we must remember that our positive doubts need not be resolved at all, considering the crucial role they can play for creative-thinking all our lives. For example, people doubt the existence of God forever inherently. This is a positive and useful doubt to cherish. We can benefit from envisioning a kind (of) God as a pillar of our personal spirituality. Even most of those religious fanatics or atheists have at least their moments of doubt about God, if not lingering scepticism about their certitude. Resolving this doubt is not necessary or wise, anyway. Rather, we must learn how to use it productively for establishing our life philosophy. Instead, most of us pretend to be atheists or blindly faithful to a specific religion. A group is both when they become fanatical believers in some periods and then become atheist in other times, all depending on their needs, moods, or doubts. We hate to admit that we can never be certain about some things. Therefore, we continue to fool ourselves by accepting erratic conclusions and swing within the cycle of doubt-no-doubt forever subconsciously.

On the other hand, we may have many negative doubts that should be resolved. We may have doubts about our 'dead-end jobs,' 'life priorities,' or 'relationships.' We cannot live with these doubts forever and we cannot tolerate a cyclical process of doubtfulness and certitude. The anxiety of not knowing the nature of our niggling doubts hurts, while mixing our positive and negative doubts prevents us from building our convictions. For example, when a marital relationship is not working, we go through a long period of doubts about: i) the validity of our reasons for labelling our relationship irreconcilable, ii) the consequences of divorce and having a single life, iii) the possibility of finding another person who could replace at least some of the simple conveniences of the existing marriage, and many other similar doubts and questions. We live with these doubts and their related anxieties for many years, in addition to the direct problems and agonies of our relationships.

Sometimes, we seem to succeed in overcoming our doubts about an issue. We feel relief, confidence, and certitude, but soon somehow lose faith in our judgment as our doubts sneak back into our heads. During these cycles of overcoming and rejuvenating our doubts repeatedly, we deteriorate our self-image and spirit, as we suspect our mental stability to understand life and make proper judgments. We resent our inability to commit our psyche to a set thought-process and life-path. In particular, in some periods of our lives, e.g., during adolescence, we encounter many peculiar dilemmas and feel overwhelmed. Those are stressful times. Weighing our options regarding any of those dilemmas exhausts our mind. Our lingering anxiety makes us feel helpless and perhaps even cause mental disorder. In such debilitating condition, we lose our power to focus on each dilemma separately and patiently.

The discussions in Volume III of this trilogy reveal the enormity of our doubts and dilemmas about life, education, work, career, organizations, relationships, etc. Unfortunately, it usually takes a long time before we can possibly resolve some of our doubts sporadically. The load of doubts and dilemmas that we always carry is heavy and they have different levels of significance and priority, too. The amount of thoughts and energy we put into them and the level of anxiety we bear in the process is huge.

Yet, analysing our doubts is the only way to regain effective control of our minds and lives. Our wisdom and common sense must somehow help us decide on the nature of our doubts one by one and pinpoint the ones that need a fast resolution and the ones that should co-exist with our convictions for creative thinking. Self-doubt, as a special category of negative doubts, must be dealt with distinctly and firmly.

Nonetheless, a few conclusions can be reached: First, we must learn to distinguish positive and negative doubts. Second, we must comprehend and internalize the messages that come from our positive doubts and the options we choose. Third, we should come to terms with our doubts in a timely manner somehow. For example, we should decide to either separate from our uncompromising partner, or try to find ways to improve our relationship, or at least determine that we can never find the information we seek to overcome our doubts. We must also learn to live with the reality that we must face at the end of our doubts, accept its possible consequences, and not change our position erratically. Fourth, we must depend on our positive doubts to circumvent the inconveniences and pitfalls of decisions or convictions that result from resolving our negative doubts. For example, we may eventually conclude that our marital relationship cannot be improved to a desired level. This is a positive conclusion for a negative doubt that has caused us stress for a long time. This would end all our struggles for making our spouse understand our viewpoints or to adjust her/his attitude in the way we like. Thus, we can relax and let go of our Ego pushing, or at least hoping, to improve things.

We may compare the mental state of a chronic doubtless (dogmatic) person with the situation of a person with legitimate doubts when he eventually overcomes his doubts. The certitude of the former comes from naivety and egoistic pitfalls, because he has never entertained the possibility of alternatives and realities beyond what he has naively pursued persistently. In the latter case, however, the person's doubtlessness has evolved only after establishing certain beliefs and conviction for supporting his conclusions. It may take this person many years of doubts, thinking, and professing before his mind is satisfied with an explanation for his questions and dilemmas. However, at the end of such doubts comes a meaningful conviction ground slowly in a long process of doubtfulness. Now it becomes a belief. We can say that true beliefs come only at the end of profound doubts. Our doubts make us search for the truth and then this truth makes up our beliefs.

We can actually detect and associate the odd relationships among Ego, doubt, and beliefs in different stages of our biological growth. During childhood when our mind is not contaminated by Ego, we are doubtful about everything and depend on our parents to guide us with the questions boggling our minds, and we really do not have any established beliefs or convictions. During early adulthood, our Ego soars and suddenly we feel the urge to be certain about everything. We think (or like to pretend) that we have all the answers and therefore we develop many strange, raw beliefs starting with the fact that our parents' beliefs and thoughts are outmoded and obsolete. [In spite of the tendency of teenagers to think and act too egotistical, in reality they are overwhelmed internally by all kinds of doubts that they actively resist to acknowledge (under the influence of their Egos). They disallow their doubts to emerge for contemplation. This mental inconsistency is the cause of further inner conflict for them.]

In our middle ages, we gain some experience and suffer the consequences of our naivety and quirks in the earlier stages of life. We now have some fundamental questions to answer for ourselves and we know that we cannot depend on others to provide the right answers. With our Ego abating somewhat, we become seriously doubtful about life, its meaning, and our role. During these years, we really do not have any set beliefs because we are doubtful about things and do not build beliefs naively for the sake of having some. We have learned some good lessons in life and realized the absurdity of our certitude about certain beliefs and convictions. Our wisdom demands that we support our beliefs with more solid reasoning and thoughts.

In the last stage of our growth, we finally overcome (or come to terms with) our doubts, or at least some of the major ones. At this time, our Ego stabilizes as we think we have finally found a bit of the truth. However, because of our experience with doubtfulness during our middle age, we might succeed in ending our lasting doubts and thus attain fundamental beliefs that can carry us during the remaining years of our lives.

The end of doubts brings relief along with a new belief or conviction. No more wrestling with some painful feelings and thoughts after we settle on a plausible resolution for a puzzling dilemma. We reach a humble sense of certitude, along with determination and confidence as soon as we overcome our clashing thoughts, accept a conclusion, and prepare ourselves for its possible consequences. At the end of our doubts, we put a stagnant period of our life behind and move on with commitment and a fresher perspective. At the end of *negative* doubts, we see the need, and find the energy, to act. And at the end of *positive* doubts, we feel enlightened and peaceful. We have made a decision and a long-term plan. We must indeed feel proud of turning a few of our fundamental doubts into beliefs and convictions that can stir our life in a positive direction more objectively. Hooray!

Naturally, our beliefs and convictions are unique and personal, as they are developed according to our particular logic, needs, doubts, personal attributes and conditioning, intelligence and genetic characteristics, psychological defects, during the long process of grinding our doubts into beliefs. At the 'end of my lifelong personal doubts' about the world's basic realities, I have found certain beliefs that I would like to share some of them with you:

1. The universe, God, Nature, or any kind of name that we may use to describe the superpower responsible for human existence is a true reality that we cannot explain except for the symptoms that we might feel personally only outside religious influences. This supernatural power flows through us and manifests in our thoughts, inspirations, perseverance, tolerance, passion, compassion, and everything else. The more we understand ourselves, the more obvious and effective this power becomes in our lives, as if it drove our spirit. Many projects that I have undertaken and completed successfully have been driven by this mysterious source of inspiration, which appears to surge both within and without me and evolves as a unique thought or sensation for various purposes. For one thing, the ideas of writing this trilogy and all the materials grouped and conversed in special formats and within certain paragraphs and words have been stirred by this mysterious influence. In fact, my muse should get all the credit! (So, if some or all of my discussions sound gibberish to you, please just blame her. She kept saying everything sounded logical and profound. She did all the editing too.)

Not knowing how destiny, luck, and this supernatural power are interrelated, or are the same, does not deter me from ending (coming to terms with) my doubts about their reality. They merely constitute the main parameters of our tentative existence for whatever purposes. Strangely enough, these beliefs have evolved in spite of some related but unresolved doubts. For ex ample, I still have major doubts about any notions of reincarnation, afterlife, or the existence of any God in the format we have been conditioned to envision. Though, I do not deny a very remote possibility of some form of non-physical existence, which we are unable to even speculate about.

2. **The vanity of our socioeconomic systems** and the high likelihood of our doomed destiny has been a depressing theme throughout this trilogy. Unfortunately, this gloomy destiny seems certain and unavoidable in my opinion, despite the sadness that my pessimism gives me. Therefore, I do not wish to dwell on this matter any more beyond everything I have already said in this trilogy. I am sad enough about this matter already!

3. The impurity of human nature is no longer a doubt in my mind. I believe that no human being is as perfect as our high imagination of humanity likes to suggest. We surely do good deeds and enjoy many generous and angelic experiences during our lives, or at least witness them in others. However, we are never free from our satanic urges and needs, and thus cannot fit the image of piety that we desire to see in human race. We do not like to see our own defects that cause us serious damage. However, we are too impatient with other people's flaws that pain us too much. Accordingly, our inner conflicts and constant personality clashes ruin our spirits too. This is a double jeopardy: We do not know how we hurt ourselves personally and how much we suffer from our desires to depend on others and love people who keep proving their malice. Moments of relief, however, also emerge in our lives sometimes when others show mercy or when our selfless love invigorates us.

4. Our relationships can never be as complete and civil as we expect them to be. This can be considered an extension of the previous conclusion about human nature in general, except that in relationships the imperfections of two intimate individuals clash faster and compound the impossibility of reconciliation. Our social values and structure support the expansion of Ego, which inhibits partners' understanding of their real needs and learning compassion. We are becoming increasingly alienated toward one another while our perceptions of life's realities and our true needs get more complex. Under these circumstances, finding a fit relationship is like drawing two pieces of a jigsaw puzzle from amongst millions of pieces and praying that they fit together just by luck. We keep turning the odd pieces around and to sides and try to push some corners and press them against each other, hoping they would click together. However, all these efforts only bend the corners and destroy the edges, and eventually the pieces get ruined and out of shape. We must be extremely lucky to find even a relative match, and since this is a rarity, we must prepare ourselves for the challenges of companionship on the one hand, and finding other means of compensating for this shortfall in our lives on the other hand. We must learn to live independently and alone when necessary.

5. The value of our experiences for our children was a major question and doubt in my mind when I began writing this trilogy many years ago. I sincerely thought that perhaps some of our struggles to understand life, social structure, and opportunities for a fulfilling existence could be documented and useful to our children. Now, I have overcome my doubt and believe that my children, like most other humans, are not interested in what others think. They are as much doubtful about our experiences and conclusions as we are sceptical about the viability of the social structure imposed upon them. They see us as failures and causes of the present mayhem. They think that if we had any brains, the present world situation would not have been in such a mess. They want to disassociate themselves with our understandings of life as much as we ourselves struggle with our own doubts about the purity of human thoughts, intentions, and nature. I can live with this belief, because I understand my role more clearly now and do not have to doubt it anymore. I do not have to wonder and worry whether I have done enough for my children or not. Accordingly, I acknowledge the limited, but possible, use of this trilogy for opening children's minds about life and living. In this regard, the quotation by Peter Elbow about what we can hope readers of our words learn from our teachings is relevant:

"If your readers have a stake in what you are arguing against, you cannot take straightforward persuasion as your goal. You must resist your impulse to change their beliefs. You have to set your sights much lower. The best you can hope for—and it is hoping for a great deal—is to get your readers just to understand your point of view even while not changing theirs in the slightest. If you can get readers actually to entertain or ex-

perience your position for just a moment, you have done a wonder, and your best chance of getting them to do so is not by asking them to believe or adopt your point of view at all." Writing With Power, Peter Elbow, Oxford University Press, New York, 1981, page 203.

Therefore, the best I can hope for is that my children care to read this book patiently and spend enough time to understand the meanings that I have tried to convey in my messages. And the best I also like to hope for is that they would overcome their natural urges to contradict any new ideas contrary to mainstream values. I hope I have done a *wonder*, according to Peter Elbow's standard at least!

The end of our doubts rejuvenates our beliefs, and the end of our doubts in many occasions is...

...the Beginning of Decisions

Naturally, many aspects of life are imposed upon us and we have limited power to escape these constraints and seeming facts of life. These dynamic forces dictate our wellbeing and the framework within which we are allowed to function. Only our sensible decisions and commitments might help us fit and survive within the erratic limitations of life. Otherwise, our lives would be merely a big load of disappointments, stress, and sufferings. Especially, the decisions and personal commitments made after a period of analysing our 'doubts' usually lead to significant life changes. They reflect our impression of the world and our strategy for living.

In the final analysis, we must make two types of decisions effectively: The ones that boost our spirits and resilience, and those routine decisions required for sustaining our needs, ambitions, interactions, and relationships. The best we can do for living within the untidy rules and hostile elements in society is to make profound decisions and firm commitments to our spirit. We must strive to make timely decisions to defend ourselves and travel through the stages of life as calmly as possible. With our decisions and commitments, we also hope to achieve at least some personal growth that every human being inherently seeks along with a sense of self-actualization.

Although most of our routine decisions are driven by the rigid rules of socioeconomic systems, some even more potent forces in the universe can help us subdue the pressures of these systems on us. We must only learn how to keep our spirits intact. Our high spirits can help us withstand social pressures, make good decisions regarding 'self,' and try to be a better human being. The ideal would be to bring some sense of humour into our lives and brighten up the world around us. Maybe we could even build a strong character to laugh life off.

Thus, while we seem to be stuck to the value systems of our societies, our decisions for the right path of life might open up some opportunities to find our individuality and independence away from our mundane struggles for survival. For one thing, we could reconsider our criteria of happiness and concentrate on finding the peace of mind. We could learn 'self' driven gaols and seek 'self' control, instead of imitating the popular patterns and practices of society within our doomed culture in search of more pleasures and sexuality.

Once we make a decision, a great sense of relief replaces the anxiety of duelling with our doubts for so long. We feel ready to move on regardless of the potential outcomes, though some flares of uncertainty and anticipation still prick our mind. Of course, we must still work on implementing our decision with perseverance and high hopes for the best outcome. We must also be prepared for unpredictable repercussions beyond our imagination and wisdom. After all, peculiar results or situations could surprise us and make us lose our temper, confidence, and faith. In particular, it feels quite devastating when our plan goes sour after doing our homework with due diligence and making a seemingly good decision. The longer and deeper the effect of a decision, and the more sincere our commitment to its success, e.g., in a marital relationship, the more its failure feels disheartening. Yet, these simple warning clues do not occur to us readily when we make our decisions emotionally and often hastily and then face bizarre outcomes and lifelong disappointments.

In a nutshell, we must i) be proactive and timely with our decisions, ii) choose the right criteria to gauge their accuracy, iii) modify a decision later if possible and necessary, iv) never look back at a decision in the hindsight to blame ourselves for unexpected results—though we could try to learn a lesson for future. Depression and self-pity for our failures would only waste the mental energy and creativity we need to move forward. Losing the control of our mind and nerves over bad decisions cannot remedy the situation. Nor should we blame others for our decisions. If we do not do our due diligence for our decisions or allow other people's undue influence taint our judgment, we are responsible for the outcome nevertheless. All these cautionary points are for reiterating the grave importance of staying realistic and proactive with our decisions at the outset. Especially, the phrase "I told you so" is quite prevalent in families, especially between marriage partners, when they antagonize each other for the outcome of decisions made by one partner or because one partner's suggestions were ignored.

We probably learn from our experiences that all our decisions are eventually subject to the ultimate rules of the universe. Therefore, it helps to keep some faith in fate. The rules of Nature would definitely supersede the superficial laws of man, which are mainly created for protecting and promoting our selfish needs. We seem to have the upper hand by the way we pollute and destroy our immediate surroundings. However, the inherent laws of Nature and the forces of the universe always dictate the final outcome. We are linked to the laws of Nature more than we are part of our societies and the artificial rules and values of man. The only problem is that we do not quite appreciate this connection and the inner power in all humans, nor do we make enough efforts to grasp the strength of our spirit and insight. If we did, we may come to different conclusions and decisions about our existence and lifestyles.

On the other hand, deep down, we also mistrust destiny's goodwill, especially when we face so much agony in life every day after making our conscious and faithful decisions as diligently as possible. We often reach this level of pessimism about fate after facing major failures, sour personal experiences, never-ending social pressures, unfairness, and people's apathy. We ask our spirit, "Why did not God make it happen as we asked for it." Sometimes, we simply give up trusting these kinds of intangible realities in a presumed 'real world.' This topic has been elaborated in a couple of places in this book. The bottom line is that nobody has proof about destiny's role, or how it operates and affects our lives.

Therefore, while it helps to believe in some supernatural power directing our ultimate fate, we must carry a bigger responsibility and role for being the best proactive decision-maker, especially regarding major life decisions, which are discussed in Volume III. This mentality would help overcome our deep (and often warranted) cynicism about destiny due to bad experiences and depression. More importantly, however, we must learn to rely on our ability to control our lives through personal power and initiative, with only a moderate faith in fate in the form of a positive doubt. In fact, it seems that destiny works better in conjunction with our full awareness and participation. Maybe our personal high consciousness is actually connected to the universe's consciousness, after all! Maybe all we need is just to learn how to focus and reach a higher personal consciousness through self-awareness and positive doubts. However, our personal power cannot grow through egotism and domination of others. Rather, it erupts naturally from a well-nurtured spirit and our sincere desire for inner connection with the universe eternally. It requires building our beliefs by pondering all the points raised in this volume and always honouring the sanctity of human spirit.

CHAPTER SIXTEEN
Decisions plus Destiny

We like to be in control of our lives, yet our regular failures and disappointments make us doubt the value of our arduous decisions, plans, analyses, and sacrifices. We cannot help wondering why things keep going wrong despite all our efforts and talents. We usually blame our destiny, bad luck, unfairness in the world, or other people's malice and stupidity, which are all indeed real factors affecting everybody's life. Why has God created such an imperfect world for humans *specifically* is mind-boggling! In fact, humans' controversial character offers a bizarre dilemma when we consider the amazing coordination and precision needed for the creation and survival of the universe itself, the planet Earth, and even the inner workings of human body and brain. On top of this already odd phenomenon, humans' inherent keenness, and inability, to find a simple purpose for living, to end their lifelong confusion and evilness, appears like a designed scheme for perpetual human torture, something that at least other animals seem not to bear. We envy their simplicity and peace. Compared to their natural serenity, our irritating, innate need to know the reason for humans' chronic misery feels like still another evidence about this colossal imperfection of human life. Why are we so keen intuitively, or feel obliged, to justify our existence regularly? Why should humans' thinking ability (disability?) cause them more suffering instead of a lasting tranquility that could make even animals jealous?

A plausible conclusion is that humans' measly existence, amidst the perfect universe, is only a miniscule, irrelevant, and accidental by-product of the creation with no particular design other than their physical form. In that sense, human life has no specific purpose either—neither in the big scheme of existence nor at a personal scale as a thinking species. This sad conclusion, however, contradicts the discussions in other parts of this trilogy about the sanctity of human spirit and existence. Unfortunately, this conflict is merely another life dichotomy we cannot avoid, as we have both positive and negative perspectives about humans' role in the universe. We must quarrel with this major conflict, doubt forever, and whine hopelessly. This and many other dilemmas and dichotomies in human life have become the sources of our misery, no matter how these conflicts have been created and why. Whether our thinking (dis)ability or our genetic characteristics makes us so helpless in finding peace does not matter at the end as long as we cannot overcome this debility somehow.

Regardless of humans' role in the universe or ability to figure out the purpose of their existence eventually, we cannot ignore the impact of some hidden forces that randomly work in our favour or against us throughout our lives. All these forceful, uncontrollable factors (plus our nagging existential questions) keep us bewildered and unhappy. So we just accept our inability to grasp or fight these hidden forces. Dwelling over God's plan and wisdom regarding human life would only raise our tension and depression. The ongoing quarrels among scientists, philosophers, and spiritualists would not lead to a satisfactory solution, either, but only add to our confusion because we are such an imperfect, curious species. The book, *War of the Worldviews*, by Deepak Chopra and Leonard Mlodinow, reveals humans' struggle for answers that do not seem to be forthcoming anytime soon.

Considering our seeming helplessness within this mysterious environment, we often feel that it is easier to trust fate patiently *somewhat*. All that hardship and fighting every step of the way to implement our decisions and desires is stressful and frustrating, after all. On the other hand, we notice that our bad decisions or indecision, while duelling with our doubts or trusting fate, have contributed to our doomed destiny too. We admit our past major mistakes when we become a bit more objective and a bit less fatalist. We acknowledge that our regrets or misfortunes are normally the result of bad decisions in the past, most likely our own, or someone else's.

So, in the end, we feel obliged to make good decisions as rational people, despite our faith in fate. We have this instinctual need to control our lives no matter how much we trust fate. Heck, we crave to control other people's lives, too, if we could. We all like to be leaders and proactive. Thus, we try to make good judgments and understand our options and choices. Few of us have the patience and courage to depend on destiny alone, not to mention the impression of naivety that dependence on fate alone gives to others. Therefore, we strive to strike a balance without knowing how best to achieve it. We just do our best and hope that thc right combination of 'destiny' and 'decisions' would give us a better chance for survival and happiness than depending only on fate or ignoring it. Few of us have the courage and arrogance to deny fate completely, as dismissing fate as a major factor reveals our shortsightedness. What other rational choice do we have? Relying fully on fate or trusting only our wisdom merely shows our naiveté, stubbornness, and arrogance. Yet, finding that right balance always remains difficult and personal. All along, our lifelong doubt about trusting fate patiently or making more decisions and plans proactively drains our mind and spirit, usually with little results.

Some good examples of destiny and decisions working together mysteriously were given in Chapter Eleven, where some of the author's life experiences were discussed. They demonstrate how proactive decision-making had been necessary to implement risky and adventurous plans, but more importantly the fact that without certain divine interventions those plans would not have materialized. At the same time, the overall tally of the author's life, as given at the end of that chapter, shows the unreliability of both our decisions and fate. Ultimately, we must carry all these doubts and many disappointments our whole lives no matter how much we trust fate and our decision-making ability. Yet, as mentioned in several places in this trilogy, we must always remember that one simple (maybe innocent) mistake, or a wrong turn, can ruin our lives forever.

The first thing we learn quickly for decision-making is to be careful with the information we need. Especially, in our greed-driven societies, we could be deceived or tempted by the corrupt information that is maliciously or carelessly communicated to us. For example, we learn to be doubtful about the information that so-called professionals like investment advisors, real estate agents, insurance and stockbrokers, car dealers, lawyers, mechanics, and many others give us, including the advice of incompetent or greedy surgeons leading to unnecessary operations. A major problem, which aggravates our chronic doubts, is that we have a hard time distinguishing the right advice from misinformation or false information.

All along, we also like to test the power of our logic and common sense, which we depend on for making right judgments and decisions. We want to find and analyse the factors relevant for decision-making. Meanwhile, most of us learn that in the large scheme of things, and considering our wide misperception of reality, no absolute answers exist for most fundamental questions. Our doubts, and the reasons behind them, are quite valid. Everything is relative in terms of time, place, circumstance, and external factors, including other people's actions and decisions based on their peculiar outlooks, tastes, perceptions of life, judgments, timing, and the pressures of the prevailing socioeconomic conditions.

Ultimately, we can be certain only about two things in this world: Each of us gets a physical existence at a special instance, and it reaches its end at another specific instance. Beyond these two certainties, everything else occurs to us in the context of perceptions, questions, hopes, uncertainties and doubts, while we feel obliged to understand them, find the right answers, and make the right decisions.

Types of Decisions

Everybody with some level of consciousness intuitively feels the need to make many decisions by i) playing an active role, ii) letting someone else make them for him/her, or iii) leaving everything to fate (to live in the now). One of these three choices prevails either through our conscious decision or by the force of nature and time. Yet, common sense dictates that playing an active role is more sensible than waiting for things to happen to us without adequate control and preparation. Active decision-making has special requirements though, including solid decision criteria, a reliable information base, ability to choose and analyse *real* facts, a solid value system, as well as time and patience to assess all the relevant factors.

Making a decision does not always mean taking actions or risks, however. Rather, even a passive decision not to proceed with an action is indeed a sign of firm commitment. Decision-making is only for taking charge of a question or situation and acting upon it in a timely manner rather than procrastinating with crude excuses. Of course, we are conditioned mentally to give a higher significance to active decisions, while passive decisions might come across as one's inability to take action or accept risk. This mentality sometimes even forces us into a bad decision just to feel like a proactive and decisive person.

An active decision leads to a specific action or effort that normally brings challenge, change, and vitality. For example, we may be contemplating for some time to buy a house. All the information about the market condition and personal income are available, but of course, there are always uncertainties about the future. Perhaps mortgage rates are low, so we favour the decision of buying a house seriously. In this case, a decision to buy a house is 'active' because some actions and risks are taken. A decision not to buy is 'passive' simply because we do nothing, perhaps in fears of losing our job or interest rates going up after we took on a large mortgage.

Nevertheless, a passive decision is much preferred over *indecision* that only reflect our inability to commit ourselves one way or other, until it is too late; e.g., market conditions change adversely, or we use our down-payment on some other project. A passive decision shows individual's ability to assess the situation, chose an option, get mentality ready for the worst outcome, and move on.

At the same time, the merits of active decisions over passive ones depend on our vision of life, perception of our real needs, priorities in life at certain points, and willingness to accept unexpected hassles. Our personality and degree of risk aversion goad us to be an active or passive decision-maker in general. For active decisions, we gauge the chances of rewards in line with the level of risk. We try to project the expected outcome with the use of available information and insight about future possible events. Yet we must still prepare ourselves for a completely different outcome. On the other hand, passive decisions eliminate the hassles and stress of active decisions at the cost of bypassing potential opportunities and rewards.

The possible advantages of active over passive decisions depend also on the type and timing of a decision. Major life decisions, in particular, have much higher consequences, either positively or negatively, depending on the timeliness and effectiveness of our decisions. For example, we appreciate the gravity and difficulty of a decision about marriage, compared with a simpler one, such as a decision on the kind of automobile to buy. Overall, however, the significance of an active or passive decision lies in our ability to gauge the value of potential rewards, risks, and the advantages of avoiding unnecessary headaches, compared with the possible loss of opportunities (especially for major decisions).

A similar analysis of opportunities and risks can be made for our indecision too. However, the main drawback of indecision lies in the frustration of not knowing what we really want or must do. The problem of indecision stems mainly from our inability to take charge of our life direction. We may pretend or presume that our indecision implies our complete faith in destiny and letting things happen naturally. However, trusting faith is different from allowing all kinds of external sources and forces interfere and impact the direction of our lives. Our *common sense* often indicates that it is unwise to remain passive and let our future be severely affected by outside forces when we have enough intelligence and willpower to play a role. The minimum advantage of our decisions is that they often offset the impact of adverse external forces (mainly other people) that continually interfere with our lives for their own benefits. We cannot consider these influences and interferences a logical and inherent part of destiny. An extreme example is our inability to decide about our career or our real interests in life. Indecision is normally associated with chronic doubtfulness, low self-image, and a lack of confidence in personal judgment.

Decision-making Factors

Uncertainty is the main factor affecting our decisions and actions, because we abhor *risks* and *disappointments*, which are actually two other decision-making factors by themselves. Life outlook, personality, and the tension of indecision are other factors playing their roles in decision-making process. For example, many people are consciously or ignorantly less concerned about future when they place a high value on the present—living in the now, perhaps. However, most of us are usually concerned about the long-term implications of our decisions and their impacts on our future. We prefer to work harder, and forego the luxury of living in the now, to secure a longer-lasting peace of mind and a higher stability for our future. There is always going to be a trade off: We must work hard and accept some form of inconvenience now, for enjoying a less stressful life in the long run, compared with situations where people prefer to 'live in the now' fully or somewhat. The latter group is either ignorant about, or willing to accept, the risks of their lax personality and dealing with more uncertainties all their lives. Again, it is hard to say which group is right or luckier in terms of their life philosophy.

Nevertheless, our approach, mentality, and diligence are other important factors that influence the outcomes of our decisions. Our brains' constant effort to predict and assess our choices is for gauging risks versus the value of success, and then using this information to adjust the criteria for future decisions or correct the previous decisions if possible. We inherently strive for consistency and harmony in our lives regardless of our personality, even if we are an easygoing person wishing to live only in the now. After all, everybody feels elation or defeat depending on the level of turmoil and tension in his/her life. Therefore, we prefer to use uniform and reliable criteria for our decisions, based on our level of intelligence, convictions, beliefs, and personal philosophy.

In reality, however, most people are rather eager (or maybe even hasty) to make their decisions quickly and move on. Indecision feels unattractive and often a sign of self-doubt. Besides, we are often impatient. We abhor the tension of analysing our options and wrestling with the *unknown* for too long. We also like to mitigate the chance of feeling *too guilty* (afterwards) for selecting the wrong option, especially after lengthy contemplation. The more we fuss over a decision, the more we must struggle with the unknown and guilt. Thus, we prefer to suppress our doubts, move on fast, and feel the least amount of guilt if the outcome did not turn out as expected. We learn to always blame destiny, bad luck, or other people somehow for the agony of defeat after our hasty decisions. That is an easy way out and less stressful than practicing patience and dealing with all our doubts and life options more seriously all the time. It feels less stressful in the short run to be a decisive person; no responsibility and no burden of exhausting our brains. Right? Wrong? Again, we cannot say what a more logical approach is, because people have different personalities and preferences. No one can dictate a particular strategy as a standard of human rationality.

But one thing is clear: The outcome of many decisions made today do not become apparent until several (or many) years later, usually when a correction is impossible and our lives feel unbearable or at the very least unfulfilling. Another important factor is that from millions of decisions we make in our lives, about a dozen have the greatest impact on our health and happiness. We make these 'major life decisions' while pursuing the routine structure of life, as discussed in Volume III of this trilogy. At the same time, making the right decisions about these handful major life issues is becoming more difficult due to rising social complexities and our eagerness (and frustration) to prove our abilities and individualism. All these factors add up and make decision making a tough challenge nowadays.

On top of all these hurdles, most of our important decisions must be made at an early age, prior to 30 or so, when unfortunately, as a young person, we are driven by passion and sexuality, have the least experience about life, and are quite careless in our views of life beyond those youthful aspirations. As a young person, we also feel invincible and wise at the same time. Therefore, we take more risks and make hasty decisions. For example, we may end up in a lifelong boring profession because of our shoddy decisions about our education or ambitions. Most of us find it easier to simply follow social norms and values, e.g., get a degree anyway. On the other hand, many people with limited education and ambitions succeed in pursuing a less stressful life that is fulfilling or at least not boring. The point is that making the right choices is becoming more difficult, especially in a society driven by superfluous values and mechanisms like ours. Instead of thinking independently and developing our lifestyle and convictions, we naively trust the social order, even though we often notice how our modern lifestyles have proven to cause only more stress, confusion, and disappointments. We ignore that our societies are running out of both economic and moral resources.

Socioeconomic complexities demand great emphasis on the accuracy of our decisions, because our choices set the path of our lives. Our choices show the authenticity of our needs and personalities or our naiveté. The outcome of many decisions we make so mechanically, as we imitate others, often ruin our lives significantly, if not entirely, e.g., a bad marriage. We learn only years later how naïve and idealistic we had been. Especially, the mentality of 'taking life in our strides and living in the now'—to mitigate our disappointments and stress—may adversely affect the quality of our decisions. This liberal philosophical notion encourages people to undermine the truth about the complexity of life decisions (in order to live most effectively in the now). This mentality would surely cause only more frustration and suffering later.

Without making objective judgments and decisions today, we would usually face dead-ends and desperation eventually. We would get trapped in life's processes and pay a high price for our negligence all our lives. Particularly, downplaying the importance of *major life decisions*, despite the vast variety of our doubts about everything, eventually leads to self-destruction and thoughts of suicide. Yet, at this juncture, even suicide does not stand the basic test of logic, let alone a philosophical justification. At best, it reflects the frailty of any personal or common philosophy that might support suicide as an option for a healthy person.

However, usually it merely indicates our failure to make timely decisions and learn to be content with the outcome.

Blindly following the teachings and routines that society offers to everybody can mislead us completely, because social values nowadays only serve the interests of certain groups and businesses and not the public. This means that we must make unique decisions with certain level of wisdom on a timely manner for our own welfare and long-term sanity. Our decisions must be effective simply because nowadays we have greater difficulty judging the implications of lifestyles we are choosing and dreaming. Furthermore, with so much emphasis on individualism, a general formula or philosophy cannot fit everybody anymore. We need personal convictions and philosophies that can serve our unique needs, especially the psychological and spiritual ones. All these issues constitute a vast number of decision factors to keep in mind.

Decision-making Conditions

We usually regret our sloppiness in later stages of our lives for not thinking properly and making the right decisions when we had a chance. We often gain this prevalent wisdom after the fact, when it is impossible to correct the situation. On the other hand, we regularly make many emotional and hasty decisions that we also regret deeply later. Overall, the number of regrets for making a wrong decision, or for not acting when we had a chance, usually exceeds the satisfaction we get from making the right and timely decisions. Everybody realizes that success and happiness often depend on the timeliness and quality of his/her decisions. However, it usually seems easier and less risky to procrastinate, since making decisions brings more responsibility and a higher chance of failure. Our lingering doubts and laziness also make us delay or abort making a decision. In all, ten conditions help us make a decision or cause our indecision and procrastination. They are:

A. We feel ready to make a decision when:

1. we believe to have all the necessary information,
2. we are too emotionally attached to a situation and do not care about the accuracy of information or the validity of our reasons,
3. a decision is required quickly (forced) in spite of the incomplete information,
4. enough information would never become available, but we are ready to accept the risks and consequences, or
5. a combination of the above four.

B. We delay making a decision when we have doubts about:

6. the quality or validity of the information,
7. the timing, or do not see an urgency,
8. the level of risks and consequences of the decision,
9. taking risks in general and facing the unknown, or
10. a combination of the above four.

It is hard to generalize whether we normally hinder our decision-making ability by our doubts, or we actually help ourselves by delaying a decision until we are satisfied about all the required conditions and information. It all depends on our level of intelligence, personality, awareness about the causes of our doubts, and our rationality about those doubts. This conclusion appears quite useless for enhancing our decision-making abilities; it makes us wonder when doubts are warranted and when they are nuisance. One may even argue that viewing our doubts as a positive factor is absurd, because they impair our judgment and action about any decision at hand. However, exploring the sources and meaning of our doubts can sharpen our judgment and awareness, as explained in the previous chapters. Discussions in the previous chapters are useful for distinguishing positive and negative doubts and using them properly for decision-making.

Unfortunately, it seems that most of us are poor decision makers in terms of not realizing the right conditions and timing for our decisions and the causes of our doubts. This general awareness (including the ten above noted conditions for decision-making) provides a platform to think more systematically when a decision is required. It also helps to analyse the causes of our hasty decisions or procrastination. Naturally, a calculated decision to 'not make a decision' is preferable to procrastinating in a state of doubtfulness for a long time. Doubtfulness appears like ignoring the need for a decision and an inability to develop options and solutions. Our goal, of course, is to bring all relevant information to a conscious level and process it. If the decision is to 'do nothing' after a careful processing of information, that would be a worthy 'decision,' though perhaps not an effective one. At the end, it may only serve us to overcome the state of doubtfulness, but most likely does not eliminate our doubts.

Decision-making Elements

Knowing the main elements of decision-making can also increase the quality and integrity of every decision. Therefore, the following decision-making elements are reviewed briefly:

a) The evidence and criteria for measuring it.
b) The validity of decision objectives.
c) Our understanding of legitimate incentives.
d) Our overall commitment and motivation.
e) Our timing.

The evidence and criteria: Naturally, the strength of the evidence that supports our decision affects its quality and integrity. However, the means of validating the criteria and assessing the evidence through analysis and common sense are even more important. We need impartial and unbiased criteria to establish the soundness of the evidence, while curbing our soft emotions too. Otherwise, we use evidence only to justify our prejudgments, misperceptions, temptations and crooked logic. For example, when we determine in our mind that our relationship with our spouse is doomed, we choose any evidence that can support our decision, and use our biased criteria to present and assess only certain kinds of evidences. Thus, we often end up making a wrong decision, while the outcome only reiterates our egoistic attitude to ourselves and others.

The purpose: Every decision has one or more objectives, but usually, we ignore or undermine the right ones or adopt false purposes that change the whole scope of the decision. We do this often due to our emotional and hasty reaction to an event or situation. For example, when we are angry with our children or spouse, we may conclude that they are intentionally hurting us or ignoring our individuality or authority. Therefore, we decide to retaliate in our own ways, and thus create a tenser relationship with lesser chances of understanding the real issues concerning everybody. In fact, in situations like these, we may be in fault for two things. First, we may have misunderstood the objective of our spouse's or children's comments, or have been agitated by the way they have presented their points. Second, we adopt a false objective (e.g., retaliation) to develop a decision (which we think is necessary). In such circumstances, especially when we are emotionally pressed or depressed, we must avoid making judgments and decisions before we get a chance to cool down and understand the objectives of the parties involved, but more importantly validate the purpose of our decision (reaction).

If a decision is not supported by legitimate and constructive intentions, not making it would definitely be to our advantage. In the end, we would maintain our physical and mental health better by not wasting our lives on decisions with negative or irrelevant purposes. Also, we give ourselves a better chance for improving our relationships by not responding to other individuals' vindictive challenges.

Sometimes, problems arise from our unrealistic or irrelevant objectives. For example, we may decide to pursue higher education for getting rich. This objective is both unrealistic and irrelevant for the decision of pursuing higher education. It is unrealistic, because higher education is not a guarantee for finding opportunities to get rich. And it is irrelevant, because the purpose of higher education is to concentrate on the use of our potentialities in the service of humanity, for self-actualization, etc. As another example, a marriage decision is not for making a change in our lives, satisfying a bunch of egoistic personal needs, or having somebody in our lives that we can depend on financially or mentally. It probably is not for having children per se either, never mind for the purpose of sex. All these false objectives create a wrong mental vision of our purpose and criteria for making decisions, and thus failure becomes inevitable.

The incentives: Any decision has its potential consequences, which we must predict as best we can. We must be willing to take the risks of being wrong, while looking forward to some kind of a positive outcome. Therefore, some incentive usually drives our decisions, although sometimes we make a decision without any tangible incentive attached to it—merely out of pride or egoism or fear. On the other hand, even our major decisions may have to be made with limited information or options, which means our incentives are tenuous and merely speculative. For example, if we have limited choices or financial resources to get the desired education, we are forced to compromise and pursue an education and career that may end up being a waste of our lives, or conversely result in a successfully quiet life. Yet, initially, incentives are not quite clear and valid. Nevertheless, a vision of some tangible incentives increases our motivation for accepting the risks and hardship that are usually necessary for accomplishing the objectives of our decisions.

The incentives and objectives of a decision imply different things, although they are closely related and sometimes the same. The purpose of a decision is to accomplish a goal, but incentive is the reason substantiating that target. Our incentive determines why we pursue this objective and what happens when we get there. Another way of distinguishing the purpose and the incentive is to think of them as 'what' and 'why' of every decision respectively. The purpose is *what* we aim for. And the incentive is *why* we do it. Both 'what' and 'why' of making a decision should be valuable and unselfish. Distinguishing what and why is also important.

Like the purposes of a decision, incentives should be legitimate and relevant too. The incentive of 'seeing somebody suffers' as a result of our decision is not legitimate or relevant. The incentive of making a lot of money with a certain investment decision is not relevant and important for finding the ultimate purpose of life, i.e., peace of mind, either. Maybe what we do with the money creates a better vision of an incentive for our decision. For example, we may envision a relaxing vacation with the money we earn for the extra work we do. The value and vision of an incentive reduces the level of stress that a decision and subsequent efforts cause. Our decisions cause stress if we do not have a legitimate and relevant purpose. We usually have many false incentives like making 'more money than we ever need,' or 'taking revenge.' However, these types of criteria cannot be legitimate *purposes* or *incentives* for planning and working too hard.

We get our life energy from our achievements. We need to achieve something in order to fuel our journey forward. This inherent, strong need makes us seek all kinds of adventures. Sometimes, we even adhere to negative activities and thoughts (with no legitimate purpose and incentive) in hopes of feeling successful and getting the life energy that we need. We create artificial and perhaps illegitimate incentives for ourselves and subsequently make decisions that have no value for enriching our lives.

The commitment: The overall commitment and motivation for our decisions and subsequent implementation of their details are naturally important for achieving good results. Commitment and motivation result directly from the three factors of evidence, purpose, and incentive. Usually when we use these factors properly in decision-making, we gain enough momentum and motivation to make a good decision and also pursue it methodically—unless a person is lazy or too passive by nature. Involvement and ownership of a decision are other factors that make our decisions successful. Sometimes, we only appear to be involved with a decision, whereas in reality we are participating only because we have to, or only like to pretend that we are interested. Sometimes, we are actually interested in the success of a decision, but do not have the time or patience to spend on the required work. Thus, we delegate it to somebody else and hope that we get the exact results. Often, we do not have the right criteria for making important decisions, and perhaps even depend on the judgment of others, e.g., about a person we want to marry.

On the other hand, we sometimes impose our decisions upon others, or do not create the atmosphere required for teamwork and involvement of people who have, or should have, some say or interests in the decision. Again, like the example of choosing a companion, we may dominant the situation and prevent the full participation of our partner in discussions and decisions that would affect the important decision of marriage. Thus, we face sad consequences and sufferings when not all related parties seem fully involved and committed to the decision for the right reasons. They are there for the wrong incentives and reasons; and we do not realize it until it is too late. In fact, if the persons who should be involved and active in decision-making show reluctance to express their viewpoints, or submit to our whims casually, we should consider it a sign of imminent failure of our decision if we go ahead with it. This lack of commitment would taint the process. Sooner or later, the voice of opposition or indifference would surface and ruin the outcome.

Normally, we associate 'decision-making' with free will, though in reality many decisions are a form of compromise or coercion—usually in inconspicuous manners. When people are not responsible for their decisions, they are less inclined to take ownership of them and implement them. People's level of commitment to any decision, and its success, is necessarily a function of how much they have contributed in developing it. In all, the chances of success of any decision depend on the level of initial work, including our doubts, that has gone into it.

The timing: The 'timing limitation' discussions in Chapter Nine shows the importance of timing as a major decision-making element.

Decision-making Criteria

All our decisions, e.g., what to eat, where to go, what kind of education to get, whom to marry, etc., must be logical. Thus, we set certain criteria based on our personal tastes, preferences, and life paths, which give different emphasis to material things, physical pleasures, and soul-searching goals. We build our decision criteria consciously or subconsciously to gauge our decisions prudently and pursue our primary goals consistently in line with a personal life philosophy. Our decision criteria also depend on the nature of decision, including its importance, risks, timing, plus all the decision factors, conditions, and elements discussed in this chapter. Every decision has its own objective and consequences, yet all our decisions have a few common, ultimate goals, e.g., our lifelong health, success, and happiness. We make all our decisions according to the values (criteria) that make sense for the life path we follow and fulfil our long-term needs.

Intuitively, we all seek a life path that can bring us a manageable routine and peace of mind. We all imagine that our choice is correct and that is the best option for reaching our ultimate goals.

However, so far most of prevalent life paths have failed to bring humans a real sense of success or lasting happiness. Our life paths and the decision criteria supporting them have not given us even some solace. In fact, our value systems and cultures are preventing us from finding even some basic peace of mind, let alone ultimate happiness. Meanwhile, our raw positive thinking and obsession to find happiness have caused everybody more confusion. They have only made us raise our expectations from life instead of learning the reality of living in our complex and callous society with all the hardships we must overcome.

Contrary to what we like to believe, happiness and success are not absolute states to reach on a permanent basis. We cannot grasp even their meanings and pinpoint a path toward them. Instead, we have invented some decision criteria for various issues in life, such as getting good grades at school or accumulating wealth as measures of success and eventual happiness. We teach our children to work and compete hard. Yet outside these elementary definitions of success and happiness, we have really not been able to formulate some good ideas to share with others about real success and happiness. In fact, it is depressing and surprising that we have not, as human beings, been able to come up with a more practical way of sharing peace and contentment among us. Our philosophers and prophets in the last few millenniums have failed to offer guidelines that could help us be better human beings and thus suffer less. We have failed collectively as humans, too, to overcome superstitions, religious fanaticism, greed, and superficialities in order to find a more meaningful and peaceful life for all.

Theoretically, at least, we expect that a structured process of thinking would help us choose a suitable life path and the right decision criteria for a more meaningful means of success and happiness. The objective is not to restrict personal intuition and creativity, but rather increase all of those by providing the framework and philosophical background that would encourage individual thinking. We need some tools to develop useful decision criteria that can support our major decisions at least.

As a first step, perhaps we should change our mentality about 'happiness,' in order to make our life decisions easier and more realistic. Maybe choosing a simpler goal like 'peace of mind,' as the ultimate criterion for making our major life decisions, is more sensible. In another word, regardless of our criteria of success, our ultimate objective should be 'to achieve peace of mind'—contentment—and not necessarily happiness. How either happiness or peace of mind is found still depends on individuals' perception of these concepts, and his/her point of reference in life. Many people, in fact, think of 'pleasure' when imagining happiness. On the other hand, 'peace of mind' demands a simple lifestyle to increase one's independence and chances of living with minimal stress and worries. This requires contentment instead of pleasures and power. Nonetheless, 'peace of mind' would be an easier target (criterion) to define and pursue, compared to 'happiness,' which is only a myth. The only obstacle for pursuing 'peace of mind' is that one should develop a solid foundation of thoughts and seek a simpler lifestyle.

A Warning for the Youths

Every generation must make finer and timelier decisions to survive financially and emotionally. They would face more doubts and challenges, including a harder time to communicate with their parents or among themselves as friends and marriage partners. Worst of all, they do not have right decision criteria to make their major life decisions properly. They must make their major life decisions when they do not have enough wisdom, patience, and guidance, but a lot of bad influence. Thus, their fluid decisions often derail the course of their lives. They spend many years at universities and colleges and then end up following a different profession they do not enjoy for rest of their lives. They make their marriage decisions according to superficial values that society endorses nowadays. The decision criteria they use for all these major life issues usually lead to intolerable conditions that often cause them confusion and depression.

Sometimes, we resort to others, directly or indirectly, for insight to make a decision or to escape our depressing lives. We may seek the advice of our parents or a friend or perhaps even a stranger or fortune-teller if we are desperate. Some of us are ultra conservative and fear the risks involved in every decision. And, of course, in some situations, we are in such deep emotional turmoil that our decision-making ability is either numb or distorted—for example, in love related situations. Our inability to make a decision or take action is obviously due to inexperience or bad experiences. However, it mostly shows that we have not built a proper foundation for thinking and setting our convictions. We have not chosen a proper life path and decision criteria.

Depending on the outcome of our decisions, we end up living with a sense of success or failure for many years. Along with our senses of guilt and regret, we also feel our responsibility for not assessing our life options and their consequences adequately. Accordingly, our spirits squash and our doubts become more complex and confusing. Sometimes, we can change the course of our lives when we are in our mid-life or old ages to pursue a more authentic lifestyle and find a relative peace of mind. However, the problem is that at those ages we are usually trapped in binding circumstances caused by our earlier decisions. We would have a hard time escaping those traps, and it would take a longer time to readjust and learn the new meanings of life and means of living. Our decision-making options deplete fast as we age.

Nevertheless, we (must) feel responsible for the outcome of our decisions, instead of trying to blame external factors and destiny. One way to ensure that we have fulfilled our sense of responsibility is to enter into a clear and conscious contract with ourselves regarding every major decision after doing our best to project its expected rewards and risks. All along, we remember that the 'future self' would always find the 'present self' accountable for the decisions made today and condemn his/her carelessness or ignorance harshly.

The main point to remember is that often we surprise ourselves to find out, at a later stage of our lives, how perfunctory our definitions of success and happiness had been. After many years of suffering in pursuit of wealth or love, our criteria of happiness and success prove misleading and futile. How foolish a person feels when s/he reaches that devastating conclusion! So many precious years of lost youth, wasted efforts, fruitless thoughts, and unnecessary concerns! If only I knew! What if my parents were intelligent to direct me at least to the books that could give me a better appreciation of better things in life rather than passively passing on their materialistic values of our so-called civilized social living? What if I had some friends, books, or other sources that had shown me the wisdom of thinking for myself? What if I had realized what decisions were so important and how critical they would prove to be with time? Quite often, we feel sad for not having enough time and energy to change many things that we wished we could have done differently. However, if we get a one-in-a-million chance to communicate with our children to set their targets right, at least they may have less regrets later.

Epilogue

Regardless of the possibility of God's existence and the minuscule chance for afterlife, the power of human spirit is a plausible reality. Our spirits manifest regularly during our selfless rituals, and sometimes the sensation becomes heavenly during self-actualization experiences and moments of awakening. Almost everybody is familiar with this sacred feature of humanness, which might also be our main point of distinction from animals. Without our spirits guiding and empowering us, we soon perish under the pressures of life's hardships and self-inflicted pains. Yet, nurturing and keeping our spirits high is a difficult undertaking when we must live in such substandard environments. Our experiences, friends and family, as well as social rules and hypocrisies drain our spirits and we never get a chance to find a relative sense of freedom, let alone a notion of spirituality and connection to the real world. As discussed in Volume III, our educational systems, work environments, and family relationships cause us stress and confusion. We feel entrapped with no chance to build our identity and appreciate the strength and sanctity of our spirit. We simply plough on through a superficial life structure and become more arrogant and demanding, but also too shallow and purposeless.

Meanwhile, we cannot avoid many questions boggling our minds, such as, "Will we ever change our mentality and adopt a more natural lifestyle, nurture our spirits, and earn the wisdom for living freely? Will we ever give ourselves a chance to explore the real world and grasp the truth of existence? Will we ever tame our Egos and neediness in order to find our 'self'?" Unfortunately, the history and all the new trends in human mentality give a resounding answer 'no' to the above questions. We are too naïve and absorbed in our illusions to learn anything from our stressful experiences and social havoc that is getting more out of hand every day. The effect of keeping the large population on the globe in dark and ignorance, through religions and politics, has brought us to this abyss. There seems to be no way out of this mess while the rich and elite groups are in charge of educating and exploiting the other 99% of the population. Our occasional resistance and forewarning are answered with hostility and various disgraceful labels. Yet, many people cannot easily give up even when their intentions are misrepresented, ridiculed, or dismissed. They are too spirited to lose hope. The mass is somewhat responsible, too, mostly for submitting to the hypnotizing impressions of a modern existence with all kinds of self-gratifying immoralities. Their stubbornness to remain ignorant in their shallow shells with their religious ideologies or demented social values cannot be resolved in any rational way.

The irrational way is, of course, to wait for the final demise of social life and human spirit. It will certainly happen when all our illusions of pleasure and extravagance get fully obscured by the burdens of living and pretending. Nevertheless, as it seems at this point, perhaps we have no other viable option for our salvation, but only wait for that final blow in our faces to understand the irrationality of our lifestyles and mentalities. We do not have the courage and motivation to change our lives and resist the alluring symbols of modern life. How can we do this to ourselves?